Under Cover

**Thirty-Five Years
of CIA Deception**

Under Cover

Thirty-Five Years of CIA Deception

by Darrell Garwood

Introduction by Tom Gervasi

Grove Press, Inc./New York

First published in 1980 by
Dan River Press
Stafford, Virginia
Originally published under the title *American Shadow*

First Black Cat Edition 1985
First Printing 1985
ISBN: 0-394-62073-9
Library of Congress Catalog Card Number: 83-49378

Library of Congress Cataloging in Publication Data

Garwood, Darrell.
   Under cover.

   Originally published: American shadow. Stafford, Va.:
Dan River Press, 1980.
   Bibliography: p.
   includes index.
   1. United States. Central Intelligence Agency.
I. Title.
JK468.I6G37 1985   327.1'2'06073   83-49378
ISBN 0-394-62073-9 (pbk.)

Book design by David Miller

Printed in the United States of America

GROVE PRESS, INC., 196 West Houston Street, New York, N.Y. 100

1 3 5 4 2

To PHYLLIS J. THOMPSON,
A Valued Friend

ACKNOWLEDGMENTS

Like many that have gone before, this book owes a large debt to the *New York Times*, the well-indexed film files of which were made available to me at the Brevard Community College library in Cocoa, Florida. Even though I was involved as a reporter in many of the events chronicled here, I would have been helpless without this convenient and reliable means of checking and expanding on recollections and on notes, clippings, and other scraps of information.

I am also deeply indebted to J. William Fulbright, chairman for nearly twenty years of the Senate Foreign Relations Committee, who gave me the benefit of his vast experience in the form of both encouragement and criticism after reading through the manuscript for this book. During two decades in which the CIA inflicted serious damage on the nation's reputation at home and especially abroad, I believe that Chairman Fulbright did more than any other one man toward keeping official American foreign policy on a comparatively steady and honorable course. His record speaks for itself, and it is one we can all be proud of.

Another large debt of gratitude is due Warren L. Nelson, the last and certainly one of the best of my companions in covering the Pentagon for United Press International. He gave me the benefit of his previous experience as a Middle East correspondent located in Iran and as Middle East editor located in Washington for UPI. Nelson now heads the Washington staff of Congressman Les As-pin, of Wisconsin, which has become noted for extraordinary efforts to keep the public informed.

I am also greatly indebted to Helene MacLean, who gave me a couple hundred or more commas, and straightened at least that many crooked sentences, in a final editing of the manuscript. Above all, she read the stuff with understanding and retention, so that no contradiction or discrepancy coming along had the smallest chance of survival. If the book is never read well again, a fate not as uncommon as a person might think, it will still be possible to say that it was read well once.

CONTENTS

The thorns which I have reap'd are of
the tree
I planted; they have torn me, and I
bleed.
I should have known what fruit would
spring from such a seed.
—from Lord Byron's *Childe Harold's Pilgrimage*,
Canto IV, Stanza 10.

INTRODUCTION

The virtue of this book is that it provides a record. It draws together in one place a great deal of information about the covert activities of the Central Intelligence Agency. All of this information is in the public domain, and has been thoroughly documented at one time or another. But it is not in one place. Nor can much of it easily be found elsewhere today. Much of it was once reported and then forgotten. This, as we shall see, was no accident. It dropped out of public sight and lost its place in common knowledge. By retrieving it, Darrell Garwood reminds us that it all happened. Real history should not be forgotten. It should continue to inform. This history now has a fresh opportunity to do so. It was never needed more.

What the reader will find here is by no means a complete record of covert CIA activity. It is only what present and former officials—some with high purpose and some with low—have seen fit to reveal, what former agents have managed to expose, and what Congress and the press have been willing and able to unearth. It draws on a wide variety of sources published over the past 30 years, including the hearings of the House and Senate Select Committees on Intelligence, whose findings, when they were first released in 1975, provoked wide public outrage and calls for reform, but have since been largely ignored. However, no one outside the intelligence community, and probably no single person within it, knows how much more of the record has remained entirely hidden.

It is important that we be reminded of this history, because the record of our nation's covert activities is largely a record of violations of law and abuses of power. It contradicts the principles of justice and nonintervention in the affairs of other nations which America claims to uphold. This raises several fundamental questions. There is the question of whether we find it acceptable to apply a double standard. There is the more cynical question of why we should care whether it is acceptable, so long as we can get away with it. Ultimately, however, there is the practical question of whether we *can* get away with it, or whether we all pay too high a price.

Most CIA covert action has been a violation of our Neutrality Act. Most of it has violated agreements respecting the sovereignty of nations embodied in Article 2 (4) of the United Nations Charter, which our government signed, and in United Nations General Assembly Resolutions 2131 (XX) of 1965 and 2625 (XXV) of 1970, which our government approved. All of it has been a betrayal of international trust, in which our government has refused accountability for its acts, or at least been able plausibly to deny them. None of it has endeared us to those nations and peoples that have suffered its consequences.

The public lately has been led to believe that covert action to protect our national interests is legitimate, though whenever there has been general agreement about the legitimacy of an action there has been no need to make it covert. The public has been encouraged to applaud the use of force against nations disinclined to accept the primacy of America's interests, whether its use is covert or not, and whether it seems legitimate or not, even though legitimacy has always been far more effective than force in earning the respect of other nations, while the illegitimate use of force has earned only their contempt, and has strengthened rather than weakened opposition to America's policies, both at home and abroad.

Covert action, then, like every other form of violence and use of force save that taken strictly in defense against demonstrable aggression, works not in our national interest but against it. In the long run it is self-defeating. For those concerned only with the pursuit of America's interests, this is probably a more decisive argument against its use than the argument that the interests of other nations deserve equal respect.

⟨The problem is that we have evolved a powerful intelligence establishment, composed of several agencies, some of them authorized not only to collect intelligence but also, in the wording of most presidential directives from 1941 to the present day, "to perform such other functions and duties" as higher authority "may from time to time direct." It is also privileged with secrecy. As a result, it cannot always be restrained from performing such functions even when they are not authorized. It will not easily surrender these powers and privileges.

At the same time, we have evolved another powerful establishment known as corporate America, a growing network of firms that invest in other nations, trade with other nations, and utilize the labor and resources of other nations. Its interests are global. By legitimating and protecting those interests, our government serves this establishment in the same way the intelligence agencies serve government. The national interest has thus become synonymous with private interests. These are consequently pursued no matter how much they may conflict with the public interest, or with the interests of other nations.

When such conflicts of interest cannot be justified they are hidden, and one or another of these institutions resorts to covert action. It may be a corporation acting on its own. It may be an intelligence agency acting on its own, or on behalf of corporate interests, as the CIA acted on behalf of Western oil conglomerates in Iran, on behalf of the United Fruit Company in Cuba and Guatemala, and on behalf of ITT in Chile. If it acts without higher authority it is seldom held to account, because it is working within a community of shared interests, where cooperation may be safely presumed.⟩

The participants in this enterprise do not care that such action may be self-defeating in the long run. They are not concerned with the world inherited by their children. They are working for more immediate gains. The unlimited license to do so reflects one of the most intractable problems in our society. Our leading institutions systematically violate the law because they are beyond its reach. They work in complete disregard of the public interest because they are not accountable to it.

⟨It is a delicate matter to make such conditions tolerable in a democratic society. The public must be encouraged to believe its interest is truly being served. If that is impossible, then the public must be demoralized. It must be made to feel either that it is powerless to change these conditions, or that it is chiefly to blame for them. Thus, our government's failure, in the wake of Congressional hearings in 1975, to achieve reforms in the conduct of our intelligence agencies has been attributed not to official intransigence but to public apathy.

This is a convenient fiction, used to divert our attention from the real problem. The public is not apathetic. It was not apathetic over the danger of nuclear testing in the atmosphere in the early 1960s. Nor was it powerless. It won a ban on atmospheric tests. In the late 1960s, it was not apathetic over our involvement in Vietnam. It got us out of Vietnam.

The real problem was that government refused to press for reform. The intelligence agencies and the vested interests they serve refused to submit to reform. Of course, a public neither apathetic nor powerless would not permit such negligence. Therefore, it had to be disguised, and the public misled. Reforms had to be promised. Resolute purpose had to be demonstrated, and results displayed. This flurry of activity gave every appearance of producing reform. Its true effects had to be carefully obscured. For in fact, its purpose was not to prevent intelligence abuses from being repeated again. It was to help prevent the public from learning of them again.⟩

There were numerous sensible recommendations for reform, most notably those in the Final Reports of the House and Senate Select Committees, and in the Senate's proposed National Intelligence Reorganization and Reform Act of 1978. There was no question that we *knew* what should be done.

Yet not a single measure finally taken by Congress or the Executive Branch in response to the call for reform did anything to curb the power of the CIA or any other intelligence agency to repeat practices Congress had already condemned, from political bribery, economic subversion, disinformation, subsidized revolution, assassination and coups d'etat abroad to domestic surveillance violating the Fourth Amendment at home. These remedies, instead, provided intelligence agencies with expanded authority to continue such practices, increased secrecy to prevent them from coming to light, made more severe penalties for those who might bring them to light, and broadened immunity for intelligence officials whose misconduct might be exposed.

The CIA, prohibited by the National Security Act of 1947 from performing any "internal security functions," has now been authorized by the Reagan administration to engage in domestic surveillance, ostensibly in order to collect "significant foreign intelligence" that is "not otherwise obtainable" abroad, though for this purpose it is empowered to investigate American citizens as well as foreign nationals.¹ This expands authority for domestic operations already given the agency by the Ford and Carter administrations.² It frees the CIA to resume those activities Congress had pronounced a breach of Constitutional rights. Operation Chaos, its search for foreign influence in the antiwar protests of the 1960s, was one of these. Its current search for foreign influence in the nuclear freeze movement is another. Then, as now, the only provocation that could be found for the growth of dissent was not foreign influence but the policy of our own government. Nevertheless, undercover CIA agents are now free to infiltrate domestic political organizations.

Though its 1947 charter had also denied it any "law-enforcement powers," the CIA has now been authorized, along with every other intelligence agency, to "participate in law enforcement activities" in order to "investigate or prevent" a variety of occurrences, including "international terrorist" activities.³ These, because they may occur not only under Communist sponsorship but on behalf of a broad range of ideologies, present a more plausible threat than Communism in an age when our nation's policies meet with increasing hostility around the world, Communist inspiration for which is most of the time demonstrably absent. Therefore, international terrorism has replaced Communist subversion as the primary threat to our nation's internal security.

While there is no more evidence of this new threat than there was of the old one, it receives extravagant attention. That is because public warnings of its imminence have been a useful tool of political coercion. Though most of the violence in our nation has been in defiance of change or in support of official policy, the potential for violence may be imagined of anyone. It is therefore promptly suspected of any organization seeking change and opposing official policy. This raises the threat of domestic terrorism. It must be portrayed as international terrorism in order to imply that no disagreement with official policy would arise without foreign influence. This suggests, in turn, that no reasonable basis for disagreement exists. The reasons nevertheless presented for disagreement may then be more easily discounted. For it is not violence but the power such reasons may have to affect opinion, and so diminish support for their policies, that officials truly fear. Terrorism is the metaphor they supply for this real threat, justifying the measures they plan against it.

To make it seem more plausible that those who openly disagree with official policy may resort to violence, the few incidents of violence attributable to them are heavily emphasized in official commentary over the unremitting flow of violence from organizations like the Ku Klux Klan or the Labor Party of Lyndon LaRouche. If this distortion remains unpersuasive, evidence is fabricated. We now know that much of the violence attributed to the Weather Underground was planned by law enforcement agents.

The construction of innuendo serves to associate political activities of any kind, no matter how peaceful and lawful, with criminal intent, so that any activities discomforting to those in power may be declared hostile and possibly dangerous. In this way, the legitimacy of any efforts to bring about change may be denied. This curbs such efforts, and inhibits the expression of dissenting opinion. It discredits dissent, and so absolves those in power of any obligation to heed it.

Government officials have every reason, of course, to anticipate violence on a wide scale when they plan to remain unresponsive to the will of the people. If violence then results, they are not concerned with the failure of democracy this signals. They are concerned with the threat it poses to law and order. By portraying all violence as terrorism before it has even occurred, they imply that it can never have justifiable cause. In this way, they not only deny their own role in producing it, but also deny the people their guarantee of a political voice.

This is how the threat of terrorism was used to intimidate demonstrators opposed to new missile deployments in Western Europe. By repeatedly warning that any further opposition might end in violence, officials implied that all opposition would be judged criminal once any violence occurred. Terrorism never threatened the missile deployments. It threatened the demonstrators themselves. It was clear whose interests would best be served if violence did occur, and equally clear who was therefore most likely to employ it.>

In a similar way, the threat of terrorism has been used in our own country to justify investigations of <u>the nuclear freeze movement</u>, whose members officials have called naive, irresponsible and unpatriotic, and whose activities they claim may threaten domestic law and order, even though its single goal is to preserve international order and prevent an irreversible disturbance of the peace.

Officials have also claimed that the nuclear freeze movement could not exist without foreign influence. <They must sustain their apparent belief in the foreign origins of domestic opposition, not only to deny its true origins but also to provide grounds for action by the intelligence agencies against it, just as the threat of violence provides grounds for action by the police. The threat of foreign interference is a threat to national security. The

public has been encouraged to believe that such an emergency justifies the suspension of all normal constraints on official activity. While almost any official action against nonviolent opposition violates Federal law and our Constitution, the spirit of emergency invoked by a threat of foreign influence provides a moral justification the public has usually accepted for any illegal action that may come to light. Consequently, official action against domestic opposition in America always takes the form of a covert investigation to search for a foreign influence never yet found, in anticipation of an emergency not yet at hand. >

Thus, domestic surveillance of political organizations, ostensibly in a search for foreign influence or foreign agents, is indistinguishable from domestic surveillance of foreign agents. The former activity easily may be disguised as the latter. Our intelligence agencies have now been permitted to engage in domestic surveillance either as a "law enforcement" action against "international terrorist" activities or as a counterintelligence effort against "clandestine intelligence activities by a foreign power."[4] Either purpose may be ascribed to investigations of dissident political groups, merely by raising the possibility of foreign influence upon them.

Nor is any evidence of such influence required to warrant surveillance. Actual cause for officials to believe their investigations are ultimately "directed against a foreign power or an agent of a foreign power" has been replaced, in the language of authorizing directives, with "probable cause."[5] Suspicion alone is enough.

Inasmuch as suspicion need never be relinquished for lack of evidence, no investigation need ever end. Inasmuch as investigating agents work under cover, no one may be the wiser if they do more than monitor the activities of groups under suspicion. They may create dissension within these groups to render them less effective. They may influence them to steer them in new directions, and so affect the entire political process. That is how our intelligence and law enforcement agencies, by undertaking what they need only present as an investigation, warranted by nothing more than "probable cause," may serve as a powerful weapon of political control.⟩

These and many other activities that arise from domestic surveillance are no more lawful today than they were when practiced by CIA officers responsible for Operation Chaos, or by the FBI in its COINTELPRO operations. Then, as now, Federal law prohibited warrantless electronic surveillance, warrantless searches of homes and burglaries in violation of state and local laws, the destruction or concealment of public records, opening of the mails and the copying of its contents, making false statements, obstruction of justice, conspiracy to violate Federal laws, and conspiracy to infringe upon the civil rights of citizens by violations of their First, Fourth and Fifth Amendment rights.[6] Every one of these statutes was violated by those agencies in the 1960s and 1970s. Their new charter only further frees them to repeat these violations in the 1980s.

Passage of the Foreign Intelligence Surveillance Act of 1978 promised an end to these abuses, by establishing a court to approve applications for warrants to undertake such intrusive surveillance techniques as wiretaps and "surreptitious entries." The court presumably would grant warrants based on the merits of each application. In fact, it simply receives the recommendations of the Attorney General. He offers only his assertions of "probable cause." The court does not contest these. It merely certifies that the Attorney General has made them. Its proceedings are closed to the public. In 1979, the Foreign Intelligence Surveillance Court received 199 applications for warrants. It approved them all.

As the CIA and other intelligence agencies sought and received a wider mandate to conduct operations at home and abroad in disregard of the law, they also sought tighter secrecy measures, ostensibly the better to protect national security, though of course these could no less effectively serve to better ensure that intelligence abuses remain hidden. We have only the word of intelligence officials that this is not their principal function today.

Nevertheless, a growing body of legislation, court rulings and presidential directives has now broadened government authority to withhold information by classifying it, to withdraw information from the public domain by reclassifying it, to prevent its dissemination by prior restraint, and to penalize its dissemination even though it remains in the public domain.

The CIA continues systematically to withhold information by claiming it cannot otherwise protect its sources and methods,[7] though it has never shown why its sources and methods are bound to be compromised by revealing the information they produce, nor has it offered a single example of how they have been compromised in this way. It continues to claim several exemptions from its obligation to release information under the Freedom of Information Act, but does not even suggest its release would jeopardize national security. Instead, it only asserts that disclosures would be "perceived" to be damaging, but does not acknowledge that misperceptions would never arise without its own prompting.

The Reagan administration has now proposed legislation exempting new categories of commercial, technical and organized crime data from access under the Freedom of Information Act, refusing requests by foreign nationals, and raising government fees for processing requests. Prohibitive fees for information the public has already paid its taxes to generate and retrieve have become a highly effective means of restricting access to it. The new legislation, as Vermont's Senator Patrick J. Leahy remarked, would only "make it easier for the government to hide what it's doing."

The Reagan administration's Executive Order on National Security Information[8] has also made it simpler for officials to classify information and keep it classified indefinitely. It supersedes the Carter administration's Executive Order,[9] which required officials, before classifying information, to show that "identifiable" damage to national security would result from its disclosure. The Reagan order eliminates this requirement, and allows information to be classified whenever there is "reasonable doubt" as to whether disclosure would be advisable. While the Carter order enjoined officials to balance the public interest against the need for secrecy, and to release information whenever the public interest appeared to outweigh that need, the Reagan order gives no such direction. While the Carter order provided that documents automatically be reviewed for declassification after they reached twenty years of age, the Reagan order restricts such review to only those documents specifically requested by the public. Thus, most of the 617 million pages of material now held classified by 155 government agencies may continue to be classified simply because the public doesn't know it *exists*.

The rationale for withdrawing information that is already in the public domain first emerged in 1979, in our government's unsuccessful pursuit of a permanent injunction against publication of Howard Morland's article "The H-Bomb Secret" in *The Progressive* magazine. In his article Morland had based his deductions about the design and manufacture of thermonuclear weapons solely on information available to the public. His purpose was to show that there was no "secret" about how such weapons were made. Instead, the aura of official secrecy surrounding them had been used for decades to discourage public inquiry into nuclear weapons policy, freeing the government from its responsibility to show that its policy decisions were compatible with the public interest.

The government did not deny that all the information Morland had drawn upon for his research was in the public domain. But it argued that under the definition of "Restricted Data" in the Atomic Energy Act, any information about "the design, manufacture or utilization of atomic weapons," even if publicly available, must be considered "inherently inadmissible" to the public domain unless the government has taken specific measures to place it there. Such measures themselves may later be reassessed. In this case, the government claimed the information Morland obtained had been improperly declassified.[10]

By this line of reasoning, the government meant to disclaim responsibility for any prior action on its part, whether accidental or deliberate, that might have made such information available, and to shift the burden of liability for its disclosure, or even for the disclosure of inferences drawn from it, to the public and press. This implied, in turn, that government deemed itself the sole arbiter of what was in the public domain at any time, and might freely remove from it any information it wished, no matter how widely disseminated, including information it had previously disseminated itself.

After two newspapers published much of the same material included in Morland's article in order to challenge the constitutionality of efforts to prevent its publication, the government abandoned these. But it did not abandon the concept of inherent inadmissibility. If it could not successfully withdraw information already available to the public, it might still *declare* this information inadmissible, and so discourage publication of further references to it. It has since moved to apply this concept not only to nuclear weapons data but to any category of information it chooses. That is why the president, or any agency head or official so authorized, may now "reclassify information declassified and disclosed," without qualification.[11]

It might seem futile for our government to instruct that material so widely available be treated as though it were not, unless it could also enforce such treatment by penalizing its further dissemination. That is precisely what it has now begun to do. In 1982, the Senate enacted the Intelligence Identities Protection Act,[12] which punishes by fine and a prison term of up to three years anyone who discloses "information that identifies" a "covert" American intelligence agent, even though identifying information is drawn from public sources, whenever there is "reason to believe" this might harm our foreign intelligence activities. In effect, as the American Civil Liberties Union has observed, this law "penalizes the publication of information that is already public."

The identity of an agent can only be "covert" when no information is available to expose it. It cannot be covert when such information exists in the public domain. That information cannot be "exposed." It can only be given greater prominence. If it cannot be withdrawn from the public domain, it will certainly continue to be available to those with sufficient interest and resources to find it—for example, foreign intelligence organizations. Their access to it will not be diminished by a law which cannot expunge it but can only penalize American citizens for giving it greater prominence. This law therefore cannot achieve its ostensible purpose. It cannot improve protection for truly covert agents, whose identities were already fully protected. It cannot improve protection for agents who were never covert, and who remain identifiable because the information identifying them remains public.

The identities of thousands of CIA agents have been given greater prominence over the past decade by several researchers and journalists who had grown concerned about intelligence abuses and sought to prevent their recurrence by fully informing the public of what the public record already showed. All this they did without benefit of access to classified information. Were a law needed to prevent them from doing what they intended as a public service, there ought to be some evidence that their work has not been in the public interest. It should have led to a long list of American agents who came to harm as a result. Yet throughout this period there has been not a single instance of one who did.

Some of our agents have certainly come to harm—not because of any attention they received from the public or press, however, but because they stood in harm's way. CIA Middle East expert Robert Ames and other agency employees died in Beirut in 1983 because they were in the American embassy when it was bombed. CIA station chief Richard Welch died in Athens in 1975, but not, as the CIA later insisted, because journalists had given greater prominence to his identity. He was not even trying to hide his identity. In fact, he made himself much simpler to identify than any amount of attention from journalists could, by insisting on living in the same building previous station chiefs had occupied, despite cabled warnings from the CIA that in a city full of violent anti-American sentiment this building was well-known as a CIA residency. Those who assassinated him when he returned to it one evening did not have to know his name.

Nevertheless, the CIA arranged for exhaustive press coverage after Welch's assassination to complain about all the press coverage before it, though in fact there had been only one story about him, identifying him as a former station chief in Peru. The press did not learn of the CIA's cabled warnings to Welch and his refusal to heed them, because the CIA never mentioned them. Its warnings only later emerged in Senate testimony. This combination of emphasis and omission enabled the CIA to blame Welch's death on what it portrayed as an irresponsible press. The public remained ignorant of Welch's own recklessness, and of the long record of CIA activities in Greece that had inspired much of that nation's animosity towards the United States.

By nurturing this single misrepresentation, the CIA was able to build a false atmosphere of permanent vulnerability, in which it seemed that the safety of its agents somehow lay at the mercy of the American public and press, rather than on the effectiveness of measures to prevent information identifying them from becoming available to the public in the first place. In this atmosphere, passage of a law penalizing the public for further discussion of what it already knew seemed more urgent than any genuine attempt to improve the protection of intelligence identities.

That this new law addresses no genuine need and does nothing to achieve the purpose its title suggests only raises the question of what its true purpose is. This is best understood by noting its effect, and the effects of the campaign waged to enact it. Its first effect was to shift public attention away from all of the intelligence abuses that had originally provoked nationwide concern, and refocus it upon the alleged abuses of the press. Having implied the press was responsible for one agent's death, the CIA next suggested this proved that the press was capable of harming any agent, and willing to do so. Preoccupation with these alleged and possible harms further diverted public attention from the real harm the intelligence agencies had already inflicted.

The next stage of the CIA's campaign was to encourage fear that "irresponsible" journalism might "impair or impede" intelligence activities, jeopardizing official policy goals, as if journalism had no responsibility to impair activities that impeded the self-determination of other nations, abused human rights and violated the law. The press was presented in potential conflict with the national interest, though at that time most journalists still distinguished between the national interest, as construed by officials in power, and the public interest they intended to serve. Suspicion that the press might abuse its freedoms led inescapably to the conclusion that its freedoms should be curbed.

❬ In this way, the CIA and other agencies mounted a direct assault on First Amendment guarantees of press freedom, without a shred of genuine evidence to warrant it, and despite conclusive evidence of extensive intelligence abuses, which the press could only continue to document if its freedoms were left unimpaired. Most legal experts agree that the publication of information from open sources cannot constitutionally be made a crime. Philip Kurland, one of the nation's leading authorities on constitutional law, warned Congress, before it passed the Intelligence Identities Protection Act, that its provisions included "the clearest violation of the First Amendment attempted by Congress in this era." ❭

Whether this precedent will be upheld or eventually overturned in the courts, its endorsement by Congress marks a major victory in the continuing psychological war the intelligence agencies wage against the American people. For the broad campaign of domestic propaganda they undertook to urge its enactment was in fact their counterattack to public discovery of their abuses. By combining systematic distortion, diversion, innuendo and accusation, they produced what seemed a new national mood in which public opinion was reversed in their favor. Welch's assassination could not have been suited better to their purpose if they had planned it themselves.

Their security allegedly imperiled by domestic exposure, our intelligence services portrayed themselves at a grave disadvantage against foreign adversaries operating in total secrecy. Secrecy, they noted, enabled our adversaries to operate beyond the law. Therefore, legal constraints of our own had to be abandoned in order to place ourselves on a fair and equal footing in the secret war. Activities normally deemed criminal became mandatory to meet this emergency. If such license led to occasional abuse, surely this mattered less than the overriding interests of the nation.

This argument also implied a justification for past abuses, should the intelligence community ever be obliged to acknowledge them. Those who had committed them were portrayed as dedicated public servants performing a necessary task made thankless by malicious denunciations at home from critics who could not prove their charges. The incontrovertible evidence for those charges, much of it forcefully redocumented in this book, began to seem inconclusive. Those who presented it were systematically discredited. Since the true causes for their concern had to be denied, they were presumed, as always, to be under the influence of foreign propaganda, which in turn was always portrayed as more clever than ours.

In time, the original charges against the intelligence agencies seemed less substantial, the nature of their wrongs less clear. Public and Congressional certitude gave way to doubt. Editorials appeared reprimanding the public for its suspicions, or telling the public that it no longer entertained them, even though opinion polls showed a continuing rise in distrust of government. In the most influential media, and in most quarters of Congress, suspicion was soon displaced by gratitude towards our nation's shadow warriors, common sense by loyalty and gratuitous fears of the dangers they faced, and anger by sympathy for their plight.

This campaign, launched in the midst of the Congressional hearings on intelligence and conducted over the next several years—the same span of time in which America was stirred to a resurgence of militarism and a more aggressive foreign policy—brought national discussion of intelligence abuses almost to a halt. Public concern with most of these abuses appeared to subside. Many of them, it seemed, were soon forgotten. As Jacques Ellul, the eminent French authority on propaganda, had foreseen: "Well-known facts are simply made to disappear."

Calls for reform were no longer heard. The press suspended most of its investigations of intelligence. Its mind-set had been recalibrated. Even its opinion polls no longer asked the questions which might provoke answers it no longer wanted to hear. Editors denied they were avoiding such questions. They explained that the public was no longer interested in them. Yet no poll had been taken to determine whether that was true.

The result of this campaign, a powerful inhibition against further inquiry, significantly reduced the likelihood that further abuses would ever be brought to light, and helped to ensure that no further reforms of intelligence would be attempted. All this had been done without the mechanical imposition of censorship. It thereby avoided visibly disturbing the appearance of normal freedom of thought and expression.

Passage of the law itself, an acknowledged act of censorship, has had an even more powerful effect. The work of a great many scholars and journalists who ignored this apparent change in the national mood, and continued their research on intelligence abuses, has been severely impeded. It has been almost impossible for them, as it was intended to be, to document current intelligence activities without naming names. As a result, little of their work has since appeared. What has appeared has been far less persuasive than it would have been had names been added.

Many other books and articles about intelligence, of course, continue to appear, and many are filled with the names of intelligence agents present and past. But officials have had no objection to these. For they all adopt or reinforce official views. None has a critical word to say. This law is not for them. Its only purpose is to suppress criticism and dissent. As one former CIA agent remarked: "It's like traffic enforcement. They can stop any car for speeding, but they only stop the blue cars."

A remaining problem for the intelligence community is the danger that current or former officials and agents may leak information to support their disagreement with official policy, or simply because they believe the public has a right to it. While the press has now been better trained to minimize the importance of information which contradicts official views or disproves official statements, it must still report significant information whenever its failure to do so risks a collapse of faith that it serves the public interest. Thus, major intelligence abuses may still come to wide attention.

The courts have not proven reliable in preventing such disclosures by prior restraint, because their cooperation has only been obtained when it was possible to demonstrate that disclosure would jeopardize national security. That has rarely been the case. What almost every one of these disclosures has jeopardized, instead, has been public support for officials in power. That is because almost every disclosure has revealed official abuses. Since these disclosures have thereby done more in the long run to preserve the nation's security than harm it, our government has seldom been able to support claims to the contrary.

When our courts have been unable to deny public access to information on national security grounds, they have vigorously upheld the public's right to it. In 1971, when our government sought a permanent injunction against publication by the *New York Times* of portions of a classified Pentagon study of American policy in Vietnam, which came to be known as the Pentagon Papers, it cited "immediate and irreparable harm" to the "national defense interests of the United States and the nation's security." Daniel Ellsberg and Anthony Russo, who supplied this material, were indicted on charges of conspiracy, espionage and theft of government property. But the Supreme Court could find no danger to the national security by placing this information in the public domain. It held that the right of a free press under the First Amendment overrode any other legal grounds to prevent its release, and ordered the *Times* and the *Washington Post* to resume publication.[13]

Officials continue, nevertheless, to insist that many

leaks have damaged the nation's security, though they have not produced a single example of one that did. They ask the public to take their word for it—which the public might feel more obliged to do if it did not already know, largely as a result of leaks, that the same officials often lie. These officials continue to discredit subordinates who leak information, accusing them of disloyalty and belittling their motives for disclosure by portraying them as personally embittered. This neglects the possibility that they may be embittered because they have learned of decisions and practices heavily damaging to the nation's welfare, as the record of such disclosures almost invariably shows. It neglects the possibility that they may feel a higher loyalty than simple obedience to the administration currently in power.

It also neglects the fact that most leaks are officially authorized. They issue with impunity from the highest levels of government, exactly as often as presidents, cabinet members, intelligence chiefs and the heads of other agencies deem it expedient. When these officials insist on the right whenever they please to release information previously withheld from the public, but deny the same right to their subordinates, they seek absolute control over information, and make themselves the sole arbiters of the need for its protection.

Absolute and arbitrary control of information, exercised by a few dozen high officials, fails its ostensible purpose of safeguarding national security. The several thousand government employees whose duty it is to protect such information, most of whom are far more qualified than their superiors to judge what consequences its release may have, grow only more cynical as they see these officials violating standards they themselves must uphold.

The only purpose well served by total control of information is the control of public opinion. It permits those who appoint themselves the arbiters of information to leak it on a selective basis in order to gain support for their policies, while at the same time they may prevent further leaks from revealing that these same policies are insupportable.

President Reagan has come closer than he may know to admitting that he means to establish precisely this kind of control. In 1983 he acknowledged to a group of newspaper publishers that the information he meant to protect was "not necessarily classified." It included "options" of policy under his consideration "that sometimes, someone down the line leaks." He found this "very disturbing" because it led to "great problems." He added: "I want all options on any problem that is confronting us before I make a decision. We run our Cabinet a little bit like a board of directors. The only difference being, we do not take a vote."

Our government is not a private corporation. Its major decisions are not the exclusive province of a board of directors or a chief executive officer. They are subject to the consent of Congress, ratification by the courts, and ultimately the support of the public. This president would not worry about the management of information if he thought the public did not hold that power. He would do as he pleased, and not attempt to hide it. Instead, he asserts the right to withhold information about some of the options before him. He has no such right. The people deserve to know those options too. By claiming a right to deny them this knowledge, he demonstrates his intent to do as he pleases and *hide* it.

There is no reason why a president should hide information he concedes is not classified, and no reason why he should find it disturbing when that information is disclosed, if the only result of its disclosure is that the public informed by it continues to support the decisions he makes. Great problems can only arise when the public does not support these decisions.

Therefore, this president anticipates that he may wish to make decisions he knows the public would not support if it were fully informed. He has no right to make such decisions. But he means to disregard that limitation on his powers by keeping the people uninformed, thereby denying them their right to deny him support. This is a stunning rejection of democratic principles. He might as well have said he will not commit himself to serving the public interest, and will not be held accountable for his actions.

However, to achieve the more perfect immunity it now seeks from public accountability, our government must obtain more perfect control over public opinion. This it can only do by improving its control over the flow of information to the public. That control remains uncertain unless it can find a more reliable means of preventing unauthorized leaks. Its past efforts to do so by prior restraint or the threat of prosecution have largely failed, because its grounds for such action have always been the harm it claims disclosure would do to the nation's security. Since that harm has always turned out to be fictitious, this claim has rarely justified prior restraint or any earlier decisions to classify the information disclosed. This record only confirms that information is seldom justifiably classified.

As a result, the government lost its case against the *New York Times*, abandoned its suit against the *Progressive*, and won only a limited judgment deleting passages from *The CIA and the Cult of Intelligence*, a book by John Marks and former CIA officer Victor Marchetti.[14] It had originally sought to ban the entire book's publication. If its efforts at censorship were to be more effective, it had to find other grounds for them. It had to avoid efforts based on the claim that the information it sought to withhold was justifiably classified, because in all likelihood it would be unable to show why. This would only further emphasize that its true motives for withholding information, as our current President even admits, may have nothing to do with protecting the nation's security.

However, in its attempt to prevent publication of the book by Marks and Marchetti, the CIA developed a promising new argument, and gained a more favorable interpretation of it from the court than any legal precedent had granted. It could not deny that most of the information in the book was in the public domain. Nor could it demonstrate, as the court required it to do, that much of the remaining information had ever been classified. Consequently, the court cleared all of this material for publication.

The CIA was able to satisfy the court that some passages in the book did contain classified information. However, it next faced the prospect of having to show that this material was *justifiably* classified. If it could not do so, Marchetti's First Amendment rights would compel its publication. To avoid that outcome, the agency argued that it had no intention of testing the First Amendment, and meant only to enforce a private contract with Marchetti which prohibited disclosure of classified information he had gained in the course of his employment. It held that by signing such an agreement, which mandated prepublication review of all his writings, Marchetti had waived his First Amendment rights.

The court accepted this narrow interpretation, circumventing what would have been a perfectly legitimate test of whether disclosure was harmful, and neglecting an abundance of legal precedent which had established that the First Amendment precludes granting any relief to the government,[15] and that the Constitutional rights of employees cannot be waived by contract.[16] Marchetti did not *voluntarily* waive his First Amendment rights. He signed a secrecy agreement which required that he purport to waive those rights because it was a prerequisite of his employment. He could not have waived those rights had he intended to. They do not exist simply for his own protection. They exist for the benefit of the public at large.

The CIA has since repeatedly argued the primacy of private contracts over Constitutional guarantees, and gained acceptance of that argument in the courts—especially in the Fourth Circuit Court of Virginia. This has enabled it repeatedly to discourage, delay or penalize publication of other works by former employees, while avoiding the need to establish whether they even disclosed any classified information, let alone whether that information was justifiably classified. It has repeatedly applied this standard only to its critics. Its supporters continue to publish their work with impunity, and often with the agency's active assistance. They invariably disclose much more information than the CIA would allow its critics. That is why, paradoxically, their works become a valuable primary source for subsequent critics.

In 1978, after former CIA agent Frank Snepp published *Decent Interval*, a book critical of the agency's role in

Vietnam, but which he had not submitted for prepublication review because he knew it contained no classified information, the CIA used this same argument to win a civil suit confiscating all royalties and other proceeds from its publication, citing his failure to present his manuscript for review as a breach of contract, even though it *acknowledged* that the book contained no classified information. On appeal, the Supreme Court upheld this decision, asserting that Snepp had "breached a fiduciary obligation" and was therefore liable for the "proceeds of the breach."[17]

The agency filed a similar suit to obtain all profits from publication of *In Search of Enemies*, a book critical of its role in Africa by its former Angola Task Force chief, John Stockwell.[18] For many years it delayed publication of Ralph McGehee's *Deadly Deceits*, a book critical of its activities in Southeast Asia, by making McGehee, a former career employee, prove repeatedly that every item of information in his book had already been officially disclosed elsewhere.[19]

Thus, by claiming its right to seek relief for injuries never sustained, the CIA developed a highly effective though unconstitutional means of eliminating unwanted disclosures and suppressing dissent. The problem was that it could only be used against CIA employees. In other intelligence agencies, and in the intelligence offices and bureaus of other departments of government, employees signed similar secrecy agreements. But with those exceptions, the vast majority of the government's employees, who were privy to its internal workings and could therefore still tell the public more than key officials wanted the public to know, were bound by no such private contract which could be used to silence them.

So the Reagan administration decided to create one. In 1983 the president signed a directive which required all of the 127,500 government employees with access to "sensitive compartmented information" to sign a nondisclosure agreement whose provisions included submission of all of their writings to the government for prepublication review—without limitation on the length of time this requirement would remain in force, so that it remained in force *for the rest of their lives*, and submission to lie detector tests during investigations of unapproved leaks, with the promise of "adverse consequences" for those who would not consent to them.[20]

The president did not offer to sign this agreement himself. Nor did any of his key officials. Congress delayed approval of his directive. Early in 1984, in an effort to allay growing public suspicions over its real purpose, the president let it be known that he would not press for its approval. It was not clear whether the public whose support he sought for reelection realized that the moment it reelected him he would press for its approval again. If it does become law, his administration will gain the total control over information it seeks, preventing all of those in government most qualified to contradict official views and disprove official statements from disclosing any information which might do so.

Thus, in the evolution of means to insulate government from public control, the CIA pioneered a method which the entire Executive Branch may now adopt. Congress has the power to prevent the spread of censorship and secrecy agreements to government at large, but can do nothing to eliminate their continuing use within the intelligence community, the First Amendment rights of whose employees have already been effectively denied.

Nor has Congress been able to implement the oversight role it promised to strengthen a decade ago. Intelligence abuses continue unabated. Secrecy measures designed to conceal them continue to multiply. Congress has little power to prevent this because the intelligence agencies have successfully waged another kind of war to remain immune from Congressional control. This, too, is an information war. It is also a war of political influence.

The CIA is required, of course, to provide Congressional oversight committees with full access to any classified information they request. The felicity of this arrangement is that these committees seldom know what kind of information to request. They have no way of knowing how much information they may be unaware exists. For the most part, whatever they do not request they will never receive.

What may at first seem an exception to this is that the CIA is nominally required to give Congress prior notification of all covert operations. This, however, has not always turned out to be prior notification, because sometimes Congress has only been notified of operations after they were already under way. That places its committees in an awkward position, of course. If they disapprove of such operations, they have only the options of keeping them covert, and thus tacitly endorsing them, or revealing them and exposing the nation to greater embarrassment than it might have suffered had they been notified in time.

The committees also have no way of knowing how often they may not be notified at all. The CIA may only notify them of operations it believes they are most likely to discover on their own, so that whenever they do the agency is not then found in contempt of the law.

Even when such operations are discovered, the CIA can still minimize the effect of their exposure by continuing to *declare* them covert, as President Reagan recently declared CIA support of anti-Sandinist forces in Central America to be, after reports of it surfaced in the press. This is useful in two ways. An open admission of covert action *implies* its legitimacy by suggesting that its proponents believe there is nothing to hide. At the same time, by declaring that what has become overt remains covert, and therefore may not be discussed, it blocks thorough public examination of its legitimacy by hiding whatever there is to hide.

Meanwhile, there is nothing at all to prevent the CIA from refusing to inform Congressional committees of operations it believes they will never discover. These would certainly include operations most likely to meet with their disapproval, which the agency felt it could not rely on them to keep secret once they were informed.

Thus, because secrecy gives the CIA discretionary control over all of the information it provides, Congressional committees, if they expect to learn anything at all about the agency's activities in order to exercise what restraint they can, must prove themselves trustworthy. To the CIA, the only trustworthy Congressmen are those who demonstrably believe that the intelligence community should not only gather information but have an operational role, and that those responsible for its operations cannot be effective unless they are free to operate beyond the law.

The most trusted Congressmen, consequently, are those least likely to call for restraints on such activity. The least trusted are those given the least access to information. In this way, secrecy wholly corrupts the oversight function of Congress. It gives greater power to those under regulation, and places them in a position where they may decide how effective that regulation can be.

This means that in time they also help select who regulates them. For the Congressmen who survive on the oversight committees are those best able to accumulate intelligence expertise. They cannot acquire this knowledge without cooperation from the intelligence agencies, and they cannot obtain that cooperation without holding views these agencies find compatible. As vacancies on these committees occur, freshman Congressmen appointed to them are carefully vetted by their senior members to ensure that their views are also compatible.

Increasingly, then, the intelligence oversight committees become merely an extension of the intelligence establishment itself. Even in 1976, at the outset of calls for intelligence reform, one of the original committees investigating intelligence, chaired by Representative Otis Pike, already felt itself to be so much a part of that establishment that it began investigating *itself* to determine how it had leaked classified portions of its report to CBS correspondent Daniel Schorr.

While Congress has done little to bring the intelligence community under effective control, it has done much to further immunize it from public accountability, expanding its power to hide its activities and punish those who expose them, limiting its liabilities for exceeding the law, and reducing the rights of those it investigates and prosecutes.

The Foreign Intelligence Surveillance and Agent Identities Protection Acts were passed by both Houses of Congress and have become law. Additional measures passed by a Senate currently controlled by the party in power, and pending approval in the House of Representatives, include institution of the death penalty for those convicted of "terrorism" and "espionage," denial of bail to those whom Federal judges deem a "danger to the community," elimination of parole for those under Federal sentence, restricted use of the insanity defense, and the admissibility in Federal criminal trials of evidence obtained in violation of the Fourth Amendment, whenever investigators state they had "reasonable good faith" they were not violating it.

While some of these provisions might discourage genuine acts of terrorism and espionage among the very few inclined to them, they could also serve as a powerful inhibition against dissent among the growing numbers of those critical of official policies, who fear they may come under investigation ostensibly on the suspicion of "terrorist activities."

Not only have the intelligence agencies circumvented Congressional oversight. They have intimidated the press. This required more than persuading the press that its probes into intelligence were unwarranted and dangerous. Its attitudes and procedures had to be challenged too.

The press was warned against advocacy journalism. Whenever it expressed its views, the possible role of its own convictions in forming them was ignored. Thus, any positions it took on policy issues could always be ascribed to outside influence, and thereby held damaging to its credibility. It was urged to resist such influence. Its credibility suffered, however, only when the positions it took were opposed to official policy. It was not urged to resist influence from groups supporting official policy.

Criticism of official policy was held to be the mark of an adversary press. An adversary attitude was never acknowledged to be the possible consequence of official actions. It was attributed entirely to prejudice. This prejudice was formed, again, by outside influence. Officials accused the press of holding an adversary point of view every time they prepared to do something which might inspire it.

A responsible press was said to be even-handed, reporting every position on an issue without taking one of its own. Its credibility was said to improve the more its reporting remained objective. This meant never allowing opinion to shape its presentation of the facts—even though certain facts unavoidably led to conclusions which formed opinions which did shape the presentation of facts, whether they did so consciously or not, and whether they were acknowledged or not.

The press, then, was said to have only one duty. This was to report the facts, and not interpret them so that the public might judge them on its own.

This indoctrination proved beneficial not only for the intelligence community but for government as a whole. It helped coerce many journalists into more favorable treatment of government. Those moved to critical views grew more cautious about expressing them. This automatically gave greater prominence to favorable views. The cult of objectivity produced its desired emphasis on fact, which meant that the opinions no journalist could help but continue to hold were simply disguised as fact. This did not produce a greater abundance of fact for the public to judge. It produced dogma, and a posture of objectivity which made facts far more difficult for the public to find, let alone judge.

Increasingly discouraged from interpreting the news itself, the press looked for other sources whose interpretations it could report. Government quickly became the most generous supplier of these. Whenever government made the news, which it did exactly as often as it liked, choreographing the front pages of almost every newspaper across the nation with official announcements of its policy decisions, it also provided its own interpretations of that news. Naturally, these were considered more authoritative than conflicting interpretations. Consequently, the latter were given a minimum of attention.

In this way, official interpretations became the predominant explanation of official policy, and of the events and conditions throughout the world which policy addressed. In effect, official interpretations *became* the news.

As the press became a more reliable medium for disseminating official views with little challenge, government could begin to use it to convey less popular views. These were best left unexplained even in its own words. It could do this by taking actions which had no other purpose but symbolic gesture, and whose meaning was implicitly clear. This is what the Reagan administration did by selecting individuals well-known for believing that certain functions of government were worthless—for example protection of the environment and of human rights, and then placing them in charge of these functions.

In the same way, after former FBI officials W. Mark Felt and Edward S. Miller were convicted of repeatedly approving forced entries into homes without warrants in their agency's search for radicals in the early 1970s, President Reagan extended an unconditional pardon to both. After journalist Seymour Hersh released his exhaustive documentation of Henry Kissinger's repeated abuses of power throughout his tenure in government, President Reagan swiftly placed him in office again, appointing him chairman of his commission on Latin America. Only 48 hours after 243 American Marines were killed by a terrorist attack in Beirut, President Reagan ordered an invasion of Grenada. This demonstrated only that America could fight and win, regardless of whether in this case it deserved to win, and without any evidence that it had been at all necessary to fight.

By duly reporting these actions with little challenge to the official interpretations accompanying them, the press left the impression that the government had general approval for them, and was acting under a broad mandate, when in fact it had never even sought to determine whether it had one. That is how the press can be used by government as an instrument of propaganda, in an attempt to affect the national consensus by creating the illusion of a consensus that does not exist.

It was the CIA which first recognized the full potential of domestic propaganda, and understood that it could be used in subverting national power no less effectively at home than abroad. As long ago as 1942, the agency's primary mentor William J. Donovan, then director of our wartime Office of Strategic Services, told President Roosevelt that "the use of propaganda is the arrow of initial penetration in conditioning and preparing the people."

Even as it uses the press to reflect a false consensus, government accuses it of failing to represent the mainstream of opinion. Of course, this accusation is fair. America's "mainstream" media, for example, have consistently refused, because government has, to pay serious attention to the need for a nuclear weapons freeze, even though an overwhelming preponderance of qualified scientific opinion has persuaded the public that this is the most urgent issue the nation faces, and as a result 85 percent of the public wants a freeze. There is now an immense majority in this country opposed to official policy on the single issue most affecting it. Yet most of the press, by ignoring the authority with which that majority speaks, has ignored the implications this conflict holds for the durability of democracy.

Keeping the press on the defensive, government tells it that it represents only a minority view, as though that minority were not government itself and the elite it serves. It announces that the public is dissatisfied with the press, as though it were dissatisfied because the press is too critical of government, when it is not critical enough. The public is told it no longer trusts the press, though a poll conducted by the *Washington Post* found that when press and government contradict each other, 57 percent of the public trusts the press and only 17 percent trust the government.

Nevertheless, a distrust the public does not feel for the press has now been claimed by a government it does distrust to justify banning the press from observing the first stage of its invasion of Grenada. The government claims a majority of the public approved of this ban. But 75 percent of the membership of Common Cause did not approve it. The government has provided no proof of the consensus it claims in its favor. Yet the same press which might have found evidence to prove this invasion was wholly unwarranted, had it not been prevented from doing so, now dutifully reports the government's claim of wide public support for this censorship without challenging that claim. The myth of consensus survives even when the press is its own victim.

All this abuse and manipulation could not be expected entirely to preempt criticism from some journalists who were not intimidated by it, and who might continue to report information which challenged official views. Greater control had to be imposed over their activities, and stronger measures threatened against them. Reporters who refused to give favorable treatment to their official sources could simply be denied further access to them, and placed at a serious disadvantage in the competition for news. A broadcasting company which permitted too much criticism of government or the corporate establishment could be threatened with suspension of its Federal broadcast license. Newspaper editors could be instructed not to publish stories or pursue lines of investigation or encourage attitudes which conflicted with the interests of management or ownership.

Increasingly, individual news organizations have come under common ownership, and under the influence of that same establishment. In a 1980 survey by the American Society of Newspaper Editors, 33 percent of the editors working for newspaper chains reported they would not feel free to run a story damaging to their parent firm.

Twenty corporations now control more than half of the 61 million daily newspapers sold in America each day. Twenty control more than half the revenues of the nation's 11,000 magazines. Three control most of its television revenues. Increasingly, these corporations share common directorship. A corporation's directors are legally and morally bound to act in its best interests. Those serving on the boards of two companies at once must do their best to ensure that the policies of both remain compatible. The resulting channels of coordinated influence have been the most effective, and best hidden, means of subverting the democratic process our society has yet devised.

A Senate subcommittee report identifying interlocking directorates among the 130 largest corporations in America showed, for example, that between 1976 and 1979 six of eleven directors on the board of the *New York Times* served on the boards of 34 other corporations, including two major defense contractors and twelve major financial institutions, and that its interlocking directorates with only eight of those corporations provided the *Times* with 511 indirect interlocks with other firms, including 61 interlocks with 33 major defense contractors. It should not be surprising if those firms were exempted in this newspaper's coverage of Pentagon waste.

Reporters who ignore the tastes their editors form in response to the preferences management imposes, and who do not adopt the assumptions which give primacy to official views and constraints, are simply dismissed. Daniel Schorr lost his job for providing information from the Pike Committee's report on intelligence to *The Village Voice*, though none of it proved remotely damaging to the nation's security.

If these controls do not suffice, and the press cannot be silenced by official restraints imposed through the courts, it can still be threatened with legal action from the private sector. So it has been.

In 1982, General William Westmoreland brought suit for $120 million against CBS for alleging in its documentary "The Uncounted Enemy: A Vietnam Deception" that when he was commander of American forces in Vietnam he had arranged to "cook the figures" to underreport enemy troop strength to show he was winning the war. A Federal court decision requiring CBS to make available to the plaintiff a confidential internal study the network undertook to determine whether its documentary had violated its own journalistic standards may discourage news organizations from embarking on such self-inquiry in the future, needed though it be to maintain high standards of fairness and accuracy, and may also discourage them from pursuing controversial subjects, important though such efforts are to the public's right to know the truth about them.

In 1977, Colonel Anthony Herbert brought suit for $44 million against CBS and the producer and reporter of its *60 Minutes* report "The Selling of Colonel Herbert," charging defamation. The Supreme Court ruled in this case that the plaintiff had the right not only to examine CBS notes and files, but even to inquire into "the thoughts, opinions and conclusions" of its journalists as they prepared their story, to determine whether "actual malice" had been involved in its preparation, even though it was neither those thoughts nor any preparatory materials, but only the words finally broadcast, on which the claim of libel had to be based. The threat to penalize the press for its thoughts is an attempt to control its thoughts. This ruling has not been reversed.

In 1975, David Atlee Phillips, who had been a director of the CIA's Western Hemisphere Division, announced his "retirement" from the agency to form the Association of Former Intelligence Officers, whose 2,000 members later formed Challenge, a legal action fund to sponsor suits specifically against journalists and the authors of books and articles which "alleged" the misdeeds of intelligence agents. Former CIA director William Colby had once called Phillips a "fine *psychological* warrior" (emphasis added).

What the CIA has always done best has been to collect and analyze information. This is the function its original charter intended. It is the function the nation most needs it to serve, though the Executive Branch has not always made the best use of it. The CIA's "failure" to predict the rise of Moslem fundamentalism in Iran in 1979 was a failure by the Executive Branch to encourage the agency to tell what it knew. Instead, it told a President heavily committed to preserving the dying regime of the Shah what it knew he wanted to hear.

This is only one indication that the CIA is not quite the "rogue" organization some of its critics assume it to be. That assumption has been encouraged not only by the CIA but by the Executive Branch itself. For if the CIA has placed itself beyond the control of the public, Congress, the courts and the press, only the Executive Branch remains to exert control over it. If Presidents can claim they have no control over the CIA, then they may insist they cannot be held responsible for what it does. This is no less convenient than the CIA's own assertion that it cannot be held responsible for the actions of agents it claims it no longer employs.

Certainly, the CIA has acted without the approval of Presidents. But far more often, it has done their exact bidding. Victor Marchetti, a former executive assistant to the Deputy Director of the CIA, repeatedly documents in his book how Presidents "are always aware of, generally approve of, and often actually initiate the CIA's major undertakings." The agency has simply become a covert arm of national policy, because those in power continue to believe, against all the best evidence, that it can accomplish what diplomacy cannot do. Its activities are covert not so that they may be plausibly denied to our adversaries abroad, from whom hardly anything has ever been kept hidden, but so they may be denied to the American public, and Presidential accountability for them avoided.

Control over the CIA, then, will not come from the Executive Branch. It will only come from the public. The public can only build its case by assembling the record of facts. This is the same record the CIA has tried to make Congress ignore and the public forget, which it has tried to force its agents to keep hidden, which it has sought the help of the courts in removing from the public domain, and which it has done all it could to discourage the press from retrieving and continuing to build. By restoring a significant portion of it, Darrell Garwood has performed a public service.

It is only with this record that we may resume a debate the CIA would rather we never had: the debate over whether a democracy of the kind we presumably want can support an agency of the kind the CIA has turned out to be, and whether some means can be found to limit its role to the work we need it to do, while ensuring that the work it does strengthens rather than corrupts democratic institutions.

—Tom Gervasi
April 1983

NOTES

page

17 1. Executive Order #12333 of 1981.
17 2. Executive Order #11905 of 1976, and Executive Order #12036 of 1978.
17 /3. Executive Order #12333 of 1981, Section 2.6.
20/4. Executive Order #12333 of 1981, Section 2.6.
20/5. Executive Order #12333 of 1981, Section 2.5.
21/6. Title 18, United States Criminal Code, Sections 2511, 2236, 2071, 1708, 1702, 1001, 1503, 371 and 241 respectively.
22/7. Authority to protect CIA sources and methods is provided by 50 U.S.C. Secs. 403(D)(3) and 403 (g). Additional authority to classify information on national security and related grounds is currently established by a variety of laws, including the Espionage Statutes of 1917, 18 U.S.C. Secs. 792–798 and 952, and 50 U.S.C. Append. Sec. 781; the Atomic Energy Act of 1954, 42 U.S.C. Secs. 2162 and 2271–2281; exemptions (b)(1), (b)(2), (b)(5) and (b)(7) of the Freedom of Information Act, 5 U.S.C. Sec. 552, enacted by Congress in 1974 as amendments to the Act; P.L. 86–36 of May 29, 1959, protecting cryptographic activities and communications of the National Security Agency; 18 U.S.C. Sec. 798 protecting communications intelligence; and Executive Order #12356 on National Security Information, signed April 2, 1982 and effective August 1, 1982, which provides the basic framework safeguarding classified data and governing its release.
22/8. Executive Order #12356 of 1982.
22/9. Executive Order #12065 of 1978.
23/10. *United States v. The Progressive, Inc.*, 467 F. Supp. 990, N.D. Wisconsin, 1979, and 79-C–98, W.D. Wisconsin, 1979.
24/11. Executive Order #12356 of 1982, Section 1–602.
24/12. Pub. L. 97–200 of June 10, 1982, Section 601(c).
13. *New York Times v. United States*, 403 U.S. 713, 1971 and *United States v. Russo & Ellsberg*, 9373-WMB-CD, California, 1972. Due to "improper Government conduct" in the investigations of Ellsberg and Russo, including forced entry without a warrant into

the office of Ellsberg's psychiatrist, a Federal judge dismissed all charges against the two.

33/14. *United States v. Marchetti,* 466 F. 2d 1309 (4th Circuit, 1972) cert. denied, 409 U.S. 1063 (1972) and *Alfred A. Knopf, Inc. v. Colby,* 509 F. 2d 1362 (4th Circuit, 1975) cert. denied, 421 U.S. 992 (1975) 540–73-A (E.D. Va., 1980).

15. *Near v. Minnesota,* 283 U.S. 697, 716 (1931), *New York Times Company v. Sullivan,* 376 U.S. 254, 270 (1964), *Caldwell v. United States,* 434 F. 2d 1081, 1084–1085 (9th Circuit, 1970), and *United States v. Robel,* 389 U.S. 258, 263–264 (1967).

16. *Garrity v. New Jersey,* 385 U.S. 493 (1967), *Gardner v. Broderick,* 392 U.S. 273 (1968), *Pickering v. Board of Education,* 391 U.S. 563 (1968), and *Cole v. Richardson,* No. 70–16 (1972).

35/17. *Snepp v. United States,* 444 U.S. 507 (1980), 78–1871 and 79–265, 48 U.S.L.W. 3527 (1980).

35/18. *United States v. Stockwell,* 80–207-A (E.D. Virginia, 1980).

35/19. *McGehee v. Turner,* 78–2407 (D.D.C., 1980).

36/20. National Security Decision Directive #84 on Safeguarding National Security Information, March 11, 1983, Sections 1(a), 1(b) and 5.

FOREWORD

It seems to me the present crisis in international affairs exists not only because the CIA has largely succeeded in undermining this country's once-treasured integrity, but also, and no doubt mainly because the consequences of CIA activity can be anything up to and including the extinction of civilization, if not of the human race and perhaps all life on earth.

Consequently, although the CIA has participated with other agencies in domestic spying, drug experiments, and other illegal activities on the home front, I have been chiefly interested here in its shaping and especially its frustrating of American foreign policy. These latter aspects have seemed to me to be unique both in American history and internationally, there being no record, at any time, either at home or abroad, of any other intelligence agency that consistently pursued a foreign policy differing from and sometimes diametrically opposite to that of the government it was representing.

I have also been interested in setting forth the attitudes and practices which have permitted such an anomaly to exist in our government for two generations, and in considering whether the contradiction is bound to continue. Admiral Stansfield Turner, the Carter administration's nominee and no doubt one of the better CIA directors, promised soon after taking office to "do the indecent things as decently as possible" and to "maintain a floor of decency beyond which we will not go." But since he clearly remained convinced that indecency served the national interest, and since to him and his like-minded successors, indecency was therefore bound to seem a patriotic act, it was difficult to avoid a conclusion that we were in for more rounds of approximately the same thing.

There were of course those who claimed "solid achievements" for the CIA, but in my opinion these could not be demonstrated—they could only be alleged in general terms. As far as specifics went, even after a quarter of a century the "solid achievements" most often cited were the agency's overthrow of left-leaning governments in Iran and Guatemala in the early 1950s. In view of Iran's early and later roles in the energy crisis that afflicted us, as well as the hostage situation and Iran's present virulent anti-American stance, and in view of Guatemala's suggesting by example and aiding the Bay of Pigs—all subjects to be dealt with in this book—the reader is invited to consider whether those actions really benefited the United States.

While some curtailing of the covert activities and de-emphasizing of secrecy in minor respects could be applauded, and despite recurring claims to the contrary, no real improvement in the basic intelligence situation has been effected or planned. Instead, surfacing at every opportunity, a campaign is persistently under way to "unleash the CIA" by lifting the few moderating restrictions that theoretically have been imposed on the agency. There is no reason why this country could not have a civilian intelligence agency that would be both effective and respected, but that would require a clearing of the decks and we are far from being on course toward achieving such a goal.

Those inclined to accept the CIA's oft-repeated claim that its misdeeds have been committed on orders from the White House will find support for that thesis in Harry Rositzke's book, *The CIA's Secret Operations* (Readers Digest, 1977), but they should note that in a rare case indeed Arthur M. Schlesinger, Jr., took issue with its author on that point in his otherwise laudatory introduction to the book.

Schlesinger, incidentally, was with the Office of Strategic Services (OSS), the CIA's predecessor, during World War II, and could be said to have strong sentimental ties to the agency. He was and is, however, primarily one of the century's leading historians, and of a stature entitling him if it did not compel him, even in somewhat embarrassing circumstances, to protect readers from a major misconception.

Schlesinger wrote:

> While there is some truth in this I think [Harry Rositzke] pushes the idea of an innocent and obedient CIA, acting only on "express" presidential instruction and authorization, a good deal too far. The record, as I read it, indicates that the Agency acted on its own in a diversity of ways, some of very considerable importance. The Senate Select Committee on Intelligence Activities (the Church Committee) could uncover no specific evidence, for example, that any President ordered the assassination of Castro or even knew about it (the plotting). John McCone, as head of the CIA, was never told of the Castro assassination projects until, two years after he took the post, he read in a newspaper that the Agency had a relationship with a Chicago gangster. Even then he was given to understand that the projects had been terminated, though in fact they were continuing. The manifestly illegal CIA program of mail intercepts ran from 1953 to 1973 during the terms of four Presidents; but "no evidence could be found," according to the Rockefeller Commission, "that any briefing of any President ever occurred." Even the CIA Inspector General, the Rockefeller Commission reported, "was sometimes refused access to particularly sensitive CIA activities."

Each of the points cogently made by Schlesinger in the above will be doubly or triply backed up by illustrative events applicable to them in the accounts to follow.

PART ONE

The CIA Abroad

The Choleric Words

1

On August 18, 1960, at a meeting of the National Security Council with twenty-one persons including observers and staff members present, President Eisenhower angrily called for straightforward action to "dispose of" Patrice Lumumba, who had been unseated as head of the Congolese government but remained a potential pro-Soviet threat.

A great deal of controversy would swirl around the words "dispose of" fifteen years later when the assassination attempts directed against foreign leaders by the Central Intelligence Agency came under investigation by the Senate intelligence committee.

What did the president mean? Only one survivor from among those present fifteen years before told the later investigators the president's words sounded to him like an order to assassinate Lumumba, and even he had had later doubts about what he had heard.

John Eisenhower, who was a member of his father's staff and was present at the earlier meeting, testified that he certainly would not conclude that "dispose of" meant to assassinate "if only because if I had something as nasty as that to plot I wouldn't do it in front of twenty-one people."

All of the survivors from among those at the 1960 meeting agreed that there was no discussion of the remark and no attempt to determine what the President meant.

In the wake of Watergate, the public was treated to a

series of shocking revelations beginning with the report by Seymour Hersh in the *New York Times* disclosing massive CIA surveillance of American dissidents during the Johnson and Nixon eras. In what some believed to be an attempt to stave off a full-fledged inquiry, President Ford appointed a "blue ribbon" panel led by Vice President Nelson Rockefeller to look into the CIA's past pecadillos. The Rockefeller Report, published in 1975, discussed a number of CIA abuses, but the Senate Select Committee on Intelligence, chaired by Frank Church, came out with its own findings after probing certain areas which had been covered up by the Rockefeller Commission, such as the CIA's assassination plots against foreign leaders.

The Senate intelligence committee itself, in the course of its shelf-length series of reports, did go so far at one point as to say:

> The chain of events revealed in the documents and testimony is strong enough to permit a reasonable inference that the plot to assassinate Lumumba was authorized by President Eisenhower.

But when John Eisenhower and a long list of others vigorously protested that assertion, the committee, while declining to disavow its statement, pointed out that it also said:

> There is enough countervailing testimony ... and enough ambiguity and lack of clarity in the records ... to preclude a finding that the president intended an assassination effort against Lumumba.

Since the two statements effectively canceled each other out, Eisenhower could be said to have gotten a fifty-fifty break from the committee, and both readers and writers were left to draw their own conclusions. Eisenhower was generally regarded as a man of good character (the Lumumba affair came toward the end of his second term), and many observers felt that the so-called "reasonable inference" that with a couple of choleric words he had intended to order an assassination in the circumstances described was not at all reasonable. But there was enough evidence on the other side to keep a controversy going.

Former CIA Director Allen Dulles, whose activities were the principal ones involved in the Senate investigation, was not among those who survived to take part in later probes; but based on the record unearthed in 1975 he could not have had any doubts about the president's meaning.

The record showed that immediately after the meeting in which Eisenhower uttered the words "dispose of," Dulles authorized $100,000 for a full-scale assassination attempt against Lumumba. In so doing he illustrated one of the security system's major entrapments.

Although apparently convinced that he was operating under a presidential order, Dulles could not inform the president of this fact because that would violate the doctrine of "plausible deniability." Former Undersecretary of State Douglas Dillon testified that Dulles "felt very strongly that we should not involve the president in things of this nature."

Consequently, in an action crucial to the reputation of the country and its government, Eisenhower and others at the White House never heard one word about the matter.

"Plausible deniability" could be regarded as one of the most wretched theories ever invented. Its application here was based on the idea that in an unholy venture a president could be kept so isolated from events that when exposure came he could truthfully emerge as shiningly blameless. In practice, whether he deserved it or not, a president almost always had to take the blame for whatever happened.

But the doctrine effectively prevented the president from correcting a wrong impression, if he had left one. He also was given no chance to have anything to say about how an order should be carried out, if in fact one was involved.

As his first step Dulles set up an "eyes only" channel to Leopoldville, with the code word "prop" designated to mean that the message could be read only by its receiver. Even over this channel he could not say exactly what he meant, but he told Leopoldville Station Chief Lawrence Devlin (to whom the Senate committee gave the pseudonym "Victor Hedgman") that "we wish to give you every possible support in eliminating Lumumba from any possibility of resuming governmental position."

Devlin was authorized, and by implication urged, to spend all of the $100,000 "to carry out any crash programs on which you do not have an opportunity to consult headquarters."

"To the extent that the ambassador may wish to be consulted you should seek his concurrence," said Dulles. "If in any particular case he does not wish to be consulted you can act on your own authority where time does not permit reference here."

This was all very mysterious, raising among other things a question as to how a person would know that the ambassador did not wish to be consulted without in some way consulting him. Former CIA Deputy Director of Plans Richard Bissell testified that the Dulles cables constituted a "circumlocutious" assassination order.

Any doubts entertained by Station Chief Devlin about what he was supposed to do were soon settled by the arrival in Leopoldville of a CIA scientist to whom the Senate committee gave the pseudonym "Joseph Schieder." He was identified in the press as Dr. Sidney Gottlieb, of the agency's Technical Services Division. To Devlin's growing consternation, since never in his training had he heard of the possibility of such a presidential action, Gottlieb told him the president himself had ordered the director to kill Lumumba.

The scientist then produced rubber gloves, a gauze mask, and a hypodermic needle or syringe for handling some "pretty dangerous material" containing a deadly virus obtained from the army's biological warfare section at Fort Dietrich, Maryland. He said the material should be placed on or in "anything Lumumba might get into his mouth, whether food or a toothbrush."

The idea as concocted at headquarters of placing a deadly virus on Lumumba's toothbrush later seemed so bizarre that when the details came out they provided quite a few laughs both inside and outside the CIA.

The situation was becoming more and more confused and incredible. Its extraordinary features included: (1) a director under the impression that he was both carrying out a presidential order and protecting the president by not letting him know of the fact; (2) a prospective victim who was already out of office and with no prospects anyone knew of for regaining power; and (3) an odd twist when Lumumba placed himself under the protection of the United Nations Peacekeeping Force in the Congo— thereby involving the United States, as a member of the UN, in efforts to *protect* the same man they were attempting to *assassinate*.

The effort against Lumumba also included the CIA's first recorded use of known criminals. One was code-named "QJ/WIN" and described as "a man of few scruples, capable of assassination." The other, code-named "WI/ROGUE," was denominated "an essentially stateless soldier of fortune, a forger and former bank robber." These gentry accomplished nothing that became known in the Congo, but they furnished precedents for later extensive efforts involving crime figures against Castro in Cuba.

Devlin had placed the deadly virus in his safe, and had asked for and received confirmation from headquarters that he was supposed to follow Gottlieb's instructions. But he sensibly never found occasion to make use of the virus. The standard account is that before Devlin could do anything further, Lumumba fled from protective custody and was killed by his Congo enemies.

However, on page 105 of John Stockwell's book *In Search of Enemies* (Norton, 1978), there is a brief mention of a somewhat eccentric CIA agent claiming he had some trouble disposing of Lumumba's body. If the body was delivered to the agency it could only have been for the collection of a reward. Even without the Stockwell mention, it would be hard to believe that the CIA people neglected to offer a reward, since they were under great pressure to do everything possible to eliminate Lumumba and to spend a huge sum of money in the process. So perhaps the CIA did have a large hand in Lumumba's death after all.

United Nations investigators, though denied access to the Congo, were able to establish that Lumumba was murdered in the most brutal fashion a month before his death was announced. Since the announcement was issued on February 13, 1961, he could have died shortly before Eisenhower left office. Ten years later the Congolese government commissioned a monument somewhat taller than the Washington obelisk for Lumumba, his name meanwhile having been conferred on Moscow's leading university. The news concerning the monument emphasized dramatically the shortsighted nature of the CIA's performance in this instance, but it rated only one small paragraph deep inside the *New York Times*.

Although blunt in other respects, the Senate intelligence committee in 1975 showed a delicacy concerning an attempt on the life of Chinese premier Zhou Enlai that served to obscure for several more years what was probably the CIA's first and most important attempt to assassinate a foreign leader. The operation against Lumumba was the first for which a presidential authorization was claimed, and it would become the first to be officially documented by Senate investigators, but it was not the venture of this kind that was freighted with the most towering implications for the future of the country and the world.

Certainly Zhou Enlai was the most important individual ever known to have been included on the CIA's hit list. Yet the Senate committee's November 1975 interim report, *Alleged Assassination Plots Involving Foreign Leaders*, contained no mention of Zhou's case. Chiefly, no doubt, this was because of the loss of fifteen innocent lives in the operation, but also perhaps because Zhou was still alive and in very recent years had made important gestures of friendship toward the United States.

The committee's final report the following spring, after Zhou had died in January 1976, did contain a reference to the attempt on his life, but it was deeply buried in a fat volume and Zhou was identified only as "an East Asian leader." Even there and in that form the reference appeared to have been entered mainly for the purpose of including the CIA's obviously hoked-up denial of its part in the affair.

But despite the committee's reticence, the truth gradually came out. William R. Corson, in *The Armies of Ignorance* (Dial/James Wade, 1977, pages 365–6), made a major contribution to the subject by describing the first phase of the attempt on Zhou's life. According to Corson, Zhou was to be slipped a bowl of poisoned rice at the Bandung Conference in Indonesia, which was scheduled to unite the efforts of the then pro-Soviet forces of Africa and Asia in 1955. That was new information, and it established what would have been incredible had not Corson proceeded to nail down the facts beyond any possibility of doubt. Even Zhou, with all his historical importance and prestige, the No. 2 leader of a billion people half a world away, was not safe from the long reach of the CIA's assassination plots.

Corson said the poisoned rice was to have been served to Zhou at the final banquet of the Bandung Conference, and that the poison was to have been undetectable and devilishly concocted so that it would not take effect until forty-eight hours later, after Zhou had returned to Peking. Corson then revealed that this plan was canceled when a member of the CIA's staff with ties to the White House—General Lucien Truscott—delivered a report to Dulles in a way and under circumstances which Corson said indicated that the president would be informed if the plotting continued. This eliminated any possibility of pretense that presidential approval had been sought or received for the outrageous undertaking.

Yet even Corson's account is not entirely complete, because as usual in such cases the CIA had not given up when its first plan was canceled. The strongest possible circumstantial evidence, overwhelming in the light of subsequent discoveries, later left no room for doubt that the agency, working through the Chinese Nationalists, had used a time bomb to blow up and send crashing into the Pacific the Air India passenger plane on which Zhou was scheduled to fly to the Bandung Conference. This was how fifteen innocent people died in connection with the operation. All passengers went down with the plane, although three crew members managed to survive.

Original Chinese charges that the CIA had perpetrated this deed were labeled "vicious nonsense" by the *New York Times*. Hardly suspecting a possible monster in our own midst, the *Times* went on to say that the charges "illustrate the type of mentality and morality with which we are dealing in the case of Red China."

But an Indonesian commission appointed to investigate the plane crash was able to produce absolute proof, from watery wreckage recovered off Sarawak. It was the time bomb's clockwork detonating mechanism, the parts of which were embedded in one wing.

Then the Chinese Nationalists refused to extradite a man who was known to have been standing near the wing where the time bomb was ingeniously inserted or affixed when the plane stopped at Hong Kong, and who was reported by the British colonial government there to have boasted on four separate occasions that he was paid the equivalent of $105,600 to plant the bomb.

All of this information was from original newspaper dispatches, current with the events to which they referred and indexed by the *New York Times*. Later accounts, perhaps less trustworthy, said the bomb was carried aboard the plane, rather than planted on or in one wing, and some said the plane went down with the loss of all on board, obviously in error since the surviving crew members were still visible on the scene.

Since the second attempt on Zhou's life bore some resemblances to the Soviet action in shooting down South Korean jetliner flight 7 in 1983, it is interesting to consider whether a more balanced treatment of that incident would have been achieved had the Senate committee published the facts concerning the Air India passenger plane on which Zhou was supposed to be flying. If such facts had been readily available for comparative purposes, which they were not (the account offered here, twenty-nine years after the event, being the first attempt to make a record of the available information on the subject), an entirely different impression might have emerged.

Unlike the Soviet action which was in response to an invasion of its air space, the attempt against Zhou involved months of ice-cold planning which must have included in its calculations the passengers scheduled to plunge to their deaths with him. The Hong Kong police, who provided the basis for the rejected extradition request, called it "carefully planned mass murder," and even that seemed an understatement. By 1983, when President Reagan led the nation and half the world in condemning the Soviet Union for downing the South Korean jetliner, the Zhou assassination attempt appeared to have totally faded from public memory.

The reasoning behind the assassination attempt was clear enough. Although this proved to be an illusion—in a piece of historical irony the movement turned out to be massively in the opposite direction—the impression at the time was that Africa and Asia were organizing for service in Moscow's cause. Zhou, with a good European education acquired in Paris, with twenty-five years of experience as Mao Tse-tung's right-hand man in the Chinese revolution, and with the kind of razor-sharp mind and polished delivery needed to make political negotiations a success, was pivotal to the entire undertaking. If anything could have completely disrupted the Bandung Conference program the loss of Zhou Enlai would have been the event most likely to achieve it.

The supreme irony at the time was that Zhou was not aboard when the time bomb so efficiently hurled the Air India passenger plane into the sea as it approached Sarawak. A last-minute decision to meet with President Gamal Abdel Nasser of Egypt at Rangoon, Burma, on their way to the Bandung Conference, saved the Chinese premier's life. He lived another twenty years in the same office as premier. During that period, more so than Mao, he was by common report the most beloved as well as the most rational of the Chinese leaders.

If he thought of America's attempt to assassinate him as he neared the end of his career, Zhou must have decided that was not relevant to current problems. President Nixon went to Peking in 1972 at Zhou's personal invitation and achieved a normalization of Sino-American diplomatic relations as a result. It was an important factor—if not the most important—in Nixon's re-election.

During a brief period following the failure of the Bay of Pigs invasion of Cuba in 1961, those who had been apprehensive concerning the powers and practices of the Central Intelligence Agency could feel that at least a long step had been taken toward reforming the agency into something more consistent with the principles of democracy.

President Kennedy had appointed a four-man investigating team headed by General Maxwell D. Taylor, former Army Chief of Staff, and it was understood that the team's recommendations would substantially cut back the CIA's potential for illegal military operations. The other investigators were Allen Dulles, who was being kept on as CIA director for a decent interval and in effect was investigating himself before leaving office; Admiral Arleigh A. Burke, Chief of Naval Operations; and Attorney General Robert F. Kennedy.

As reported by David Wise and Thomas B. Ross for their book, *The Invisible Government* (Random House, 1964), the main question before the investigators was whether "special operations" such as the Cuban invasion should be removed from the CIA's jurisdiction. Wise and Ross wrote:

> Dulles pleaded that contrary to popular belief no intelligence agency in the world was split into separate informational and operational units. When the British set up a Special

Operations Executive during World War II he maintained that they ran into serious trouble and had to revert to a CIA-type system. These pleadings proved persuasive to the Taylor committee, which declined to recommend that all clandestine activities be divorced from the CIA's responsibilities. The president agreed and the CIA continued to function in essentially its old ways.

In fact, the argument that swayed the investigators—that the CIA was like other Western intelligence agencies such as the British—turned out to be spurious. In *Philby: The Long Road to Moscow* (Simon and Schuster, 1975) the two British authors Patrick Seale and Maureen McConville wrote:

> There are some countries, notably America, in which the intelligence community has a direct hand in making national policy, but Britain is not among them. Her secret service . . . is firmly under the thumb of the Foreign Office, a servant of the Foreign Secretary.

The bureaucratic status of British intelligence thus was the same as that of the American State Department's highly respected Bureau of Intelligence and Research, and bore no resemblance whatever to the CIA's sweeping jurisdiction and almost unheard-of independent authority and hidden financing.

Wise and Ross continued:

> However, the Taylor group did come to the conclusion that the Bay of Pigs was too large and too unwieldy to have been conducted by the CIA. In the future the CIA was to be limited to military equipment no larger or more complex than side arms—weapons that could be carried by individuals. In other words, the CIA was never again to direct operations involving aircraft, tanks and amphibious ships. Operations of that size were to be conducted by the Pentagon. . . . Put another way, the CIA henceforth was to be restricted to operations which were "plausibly deniable." The Bay of Pigs

was not plausibly deniable because it was too large and pervasive. . . .

These statements, highly reassuring except for the investigators' unabashed suggestion that the difference between right and wrong lay in whether or not you got caught, had barely found their way into print when an event was described in the *New York Times* as follows:

At the Ituri River eight miles south of Nia Nia in the northeast Congo, a government column of eight hundred Congolese troops and one hundred white mercenaries had been ambushed by a rebel force and was under heavy fire. Suddenly three B–26 bombers skimmed over the rain forest and bombed and strafed a path through the rebel ranks for the forces supported by the United States. At the controls of the American-made planes were anti-Castro Cubans, veterans of the Bay of Pigs invasion three years before.

The *Times* said that the pilots had been recruited by a purportedly private CIA company in Miami, and that their planes were serviced by European mechanics solicited through London newspaper advertisements. The article continued:

Guiding them into action were American "diplomats" and other apparently civilian officials. The sponsor, director and paymaster of them all, however, was the Central Intelligence Agency with headquarters in Langley, Virginia. Its rapid and effective provision of an instant Air Force in the Congo was the climax of the agency's deep involvement there.

The CIA was maintaining a "miniature war department" in the Congo (later Zaire) at Leopoldville (later Kinshasa), said the *Times*. No doubt repeating assurances readily given, the newspaper added:

This was not to compete with the real United States embassy and its military attachés but to apply the secret or at least discreet capacities of the CIA to a seething contest among many conflicting forces.

This was more than three years after Lumumba's death, but his partisans were still active in the field. Earlier in the same year at the Ituri river final engagement they had captured Stanleyville. In summarizing the matter, the *Times* dispatch credited the CIA with a "major role" in establishing Cyrille Adoula as the successor of Lumumba as head of the Congolese government.

Money and shiny American automobiles, furnished by the logistic wizardry of Langley, are said to have been the deciding factors in the vote that brought Mr. Adoula to power. Russian, Czechoslovak, Egyptian and Ghanian agents were simply outbid where they could not be outmaneuvered.

Civilian bribery, another shadowy CIA province, thus appeared to have been more effective than illegal military operations in the Congo. The latter operations nevertheless were ample enough to demonstrate that despite the Taylor committee's finding, approved by the president, the CIA by one means or another was maintaining its full potential as a more or less secret military force, available for assignments when the missions were insufficiently legitimate, respectable, or justifiable for the regular armed forces.

There was a strong tendency in Washington to think that those in high places must know what was going on, but in the murky areas inhabited by the CIA the absence of information even at the highest levels was sometimes astounding. This was especially true on the subject of assassination.

At a meeting of the National Security Council's special group in mid–1962, when the group had been augmented to include key figures from the Defense and Justice departments, Defense Secretary McNamara remarked that he supposed they should discuss assassination. This was without indicating which side of the issue he would take, and without knowing of the current activities in the field. But the subject was dropped immediately, and by telephone later the same day, for even mentioning it, McNamara was severely taken to task by none other than CIA Director McCone, who was unaware of the assassination program in his own agency. (McCone was not told of the CIA's assassination activities until nearly two years after he took office, and even then was falsely given to understand that the program had been discontinued.)

Author Thomas Powers, on page 7 of his book, *The Man Who Kept the Secrets*, reached the conclusion that the Kennedys ordered the assassination of Castro, but I know of nothing to substantiate that. In the first place the anti-Castro assassination program was under way well before President Kennedy took office.

It was true that in November 1961, JFK told *New York Times* writer Tad Szulc that he was under great pressure to approve an assassination policy, which might have been considered a belated authorization or order, and at least would have been an approval the CIA undoubtedly would have liked to extract from him. Kennedy, however, said he was resisting the pressure, and if he ever had approved an assassination policy the reader may be confident that there were those who would have made sure that we heard about that.

Those two small-time criminals who were attached to the Lumumba assassination team furnished a precedent, but they bore little resemblance to the wealthy and well-known Mafia mobsters, rough-hewn perhaps but also well-heeled, who were recruited for operations against Castro.

The recruitment was through the good offices of Robert A. Maheu, former FBI agent turned private investigator and representative in Washington of billionaire Howard Hughes. Maheu and Mafia mobster John Roselli held their first meeting at the posh Brown Derby in Beverly Hills. Roselli and Mafia figures Sam Giancana and Santo Trafficante were soon ensconced in the Fontainebleau Hotel in Miami.

The Choleric Words · 69

Giancana, using the name "Sam Gold" in his dealings with the CIA, was on the Attorney General's "Ten Most Wanted Criminals" list.[1] Castro was still permitting the Mafia gambling syndicate to operate in Havana, for tourists only, and Trafficante traveled back and forth between Havana and Miami in that connection. The mobsters were authorized to offer a reward of $150,000 for anyone who would kill Castro and were promised any other support the agency could give.

The mobsters considered a gangland-type slaying for Castro but rejected the idea because they could not provide for the assassins' eventual escape from the island. They called for a poison that could be placed in Castro's drink, with the expectation that a lone assassin could make good his escape before the poison took effect. Colonel Sheffield Edwards, the CIA's Director of Security, gave the poison assignment to the agency's Technical Services Division (TSD) and rejected the first batch of pills because they would not dissolve in water. All this was going on through the usual bureaucratic channels in the usual bureaucratic jargon within the United States government.

A second batch of poison pills was accepted by Edwards when they proved soluble in water and "did the job expected of them when tested on monkeys." The test with the unfortunate monkeys was conducted on February 10, 1961, three weeks after the inauguration and one of several dates establishing that this program was well under way before Kennedy took office. Soon afterward the CIA delivered to the mobsters the pills and what Roselli recalled as "a whole lot of money"—$10,000 or more—toward the assassination reward. In a ceremonial transaction at the Fontainebleau, the mobsters in turn delivered the pills and money to a Cuban official who had been accepting surreptitious kickbacks from the gambling syndicate. As Roselli recalled in his testimony, the Cuban was told the pills "could not be used in boiling soups and things like that, but could be used in water or otherwise, but they couldn't last forever. . . . It had to be done as soon as possible."

Thus was launched the first of the CIA's many attempts—twenty-four as counted by Cubans and eight or more according to Senate investigators—to assassinate Castro. CIA records showed that the poison involved in this first attempt was botulinum toxin. At one point Castro was reported ill and the mobsters engaged in mutual congratulations, but nothing really happened and the first project was then called off by the designated assassin himself. A dressed-up version of the escapade was that the Cuban official had lost his position and contact with Castro, but in his testimony Roselli put the matter more bluntly: he said the Cuban official returned the money and pills because he had developed a case of "cold feet."

Even years later when they revealed some of the facts concerning the CIA's assassination attempts, Senate investigators recognized defensively that there would be criticism of these disclosures. "We reject any contention that the facts disclosed in this report should be kept secret because they are embarrassing to the United States," they said, adding: "Despite the temporary injury to our national reputation the committee believes that foreign peoples will respect us more for keeping faith with democratic ideals than they will blame us for the misconduct revealed."

The Senators were still treading softly, however. "Misconduct," with its connotation of childhood pranks, was scarcely an adequate synonym for criminal activity which the committee itself had described as a violation of American principles, international order, and basic morality. Only Senator George McGovern said aggressively:

At some time we must consider the appalling prospect that the CIA was engaged in assassination attempts in Cuba entirely on its own, and perhaps in direct defiance of higher authority. If that is the case we have suffered abuses which a free society simply cannot tolerate. We must spare no effort in learning the full truth, in identifying those responsible and in developing ways to assure that this can never happen again.

Open Skies

2

On July 21, 1955, President Eisenhower stood in one of the hallowed halls of the late-lamented League of Nations in Geneva, Switzerland, to address the first session of a four-power summit meeting. He directed his opening remarks to the entire assemblage, which included large delegations from the four great powers and observers and reporters from all the nations of the world, saying:

> I have been searching my heart and mind for something I could say here that would convince everyone of the great sincerity of the United States in approaching the problem of disarmament.

The American president paused and turned to face the delegation from the Soviet Union, which was headed by Premier Nikolai Bulganin:

> I should address myself for the moment principally to the delegation from the Soviet Union, because our two countries admittedly possess new and terrible weapons in quantities that do give rise in other parts of the world, and reciprocally, to fears and dangers of surprise attack. I propose, therefore, that we take a practical step, that we begin an arrangement, very quickly, as between ourselves—immediately.

The president's unpolished prose strongly suggested that although the subject had long been in his thoughts, he was putting these particular words together for the first time:

> The step would include: first, to give each other complete blueprints of our military establishments, from beginning to end, from one end of the country to the other, lay out the establishments and provide the blueprints to each other. Next, to provide within our countries facilities for aerial photography by the other country—we to provide you with the facilities within our country, ample facilities for aerial reconnaissance, where you can make all the pictures you choose and take them to your own country for study, and you to provide us with the same facilities and we to make these examinations; and by this step to convince the world that we are providing as between ourselves against the possibility of great surprise attack, thus lessening danger and relaxing tensions. This will make more easily attainable a complete and effective system of inspection and disarmament, for what I propose, I assure you, would be but a beginning.

A more facile Soviet delegation leader might have risen with a few politely stalling remarks following Eisenhower's speech, but Bulganin did not respond at all. Nikita Khrushchev, already the boss but silent because he was not yet installed as such, was a sometime admirer of the American president, partly because General Eisenhower did not rush forward and try to take credit for the capture of Berlin after the Russians fought their way into its suburbs in World War II. But when Khrushchev did speak his tone was incredulous, as well it might have been, and he branded Eisenhower's current idea as "pure fantasy."

Washington, meanwhile, had reacted with well-primed promptitude. A Pentagon spokesman said the Joint Chiefs of Staff had made the basic recommendations behind Eisenhower's proposal. Senate Majority Leader Lyndon B. Johnson, recovering from a heart attack at Bethesda Naval Hospital said: "This is the daring, imaginative stroke for which a war-weary world has been waiting."

What the Soviet leaders and a bemused American

public could not know was that the CIA was preparing to carry out America's part with reconnaissance operations over the Soviet Union whether the Russians agreed to them or not. The later famous U–2, which could be described as a jet-powered glider with an eighty-foot wing-spread that was twice the length of the fuselage, made its first flight less than a month after Eisenhower's speech.

It is now possible to conclude that Eisenhower's grand, statesmanlike, and no doubt sincere and quite feasible proposal, which would be realized to an extent but under vastly different and more complicated circumstances through the operation of spy satellites, was being reduced to a level of political and diplomatic one-upmanship commensurate with the CIA's other operations. If we had been considering matters from that standpoint at that time, it should have been an occasion for weeping.

By the following January, in co-operation with the Air Force from which they were permitted to resign, the CIA had assembled pilots, including Francis Gary Powers, for the Soviet overflights. One of the first things Powers learned after his transfer to civilian employment was never to speak of "the CIA," because that made his new mentors wince. They much preferred to speak only of "the government," although they could stand for occasional references to "the agency."

When Powers resigned from the Air Force he and his working wife had a combined income of just over $8,000 a year. In one of the rare cases where the terms of a CIA contract were made public, it was revealed that he was paid $18,000 a year for six months of home training and $30,000 a year as soon as he and his unit of about one hundred men reached Incirlik Air Base near Adana, Turkey. After a series of border reconnaissances, Powers himself made the first flight over Soviet territory in November 1956.

Fourteen years later in his book *Operation Overflight* (Holt, Rinehart and Winston, 1970), Powers still declined to state the maximum altitude for the U–2. When he was shot down in 1960 he told the Russians he was at 68,000 feet, but in his book he said that was not the correct figure—merely close enough to be believed. If widely accepted information was correct, the U–2 of the time was capable of sustained flight at altitudes as great as 90,000 feet, a good 50 percent above other operational military planes, and initially well beyond the range of Soviet anti-aircraft missiles.

Powers's long-delayed book corrected a number of major misconceptions concerning his ill-fated mission of May 1, 1960. One was that, while approval for a series of overflights had been obtained, the White House did not know that a mission was scheduled so close to the Paris Summit Conference which Khrushchev angrily torpedoed sixteen days after Powers was shot down. It turned out that, sweating uncomfortably in his helmet and long-johns, Powers had been kept waiting on the runway an extra twenty minutes while a specific White House clearance such as had never been required before was obtained for that flight.

In view of the National Security Council's unpublicized "Special Group" which sometimes acted together or through a representative on the president's behalf, this did not prove that Eisenhower personally knew of the flight. But together with another circumstance, it ruled out any possibility that the timing of the mission in connection with the Summit Conference had failed to receive thorough consideration at a high level of government.

This second circumstance was that the flight was not one of a series, nor ordinary in any sense. It was the first and only U–2 ever charted completely across the Soviet Union, with a landing scheduled at Bodo, Norway. All other flights had returned to the base of origin. And with one other of a shorter nature, the May 1 mission represented a resumption of the flights after they had been virtually discontinued for twenty-seven months, and after Washington was well aware that Soviet radar was spotting and tracking the U–2s whenever they set forth in that direction.

Powers himself was acutely conscious of the flight's unique character and the close approach of the Summit

Conference when he took off. As he soared onto a course well above the visible skies, he thought this obvious risk of an untimely mishap was considered necessary to obtain important intelligence before the Russians could solve guidance problems in a more powerful version of their antiaircraft missile.

After his capture and imprisonment, Powers had a few second thoughts. He strongly suspected that his flight had been scheduled *because of*, rather than in spite of, the Summit Conference's close approach. The CIA was deeply committed to the iron-fist-in-the-velvet-glove theory, and had the border-to-border flight been successful, he thought it could have been used as a well-covered fist.

> We knew the Russians had radar-tracked most if not all of the overflights, so the chances were that these last two U–2 flights would not have gone undetected. Might Eisenhower or his advisers have felt it to be to our advantage, psychologically, to have Khrushchev know of the flights and to have this very much on his mind when he arrived in Paris for the talks? . . .
>
> Had the flight gone off as planned it would not have been mentioned [in Paris]. The two men sitting across the table from each other: Eisenhower smug in the knowledge that he could overfly Russia at will, and Khrushchev not able to do anything about it; Khrushchev inwardly raging but unable to protest because to do so would be to admit that his country did not have missiles capable of reaching the planes. What a perfect setting for reopening discussion of Eisenhower's Open Skies plan! . . . Eisenhower could climax his last year in office with a spectacular accomplishment, a major step toward disarmament!

Although pilots praised the U–2 as a superb aircraft, it was in fact an extremely fragile plane. Clarence L. "Kelly" Johnson, the Lockheed designing genius, had stretched every law of aerodynamics to its absolute limit and had sacrificed strength to weight reduction wherever he dared in its construction. The wings were so long that "pogo sticks" with a wheel on one end had to be attached to the wingtips and later dropped off to keep them from scraping the runways on takeoffs. Powers said the wings "visibly flapped" during flight.

For most of their flights the U–2s cruised above weather and other disturbances—indeed higher than up to ninety percent of the atmosphere—so a safe return could be anticipated if all went well at each end of the mission. But one U–2, perhaps flying at a lower altitude than usual, had broken up in the turbulence left behind by a couple of Canadian fighter pilots who merely flew up to have a look.

Something similar happened to Powers on that fateful May 1, which he remembered was a "Communist holiday," and which would make the CIA's name familiar in all parts of the world. Powers was four hours into his 3,000-mile flight, averaging about 400 miles an hour, and was 1,300 miles inside the Soviet Union, thirty or forty miles south of Sverdlovsk, when he heard a "dull thump." "The aircraft jerked forward and a tremendous orange flash lit the cockpit and the sky," he recalled. "I later theorized that I had been the victim of a near miss by a Soviet missile."

Powers had been thrown forward into a dangerous position. If he had used his power ejection seat both his legs would have been severed above the knee. As the long wings came off and he spun toward earth, he made a herculean effort and struggled out through the upper canopy. He must have been at about 15,000 feet when he left the cockpit because his parachute, set to open at that altitude, did so immediately. He landed safely only twenty-five feet from a tractor and two collective farm hands.

Seeing no chance of escape in an open expanse, Powers surrendered and was taken to Sverdlovsk in a small Russian compact. On his arrival, an interpreter was available and he was questioned by professionals from the KGB. Powers had never planned suicide and had rejected optional cyanide pills which the CIA made available for the purpose, but he had brought along a "curare"—a needle so heavily poisoned that a mere pinprick would cause almost instant death.

Although primarily intended for suicide, the curare conceivably could be used as a weapon, to jab an opponent in a life-and-death struggle. The needle was usually carried inside a case which was a replica of an American silver dollar. As Powers was floating toward earth in his parachute, it had occurred to him that this was a poor hiding place, as the shiny case would be sure to attract attention. So he threw away the case and put the loosely-sheathed needle back in his pocket.

In the course of his examination at Sverdlovsk, a KGB representative described by Powers as "one of the civilians to whom the others seemed to defer" found the needle and "after examining it cursorily" slipped it into his briefcase.

> As the questioning continued I suddenly realized that the man with the briefcase had left the room. . . . I had been afraid of that. I told the interpreter to tell him to be extremely careful with the pin. I knew that on closer examination the secret of the pin would be discovered. But I didn't want it to be found through a pricked finger and an accidental death.

As it turned out, the man with the poisoned needle was the only person involved who would experience physical danger after Powers hit the ground. Powers's own treatment was more than reasonably good from the start and it grew better as the Russians realized they were reaping a fine propaganda harvest. He was given a formal trial, was sentenced to ten years in prison, and after eighteen months was exchanged for the convicted Soviet spy Rudolph Abel.

Khrushchev had domestic as well as foreign problems in connection with the capture of Powers. Although he was vituperative in breaking up the Paris Summit Conference, his actions were confined to an agenda prepared before he left Moscow, and he was firmly accompanied on either side by Foreign Minister Andrei Gromyko and Marshal Rodion Malinovsky, chief of the Soviet military forces. Dispatches quoting "informed sources" said the Russians had gone back to a system of "making all decisions at home," and the Senate Foreign Relations Committee, in attempting to explain Khrushchev's predicament, said: "Having to some extent staked his prestige on dealing with President Eisenhower as a man of peace, the development of circumstances making it impossible for him to do so accordingly weakened his position."

Khrushchev at first said he was ready to believe that Eisenhower knew nothing of the Powers flight. He must have soon realized that this was an untenable position for the American president, since Khrushchev himself said: "If actions are taken by American military men on their own account it must be of special concern to world opinion."

Eisenhower wrote in his memoirs:

> To deny my own part in the entire affair would have been a declaration that portions of the government of the United States were acting irresponsibly, in complete disregard of proper presidential control. Moreover, to enter into a conference with Khrushchev when he could refer in pity to my "inability" to control important matters in our government, and scornfully dismiss any argument of mine on the ground that obviously I could not speak authoritatively for my own government, was out of the question.

The fact remained that Eisenhower did not say he knew of the particular flight—he only said that he could not deny knowledge—and the evidence was that he did not know of it. After extensive hearings, the Senate Foreign Relations Committee reported:

> Specific missions of these unarmed civilian aircraft have not been subject to presidential authorization. . . . Neither the President, the Secretary of State, nor the Secretary of De-

fense knew that the particular [Powers] flight was even in the air.

In his memoirs Eisenhower appeared to confirm the committee report indirectly by saying that when he was told a reconnaissance plane was missing, "I knew instantly that this was one of our U–2 planes, probably over Russia." His use of the word "knew" in the sense of divining, and the phrases "one of our U–2 planes" and "probably over Russia" were difficult to square with the assumption by Powers that Eisenhower had given a unique go-ahead for this particular flight only hours before. If such had been the case surely no guessing or divining would have been needed to tell him exactly which plane was missing.

If Eisenhower had *not* kept track of the particular flight and the many special arrangements it required, including those for the first U–2 ground crew ever sent to Norway, some interesting questions could be asked. How could the president have been a participant in reaching the preposterous and dangerous conclusion—"irresponsible," to use Eisenhower's word—that the chances of peace would be enhanced by zooming a sure-to-be-detected military reconnaissance plane completely across Russia just before sitting down with Khrushchev in the hope of discussing peace in an atmosphere of mutual confidence?

And if Eisenhower had not participated in such a decision, which aside from the evidence was the only conclusion that could be reached by a person knowing anything at all about the man, why was Powers kept waiting on the runway for an extraordinary White House clearance? Air Force Colonel William F. Shelton was specific in telling Powers that the final go-ahead had to come from the White House.

In answer to the first question, all evidence indicated CIA Director Dulles had executed a fast end run in which he made all the decisions himself. Dulles was in active charge of the overflights, and his forceful older brother Foster had died in office as secretary of state the previous year. From a largely hidden position and on a grand scale, one man was stage-managing events involving life or death for the nation and the world. And that one man had just been obliged to watch his latest global ploy collapse when Powers was shot down—though the consequences of a "successful" flight could well have been much worse.

Yet such was the protection afforded him by both secrecy and the glamorous intelligence aspects of the U-2 flights that Dulles came through this one in great shape. He was strong enough to refuse absolutely to tell the Senate Foreign Relations Committee, on or off the record, in general or in particular, just what intelligence was sought in the Powers mission. The frustrated committee, never suspecting that the flight's purpose was not intelligence at all, was obliged to report that it had been unable to obtain enough information to reach a conclusion as to whether the flight was worth its risk.

That Dulles's power was not confined to his fellow Republicans was demonstrated when President Kennedy, in his first official act after taking office, reappointed him at the same time that he reappointed J. Edgar Hoover. A man seeing great plans collapse could scarcely be expected to be equally fortunate on such a scale in two successive years, and Dulles wasn't. The Bay of Pigs operation which would prove his undoing came a year after the U-2 debacle.

While it seemed certain that Powers's final go-ahead had to come from the White House, this did not necessarily mean that the decision was made by someone other than Dulles. Schlesinger and Ted Sorensen, in their thorough histories of the Kennedy administration, had to guess at the modus operandi of the NSC Special Group that sometimes acted for Eisenhower, but presumably the procedures were similar to those under Kennedy. If so, telephone consultations and authorizations were common; through smooth arrangements made by Dulles, whoever was standing in for the Special Group at the White House that day could have been given to understand that the decision on the Powers flight should be obtained from the responsible operating agency—the CIA.

Such arrangements would have enabled Dulles to give the final go-ahead on the Powers flight if, from the vantage points at both the White House and the CIA, the coast appeared to be clear, while at the same time retaining in his hands to the last minute the power to cancel the operation if, from the same vantage points, anything appeared to have gone wrong.

Caribbean Debacle

3

Although denied a spectacular or fruitful climax to his White House career, former President Eisenhower was in excellent health and spirits on September 11, 1961, when he was host to sixty freshman Republican congressmen at his farm near Gettysburg, Pennsylvania. After a sumptuous lunch and some good-natured socializing, he agreed to answer questions posed by the congressmen and accompanying newsmen.

When one of the questions concerned his administration's share in the responsibility for the failure of the Bay of Pigs invasion earlier the same year, Eisenhower recalled that in March 1960, the CIA had been authorized to train Cuban exiles for possible infiltration into their homeland for the purpose of conducting guerrilla warfare. Eisenhower then maintained unequivocally: "There was absolutely no planning for an invasion in my administration."

In reporting Eisenhower's statement on an incredulous note for the *New York Times*, Cabell Phillips wrote:

> This disclaimer is in sharp contrast to what high officials of both the Eisenhower and Kennedy administrations have said privately about the ill-starred undertaking of last April, when Cuban refugees failed to hold a beachhead. It has heretofore been taken as fact, that an invasion of American-trained Cuban guerrillas was projected as early as last November.

Schlesinger went back into the record and found that Eisenhower was entirely correct as far as the official policy of his government was concerned. The Eisenhower decision was reached on March 17, 1960, Schlesinger wrote, and consisted of two main parts:

> On the political side it directed the CIA to bring together a broad range of Cuban exiles, with Communists and Batistianos specifically excluded, into unified opposition to the Castro regime. On the military side it directed the CIA to recruit and train a force capable of guerrilla action against that regime.

The following August Eisenhower approved a budget of $13 million for these purposes, about one-fourth the cost of the Bay of Pigs alone. Just what sort of an authorization this would be, obviously one with no limiting aspect as far as the CIA was concerned, was far from clear, but there was nothing to indicate Eisenhower could have anticipated the substitution of a larger plan. In other words it was another of the agency's gigantic deceptions.

Concerning the transition from an infiltration of guerrillas to an invasion plan, Schlesinger wrote that "the CIA people began to doubt that the guerrilla theory would work" and that "they had difficulty in contacting the Cuban underground." "Perhaps," he wrote, "the memory of the successful coup against the Arbenz regime in Guatemala played its part: Castro too might collapse under the shock of an attack in force."

The strategy and tactics used by the CIA in engineering the overthrow of Guatemalan President Jacobo Arbenz in 1954 indeed set the pattern for the Bay of Pigs operation. Arbenz had been smashingly elected in 1952 by a victory of 242,901 over 68,146 for his nearest opponent, Miguel Ydigoras Fuentes, who became president after Arbenz had been removed from the scene.

According to the State Department, Arbenz himself was not a Communist, but the Communists comprised one of four political parties supporting him and held some key positions in his government. And according to a story in the *Saturday Evening Post* (based on information leaked by CIA sources), a CIA-sponsored invasion of Guatemala was triggered by a shipment to Guatemala of Czech-made guns and ammunition aboard the Swedish freighter *Alphem*.

The lengthy and carefully detailed *Saturday Evening Post* article said the *Alphem* had been observed by a CIA agent during loading operations at Polish Stettin and had been tracked to its destination at Porto Barrios, Guatemala, where it unloaded 15,000 crates—1,900 tons—of small arms and ammunition. Shipping schedules showed, however, that the *Alphem*'s arrival was in May 1954. Since the invasion came in June and obviously had required several months of preparation, the real trigger had to be sought at an earlier date.

The true cause of the invasion was a chain of events starting on February 24, 1953. On that date, in the course of a slow-moving agrarian reform program which had taken half a million acres of private land and was paying non-negotiable bonds in compensation, President Arbenz had announced he intended to acquire the "unused" portions of the United Fruit Company's holdings on the same basis.

Involved also was Guatemala's withdrawal from the Organization of American States in protest against an anti-Communist resolution sponsored by the United States. Guatemala regarded the resolution as "a step against" its government. Following the withdrawal the resolution was adopted unanimously by OAS, with Mexico and Argentina politely abstaining.

The real trigger was Guatemala's brazen rejection on September 5, 1953, of an American protest denouncing its proposed "expropriation" from the United Fruit Company of 355,000 acres on the Pacific and 174,000 acres on the Atlantic side of the country. The protest said that the $600,000 in agrarian bonds proposed to be paid for these acres "bears not the slightest resemblance to a true evaluation." At this point the CIA did receive authorization to "do something" about Guatemala.

Living in exile in neighboring Honduras after an unsuccessful attempt to overthrow the previous Guatemalan government of President Juan Jose Arvalo, who was like Arbenz in being called left-wing, was a certain Colonel Castillo Armas. The CIA readily convinced the anti-Communist colonel that with a modest amount of military aid which the agency would supply he could redeem the past by overthrowing Arbenz.

In the colonel's behalf the CIA recruited a handful of pilots headed by Jerry DeLarm of San Francisco. Castillo Armas was then presented with an "air force" consisting of these pilots and three prop-driven World War II P–47 Thunderbolt fighter-bombers. Some newspaper accounts did refer to an existing Guatemalan air force, but in fact, there was no such thing. Even the Castro air force which would prove so effective against the Cuban rebels seven years later consisted mainly of fifteen or twenty prop-driven British and American planes of the same vintage, and in much-less-developed Guatemala three fighter-bombers could be calculated to have a terrifying effect.

In Castillo Armas's behalf the CIA also recruited a small army of 250 troops who were put through basic training on the island of Momotombito in Lake Managua, Nicaragua. When his rudimentary air and ground forces were ready, Castillo Armas entered Guatemala on June 18 and announced by radio that he would take over the government. Simultaneously his planes began bombing Guatemala City.

The small army required twelve days to march the approximately one hundred miles over rough roads to the capital, with breakdowns frequent among the few vehicles provided. Two of the three planes crashed and replacements had to be rushed from the United States. Yet in the midst of confusion and with bombing casualties reportedly light, the Arbenz government fell and power changed hands three times in fifteen days before a cease-fire was declared.

Apparently unaware of the insignificant size of the forces of Castillo Armas, and making no use of the Czech guns and ammunition if in fact they had even been uncrated, the Arbenz government was literally frightened out of existence. When the cease-fire went into effect, it was found that seven hundred members of his administration, including Arbenz, had taken refuge in the various embassies in Guatemala City. Since the embassies were small, the official refugees created a major housekeeping problem until all were granted safe conduct out of the country in September.

Arbenz was overthrown on June 27, when the trouble-plagued invading army was still three days from the capital. He was succeeded by General Carlos Enrique Diaz, army chief of staff, who after only one day in office was overthrown by a junta headed by Colonel Elfego Munson. When Castillo Armas finally reached the capital, both Arbenz and Diaz were refugees in the Mexican embassy. The junta decided to avoid a showdown by electing Castillo Armas as their leader in place of Munson, who went into exile. Arbenz went to Mexico City and eventually reached Cuba via Czechoslovakia. When he died in Mexico in 1971, the problems of his country were sadly the same as when he and his administration ambitiously took office there.

Castillo Armas declared himself president after a rigged election in which he was the only candidate. He visited the United States the following year and was entertained by both the president of the United Fruit Company and by Vice President Nixon—Eisenhower was ill in Denver, Colorado. Then in 1957 Castillo Armas was assassinated by a palace guard. Ydigoras, the man whom Arbenz had so badly beaten in 1952, was elected president by a plurality. The same Ydigoras was still in office when the Cuban rebels and their American instructors arrived in 1960 to set up Guatemalan training camps in preparation for the Bay of Pigs.

Schlesinger's suspicion that the CIA had the Guatemala experience in mind when they began planning for the Cuban invasion turned out to be accurate. In any case, as Schlesinger wrote in 1960, the "men of Washington" moved on "to a new and drastically different conception: the idea of a direct assault on Castro by landing a force of exiles on the Cuban coast."

The *New York Times* meanwhile attempted at high levels to check on the accuracy of Eisenhower's statement at Gettysburg. Most people thought that by the time Kennedy took office the preparations for the invasion were so far advanced that it would have been difficult if not impossible to cancel the operation. Could Eisenhower have been completely wrong? In addition to being president of the United States and commander-in-chief of the armed forces he was by historical circumstance, the world's leading authority on amphibious warfare.

Nevertheless, a "well informed source close to the White House" told the *Times*: "I am sorry to say that the General is in error. I not only know there were plans for an invasion when he was in office, there are documents to prove it." Kennedy was one of the comparatively few people accustomed to referring to Eisenhower as "the General," as well as one of the extremely few "close to the White House" who were competent to make the statement. Undoubtedly, this was the new president himself speaking, with his identity withheld either because he did not wish to presume to contradict his predecessor or because other reporters weren't present.

Eisenhower's memoirs had not yet appeared at the time of these exchanges, and his remarks at Gettysburg were recorded only in the press. In view of the mild furor his statement stirred up, he might have wished to deny it or provide some explanation for it. When, however, the second volume of his memoirs finally appeared under the title *Waging Peace* (Doubleday, 1965) his only comment, avoiding all controversy and here quoted in its entirety, was:

> On March 17, 1960, I ordered the CIA to begin to organize the training of Cuban exiles, mainly in Guatemala, against a possible future day when they might return to their homeland. More specific planning was not possible because the Cubans living in exile made no move to select from

among their number a leader whom we could recognize as a government-in-exile.

In contrast to Eisenhower, Vice President Nixon as a presidential candidate was acutely conscious of the Cuban invasion plans during the 1960 campaign, and thought that as a candidate Kennedy was equally aware of them. At one point Nixon became infuriated because he misinterpreted Kennedy's remarks in favor of anti-Castro Cubans as a reference to the coming assault.

Although he favored the CIA program, Nixon felt obliged in the interests of security to denounce Kennedy's supposed suggestion as "dangerously irresponsible." He said that if Kennedy's implied recommendations were carried out "we would lose all our friends in Latin America, we would probably be denounced in the United Nations and we would not accomplish our objective." The country unknowingly was witnessing the spectacle of one candidate denouncing a program he supported with the other appearing to favor it only because he did not know of its existence.[2]

As Dulles conceded after the election, Kennedy as a candidate was briefed by the CIA in accordance with established custom, but was not told of the Cuban plan. Those who tried to measure information as a quantity would have done well to consider this situation. Several pages in a history text more or less bearing on the subject could with technical accuracy be called a great deal of information, but the difference here was made by only a few missing sentences in which the gist of the Cuban plan could have been conveyed to Kennedy in seconds.

Eisenhower was leaving office and would have nothing to do with the final decision on the Cuban assault. This circumstance may have had something to do with his being excluded from receiving the CIA's choicest information. There was also a question of diplomatic nicety, since the United States maintained formally correct relations with Havana until January 3, 1961. The diplomatic tie was finally broken only because Castro left Eisenhower no dignified alternative. The Cuban dictator demanded that the personnel of the American embassy in Havana be reduced from three hundred to eleven persons, which he said was the extent of Cuba's representation in Washington.

By the time of the diplomatic break, it was obvious that Castro knew of the coming invasion. Assuming he had informants in Central America, he could have learned of the preparations for the attack from the front page of the newspaper *La Hora* in Guatemala City on October 30, 1960. *La Hora* revealed that the Cubans were being trained and equipped on a huge coffee plantation which employed 2,000 Indians and which was owned by a brother of the Guatemalan ambassador to Washington. Similar accounts of the invasion preparations appeared in the *Nation* on November 19, 1960, and in the *New York Times* on January 10, 1961.

Eventually, while interviewing Cubans for his book *The Bay of Pigs* (W.W. Norton, 1964), Haynes Johnson obtained a copy of one of those irrefutable documents to which the "source close to the White House"—very close—must have been referring in 1961. It was a lengthy directive from the CIA's headquarters to the Guatemalan camp, ordering guerrilla training to be stopped.

The directive, dated November 4, 1960, allowed an exception for "sixty, repeat sixty" guerrillas who would be used for auxiliary purposes, but said: "Use conventional arms and training for everyone else."

"The cable spelled out," wrote Johnson, "from A to Z how the change in training was to take place, employing World War II infantry assault landing tactics. It became the bible of the training camp. From that date any talk of guerrilla warfare was regarded by the CIA as a sign of weakness."

The CIA's directive was followed quickly by the arrival in the Guatemalan camp of an officer known to the Cubans as "Frank," who replaced the guerrilla warfare experts in the training command, and who was a United States army colonel on active duty. The CIA obtained support from the armed forces without going through their commander-in-chief, commandeering their brains as well as weapons, supplies, and equipment. Sixteen World War II B–26 bombers which could also be used as fighters were ordered for a rebel air force, and construction of an airstrip near the Guatemalan camp began, although air and naval operations in the invasion itself were to be carried out from neighboring Nicaragua.

At the time guerrilla training was discontinued there were 430 Cubans in the Guatemalan camp, known as *Base Traz.* The more than 1,000 Cubans who reached the camp later received no guerrilla training, and most of those who were already there had received very little. Yet in its presentations to the Kennedy administration after the inauguration, the CIA emphasized repeatedly that if the rebels were unable to carry Cuba by frontal assault, they would retreat to the mountains and resort to guerrilla warfare.

Aside from their not having been prepared for such a purpose it later was revealed that none of the Cubans had been advised of such an alternative plan. The official explanation was that the CIA feared discussion of an alternative would weaken the Cubans' resolve. According to Johnson, "The most charitable explanation that can be placed on this reckless action is that the CIA assumed such terrible responsibility with the best of intentions: it was convinced that the rebels would win and that therefore in the classic sense the end would justify the means."

To the last, President Kennedy maintained the strongest doubts concerning the wisdom of the invasion attempt. Although remarking to an aide that he had no choice, he actively considered a cancellation of the operation as late as noon of the Sunday before the scheduled Monday morning assault. CIA representatives told the Cubans that in case of a cancellation they should stage a fake mutiny in which they would "overthrow" their American advisers and proceed with the invasion. For once the government was prepared against a CIA subterfuge; unknown to the agency, the United States Navy—with ample strength in the area—had orders to intercept and detain the invasion fleet if the operation was canceled.

When Kennedy took office there were no attractive alternatives to the CIA plan. The rebel army by this time was at its full 1,500-man strength. If the army had been disbanded and the Cubans brought back to the United States, they would have undermined Kennedy by angrily contending that their invasion would have succeeded had he not betrayed them. No other country was willing to receive them; the government of Guatemala insisted apprehensively that they must leave its territory soon. Besides, except for Schlesinger, there was no opposition to the CIA's plan in Kennedy's immediate circle of advisers.

By far the strongest opposition to the plan came from Senate Foreign Relations Chairman Fulbright, who was not on anyone's preferred intelligence list but had managed to learn what was going on. On March 19 Fulbright dispatched to the White House a memorandum declaring that if the invasion was carried out, it would be "denounced from the Rio Grande to Patagonia as an example of imperialism." And if American forces were drawn into the battle, Fulbright said:

> We would have undone the work of thirty years in trying to live down earlier interventions. . . . To give this activity even covert support is of a piece with the hypocrisy and cynicism for which the United States is constantly denouncing the Soviet Union in the United Nations and elsewhere. This point will not be lost on the rest of the world nor on our own consciences. And remember always, the Castro regime is a thorn in the side but it is not a dagger in the heart.

Because of his memorandum Fulbright was invited to join the president and his advisers in a crucial meeting on April 4, two weeks before the scheduled invasion. Schlesinger recalled:

> After the usual routine—persuasive expositions by the CIA, mild disclaimers by [Secretary of State] Rusk and pene-

trating questions by the president—Kennedy started asking people around the table what they thought. Fulbright, speaking in an emphatic and incredulous way, denounced the whole idea. The operation, he said, was wildly out of proportion to the threat. It would compromise our moral position in the world and make it impossible for us to protest treaty violations by the Communists. He made a brave, old-fashioned American speech, honorable, sensible and strong; and he left everyone in the room, except me and possibly the president, wholly unmoved.

Schlesinger also submitted memoranda of opposition—two of them. He stressed the lack of prospects for effective uprisings behind the lines and the unlikelihood that the United States could disassociate itself from the consequences even if only Cubans took part in the fighting. The only other high official to express strong opposition was Under Secretary of State Chester Bowles. In the midst of the onrushing events and with Cuban D-day drawing ever closer, the Bowles memorandum was first pigeonholed by Rusk and then returned to Bowles without ever reaching the White House.

The hearts of the Cuban rebels sank when, at Puerto Cabezas, Nicaragua, they first saw the invasion flotilla scheduled to take them back to their homeland. The flotilla consisted of four age-encrusted freighters not worth much more than scrap, two lightly-armed escort vessels, one large landing ship with a false prow to make it look like a freighter, and an assortment of smaller patrol, landing, and supply craft.

The intriguing vessel with the false prow was never used for deceptive purposes but had been conceived as a modern Trojan horse, from which a body of armed men might leap onto a dock or beach when it had appeared that only innocent supplies were being delivered. As it turned out, however, there was no opportunity for artful deceptions. Instead, a nation capable of a floating wonder such as the aircraft carrier *Enterprise*, with four thousand well-kept men aboard and power silently supplied by atomic energy, was about to entrust its prestige to equipment fit for a junkyard.

To the Cubans the situation was preposterous and incredible. They had been told over and over that their CIA mentors had no connection with the United States government, and that they merely represented a group of wealthy men who were interested in fighting Communism. To a man and for reasons that lay about on every hand, the Cubans had rejected the cover story and had assumed that, while certain pretenses had to be maintained, they were in reality backed by the limitless resources of the United States.

The reason for the decrepitude of the equipment—in comparable aeronautical terms the B–26 bombers were of about the same vintage as the freighters—was not so much a lack of money as it was the idea of secrecy. A force supposed to have been assembled by private citizens had to appear to be economical and could not include advanced military equipment, which was not available on open markets at any price. Secrecy also had a bureaucratic significance: if the operation had not been thoroughly clandestine the CIA might have been crowded out of the picture by the regular armed forces.

In another and earlier day the secrecy might have held for a time. During the overthrow of Arbenz in Guatemala, for example, great publications with ample facilities for covering the news were temporarily misled into believing that Colonel Castillo Armas's "puny" three-plane air force had been supplied by wealthy coffee plantation owners. By the time the facts came out, their significance was lost on the public because the events had passed into history. But no such time lag could be expected in the wake of Francis Gary Powers and the U–2 affair; it was now unlikely that the CIA's activities would go unnoticed.

The arrival of the Cubans at Puerto Cabezas after they left their Guatemalan training camp was accompanied by anything but secrecy. Luis Somoza, the dictator of Nicaragua, headed the welcoming delegation and loudly requested that the rebels "bring me a few hairs from Castro's beard." Castro, equally aware of the rebel movements, was making extensive preparations to defend his island by land, sea, and air.

The CIA estimated Castro's air inventory at twenty-nine planes—fifteen B–26 bombers, ten British Sea Fury fighter-bombers and four American T–33 trainers. But Castro had been unable to get spare parts and probably a third of these were in no condition to fly. They were useful, though, since one of his defense ploys was to leave nonoperational planes on or near the runways as decoys while effective planes were well camouflaged in the brush. The rebels expected that Castro's air force would be completely destroyed before the waterborne landing.

A serious and perhaps fatal error in the CIA's air estimate, similar to the mistake in Defense Department assessments, ignored the importance of the T–33s. They were listed as trainers and in fact were built for that purpose. But these planes carried rockets and machine guns, and they were the only jets in the picture. Ted Sorensen, who as President Kennedy's special counsel had access to many documents never made public, concluded that the Cuban venture was "diplomatically unwise and militarily doomed from the start." But if that doom could be said to have been sealed by one technical factor, it was the subsequent failure to destroy Castro's air force or in some way to neutralize the T–33s, against which the rebel B–26 bombers were literally helpless.

In the final days before the landing the CIA redoubled its efforts to ensure that the operation would not be canceled. As the president later recounted the conversation to Sorensen, Dulles came to the White House and told Kennedy: "Mr. President, I stood here at Eisenhower's desk in 1954 and told him I was certain the Guatemalan operation would succeed. And, Mr. President, the prospects for this plan are even better than they were for that one."

Dulles here apparently was referring to his original optimism and later assurance concerning the Guatemalan operation. At one anxious point, after two-thirds of Castillo Armas's air force had crashed, he was estimating the operation's chances of success at only twenty percent.

Kennedy was told that the last opportunity to topple the Castro regime by means short of American involvement in war was rapidly fading. Although not yet operating Russian planes, the Cubans had received a backlog of MIG jets which were crated and awaiting assembly on their wharves, and Cuban pilots would soon be back from training in Czechoslovakia and the Soviet Union to fly them. Recalling his heavy burden of responsibility, Kennedy subsequently observed:

> There is only one person in the clear—that's Bill Fulbright. And he probably would have been converted if he had attended more meetings. If he had received the same treatment we received—discontent in Cuba, morale of the free Cubans, rainy season, Russian MIGs and destroyers, impregnable beachhead, easy escape to the Escambray Mountains, what else to do with these people—it might have moved him down the road too.

In the CIA's anxiety to avoid cancellation, the agency readily accepted, and even elaborated on, last-minute suggestions for modifications of the original invasion plan. One of these changed the point of landing from Trinidad to the Bay of Pigs, primarily because Trinidad was a fairly large community (20,000) and the idea of secrecy still prevailed. In addition to other advantages, the Bay of Pigs included only small resort towns, and it had an airstrip accessible only over jungle-bordered roads which the rebels could place under fire. But the Bay was eighty miles from those Escambray Mountains into which, unknown to themselves, the rebels were supposed to find refuge if they encountered heavy opposition.

Another modification—in violation of military principles because of the time lag—scheduled an air raid for forty-eight hours before the landing. The raid was designed for propaganda purposes: to soften up the Cubans with a preinvasion claim that a revolt had occurred in Castro's military forces and that he was being bombed by his own planes. (The propaganda story subsequently boomeranged disastrously, and the time lag presented Castro with an opportunity to recover from damage to his airfields before trouble on the beaches developed.)

Although the CIA would later be calling for air raids from American carriers, it appeared to accept without qualification Kennedy's repeated warnings that there must be no involvement of American armed forces. But given the circumstances, no matter how often or how emphatically that stipulation was repeated and accepted by the CIA, the chances of avoiding such an involvement had to be rated as no better than fair.

One of the most unlikely possibilities that might have been anticipated, in the midst of the strenuous high policy considerations and the ominous onrush of events, was that Kennedy would hold a press conference. But reporters were clamoring for some explanation of the widely noticed activity in the Caribbean, and the president decided to be as obliging as he could. If involvement of American armed forces was the greatest of the many dangers present, the press conference may have been the most fortunate occurrence in this misfortune-plagued period.

The date was April 12, the sixteenth anniversary of the death of President Franklin D. Roosevelt, and just twenty-four hours before the invasion flotilla would put to sea from Puerto Cabezas. The first question, posed by Merriman Smith of UPI, was: "Mr. President, has a decision been reached as to how far this country would be willing to go in helping an anti-Castro uprising or invasion of Cuba?"

Kennedy replied:

Well, first I want to say that there will not under any conditions be an intervention in Cuba by United States armed forces. This government will do everything it possibly can— and I think we can meet our responsibilities—to make sure that there are no Americans involved in any action inside

Cuba. . . . The basic issue in Cuba . . . is between the Cubans themselves . . . and I intend to adhere to that principle.

Nevertheless, Kennedy authorized participation in the Cuban battle by six United States Navy jets with their markings painted over—an operation which would have been completely transparent from the moment they fired their first shots, and which failed to come off only because they missed their rendezvous. It could be speculated in view of Kennedy's near-violation of his pledge that authorization for a more extensive American involvement might have been extracted from him had he not been on record with such a fresh and unequivocal avowal against such a move.

The avowal was reinforced by a round of applause from Latin America. One Brazilian newspaper, in seeming surprise, said "The United States is beginning to understand Latin American psychology." Another, of a high-minded conservative persuasion, said:

> The idea of foreign intervention must be repugnant to any democratic government and it is therefore repugnant to John F. Kennedy. This is the basis and secret of the prestige of the new leadership in Washington.

Reports of the applause appeared in print just as the antiquated invasion flotilla was breasting the waves beyond Puerto Cabezas, and though Washington still seethed with well-justified apprehensions there would be no turning back.

The bulk of the slow-moving invasion flotilla left Puerto Cabezas late in the afternoon of Thursday, April 13, 1961. Eight B–26 bombers, which needed four hours to fly the 720 miles from Nicaragua to Cuba, took off after midnight the next night for the first air strike. A ninth B–26, suitably riddled with bullet holes as though it had taken part in an attack, left for Miami, Florida, to launch the fake propaganda story.

At 6:30 A.M. on Saturday the B–26s bombed Castro's

three major airdromes. One B–26 was shot down and another developed engine trouble necessitating an emergency landing at Key West; thus, including the propaganda forerunner, there were two rebel B–26s in Florida. The others got back to Nicaragua—code-named "Happy Valley"—and reported successes. U–2 photographs taken in the wake of the bombings established that five Cuban planes had been destroyed, although in view of Castro's tactic of leaving decoys on the runways, some of these may have been ineffective.

Trouble with the propaganda story developed almost immediately. Immigration authorities said they were withholding the names of the Cuban pilots, whereas if they were really defectors from the Cuban armed forces as claimed, their identities would already have been known in Havana. Furthermore, the holes in the propaganda plane were not made by bullets of the same caliber as those in the plane at Key West. And Dr. José Miro Cardona, chairman of the Cuban Revolutionary Council in New York and designated to become head of a new Cuban government, commented too hastily that his organization had been in contact with the Cuban air force for some time regarding the revolt, whereas one of the anonymous pilots interviewed in Miami said the defection was a sudden decision.

Besides, if this was a mass defection capable of bombing three airdromes, where were the other planes and pilots? Also, the planes from Nicaragua carried extra fuel tanks, which they jettisoned after the attacks. The Cuban government displayed some of these along with charred rocket fragments bearing the initials "U.S.A." at a meeting of the entire diplomatic corps in Havana.

Consequently almost everyone believed Cuban Foreign Minister Dr. Raul Roa when he was granted a hearing before the Political Committee of the United Nations Assembly Saturday afternoon and declared that the air raids were American-instigated and "the prologue to a large-scale invasion." Almost no one believed United Nations Ambassador Adlai Stevenson, whose prestige was seriously undermined as a result, when he said: "These pilots and certain other crew members apparently defected from Castro tyranny. . . . To the best of our knowledge these were Cuba's own air force planes and according to the pilots they took off from Cuba's own airfields."

Dr. Roa, remembering American history better than most, said in the course of his impassioned oratory:

> The grass had scarcely turned green on the grave of Franklin D. Roosevelt—a liberal who never resorted to witch-hunting to defend the foundations of the capitalist order—when the old pretext was resurrected with the overwhelming strength of a stereotype: the "Communist influence," the "Communist bridgehead," the "diabolical expansion of international Communism." Such is the pretext invoked to destroy the Cuban revolution and restore the system of interests, privileges, coercion and bribery which the revolution overthrew. The revolutionary government of Cuba knows—and can the United States deny this?—that the Central Intelligence Agency is a body directed toward the subversion of Cuba.

When the session was over there could be no doubt that Dr. Roa carried the day. The diplomatic defeat was so humiliating, and it was so clear that America would be blamed for further bombing in Cuba, that President Kennedy canceled a second air strike scheduled to coincide with the landing Monday morning. Since this would leave Castro's air force virtually intact, the rebel army was ordered to go ashore under cover of darkness.

Although *all* amphibious landings during World War II began at dawn, the gear-laden rebels at the Bay of Pigs began going ashore at one A.M. They had to contend with uncharted reefs in pitch darkness. Many of them were in seventeen-foot fiberglass boats built for inland waters rather than the sea.

Under the circumstances, the landing itself was remarkably successful. By soon after daybreak all individuals except the casualties and the flotilla's crew members

were ashore, along with some heavy equipment and whatever ammunition and supplies they could carry. Then
Castro's planes appeared in the sky, and in the wake of
their initial attacks—except for insignificant airdrops—
the rebels received no ammunition or supplies whatever.

Almost the entire remaining fleet of rebel B–26s was
used that first morning in an effort to protect the unloading of supplies. Since their tail guns had been removed to
make room for extra fuel tanks, the B–26s were no match
even for the prop-driven Castro planes, and nearly half
of them were shot down in the early hours after dawn.

One of the Castro Sea Furies scored a direct bomb hit
on the freighter *Rio Escondido* which, with a cargo of ammunition, fuel, medical supplies, and communications
equipment, blew up in spectacular fashion—an explosion
which a Cuban described as "like the Fourth of July." The
freighter *Houston*, attacked by a T–33, had its hull shat-
tered by a rocket that did not explode, and would have
sunk if it had not grounded on a reef. The only other
ships carrying ammunition and supplies, the *Atlantico* and
the *Caribe*, fled southward to escape the bombing and straf-
ing Castro planes.

After the disastrous Monday morning encounters,
there was no chance that the rebel force could survive
without armed American assistance. The situation was not
immediately apparent on the scene and would not be
faced in Washington for another forty hours. The rebels,
meanwhile, established headquarters at Playa Giron and
set up roadblocks at Playa Largo (Long Beach) and on the
main coastal highway to Cienfuegos. They did not realize
that their two remaining supply ships had not only left the
beachhead area, they had no intention whatever of returning.

Major American naval units were standing at convenient distances offshore. These included the aircraft carrier *Essex*. After the rebels had gotten a transmitter into
operation, the *Essex* began picking up messages that went
like this: "Hello *Caribe*! Hello *Caribe*! Where are you, you
son of a bitch? I need you! I need you!" When the captain

of the *Essex* finally sent fast destroyers to search for them, the *Caribe* was located 218 miles south of the Bay of Pigs, while the *Atlantico* was intercepted 110 miles south of Cuban waters.

The *Atlantico* was persuaded to return to a rendezvous point fifty miles south of the Bay of Pigs, where it was joined by the rebel patrol boats *Blagar* and *Barbara J* late Tuesday afternoon. As rapidly as they could, the crews of the three vessels loaded five small boats with supplies desperately needed ashore. When the loading was completed in darkness, there was not enough time to race to the beachhead and unload before dawn. The crews for the small boats, who had witnessed the fiery end of the *Rio Escondido* and seen the *Houston* breaking up on a reef, refused to leave for the landing area unless they were guaranteed jet cover at dawn.

An appeal for jet cover was sent to CIA headquarters in Langley. Whoever had the night duty for the CIA, apparently unaware of the desperate nature of the situation, ordered a cancellation of the supply operation without referring the matter to the White House. The appeal was quickly renewed through the Pentagon. This time President Kennedy met with representatives of the CIA and the Joint Chiefs of Staff in a postmidnight session at the White House. Everyone present conceded that all would be lost unless the United States took positive and immediate action. Castro's forces were massing in great strength at San Blas, north of the Playa Giron area, and many of the rebels had been sleepless since Sunday.

The CIA and the Joint Chiefs urged an air strike from the *Essex* to destroy Castro's air force at daybreak. Kennedy evolved a compromise which he called "air cover for the air cover." This was the near-violation of his pledge, a provision that six jets from the *Essex* with their markings painted over would be permitted to protect rebel B–26s guarding the beachhead during the unloading operation. The B–26s would still have to come from Nicaragua, but they could call on the jets for help if they ran into trouble.

When the decision was reached almost immediate takeoffs from Nicaragua were necessary to get to the beachhead in time, but only three B–26s and one Cuban pilot were in a condition to fly. The Cubans had been flying in nonstop relays over the 1,500-mile round trip to Cuba, and flesh even more than equipment had given out. Gonzolo Herrera agreed to fly one of the B–26s alone, although the usual crew was two. Miraculously, he would survive to tell the story.

The remaining two B–26s, and two others already air-borne which joined them, were flown by American pilot instructors. This was in violation of Kennedy's orders, but so was the "air cover for the air cover." Thus, despite all the elaborate efforts to avoid such a solution, four of the five planes in the last rebel air operation were flown by Americans. As Herrera recalled, the orders dictated to Nicaragua said that "the jet cover we had been requesting had been granted." "They said the jets would be waiting for us at 10,000 feet," he remembered. "All we had to do if we needed help was give the usual signal: 'Mad Dog 4! Mayday! Mayday!'"

Due to a mixup in the hasty instructions, attributed to a difference in time zones or a communications delay or both, the rebel B–26s reached the beachhead an hour ahead of the Navy jets. When the bombers being used as fighters swept down toward the Playa Giron area they assumed the jet cover was somewhere above them. Although himself under attack and careening out of the area, Herrera heard the last transmissions from the two planes that were lost. One of them said: "Mad Dog 4! Mayday! Mayday! T–33 attacking. We are Americans. Help us. T–33 attacking. I need cover. Where are you? I am falling . . ."

There was no answer. Because of the communications mixup, the late-arriving unmarked jets could provide no cover; they had become, in effect, reconnaissance planes whose pilots could find nothing to report by the time they flew over Playa Giron.

President Kennedy said the four American pilots in the two planes that were lost had died in the service of their country. Through the Chase Manhattan Bank, their widows, whose husbands had been members of the Alabama Air National Guard, received money of mysterious origin in amounts exactly equalling the benefits to which they would have been entitled if the husbands had died in regular military service. These women were sometimes called "the CIA widows."

With the failure of the air cover scheme, the small supply boats, after standing offshore during the last day of the battle, returned to their rendezvous point in the gray hours of the following dawn. Rebel headquarters had fallen to the Castroites at 5 P.M. Wednesday. The rebels no longer had anything with which to fight and were soon rounded up. Castro turned out to be well-supplied with armed helicopters, and his forces used these to remorselessly hunt down the rebels who fled into the wild regions of the Zapata swamp.

The Castro forces took more than eleven hundred prisoners—1,180 by a later count. Of these, 1,113 were still alive and in prison when they were traded on Christmas Eve of 1962 for $10 million in cash and $53 million in medicines, baby foods, and other supplies and equipment exempted from the American embargo on shipments to Cuba. The ransom was collected by a private group in whose original formation Mrs. Eleanor Roosevelt was a prominent figure. Since another count showed that at least 1,297 Cubans had gone ashore, it appeared that fatal casualties among the rebels had been approximately ten percent during three days of hazardous operations and fighting. A final count placed the rebel dead at 114.

Six weeks later, with repercussions of the Cuban setback still rumbling across the Caribbean, the CIA was inextricably involved in yet another deadly venture in the same area. The new operation was, in fact, related in its planning stages to the Cuban affair. This time the action took place in the neighboring Dominican Republic.

Era of Absolutism

4

In 1972 when columnist Jack Anderson obtained documents relating to the International Telephone and Telegraph Company's attempts to prevent the inauguration of Salvador Allende after his election as president of Chile, there was one official communication that may have come as something of a relief to Allende's still functioning government in Santiago. It was stamped "Personal and Confidential" and bore a notation by ITT's Washington Vice President William Merriam that "this should be tightly held."

There followed an eight-page memorandum to the effect that on September 15, 1970, United States Ambassador to Chile Edward M. Korry had "received a message from the State Department giving him a green light in the name of President Nixon . . . to do all possible—short of a Dominican-type action—to keep Allende from taking power."

The CIA, which almost without exception handled cable communications at all American embassies, must have raised some eyebrows upon reading this message to Korry, both because of the agency's many attempts to prevent Allende's inauguration or, later, to overthrow him, and also because of the CIA's heavy involvement in the "Dominican-type action" here referred to—the assassination of dictator Rafael Trujillo.

Trujillo's slaying had been conceived as an act which would benefit not only Latin America but the entire Western hemisphere. Ironically, however, the "high purpose" which the CIA perceived would be served by engineering Trujillo's death had been buried in the waters of the Bay of Pigs before the shooting took place. By that time, in fact, both the CIA and the State Department were engaged in desperate and unsuccessful attempts to *prevent* the assassination they had earlier helped to set in motion.

The original idea was that the assassination of the right-wing Trujillo would achieve a political balance in the Caribbean by offsetting the anticipated overthrow of the left-wing Castro in Cuba. Here again, as in the case of Lumumba and the invasion of Cuba itself, the idea seemed to have been taken from something Eisenhower had suggested or approved (judging from statements in his memoirs) and then carried far beyond his intention.

Eisenhower wrote that he himself considered Castro "a far more menacing presence in the hemisphere," but that other governments did not agree.

> Most of his Latin American neighbors considered [Castro] less of a threat than the Dominican Republic's Generalissimo Rafael Leonidas Trujillo Molina, who at 68, after a thirty-year rule, could claim undisputed title to the world's oldest surviving dictatorship. "El Jefe," as his three million subjects knew him, boasted efficient secret police and an extensive record of mysterious deaths and disappearances. . . . We knew that until the American nations made some effective move against Trujillo they could do nothing against Castro.

During his last months in office, Eisenhower attempted to isolate Trujillo diplomatically on the basis of a 1960 report by the Organization of American States that found him guilty of "flagrant and widespread violations of human rights." In his memoirs Eisenhower wrote:

> It continued to be difficult to get a consensus among the American governments. . . . It was certain that public opinion in America would not condemn Castro until we moved against Trujillo, who, in July (1960) was accused of attempting the assassination of President Betancourt of Venezuela.

The attempt took place on a Caracas street when an automobile full of explosives (called an automobile bomb) was detonated as the president's car was passing. Only a closed rear window saved Betancourt's life; the riders in the front seat, with the windows open, were killed.

The Dominican Republic shared an island with Haiti, and in Caribbean terms it had proved to be an invulnerable fortress. Both Cuba and Venezuela had failed in attempts to invade Trujillo's domain in 1959. In January 1960, he had smashed a domestic plot against himself, imprisoning more than a thousand people. Eisenhower's second term ended with Trujillo still in full power. He was assassinated when the Kennedy administration was four months old.

For more than a year the dictator's fate was regarded in the United States as a purely Latin American affair. Unlike Allende in Chile, who was perceived as a distinguished intellectual, Trujillo had led a gangster-type life of luxury, mayhem, and plunder, which did not garner much outside sympathy for him. Then in September 1962, the *New York Times* carried a UPI dispatch from Ottawa, Canada, quoting Major General Arturo R. Espaillat, a graduate of West Point who had been Trujillo's security chief, as saying "The Central Intelligence Agency supplied the weapons for Trujillo's assassination."

The State Department reacted with denials and the CIA, as usual, had no comment. This spurred a concerted search for the facts. Many of these were supplied by Espaillat in a book titled *Trujillo: The Last Caesar* (H. Regnery, 1963). Others came in an article by Norman Gall of Puerto Rico's *San Juan Star*, who investigated on the scene in the Dominican Republic and reported his findings in the April 13, 1963, issue of the *New Republic*. Although Espaillat was pro- and Gall was anti-Trujillo there was little difference in their assessments of what had happened.

During most of his long career Trujillo had been regarded as a protegé of the United States, but for reasons that will become clear, this policy did not have the full support of the CIA. In the course of disputes over human rights under Eisenhower, the American diplomatic representation in the Dominican Republic had been reduced from an embassy to a consulate. And for months as Eisenhower's second term drew toward a close the consulate had been maintaining contact with dissidents seeking Trujillo's overthrow.

Senate investigators found that precisely on Eisenhower's last day in office (whether he saw the message before he left was not stated, but it must have been a busy day) Consul General Henry Dearborn in Ciudad Trujillo was authorized to supply the dissidents with arms including "exotic equipment" such as telescopic sights. CIA officials met with dissident leaders in New York the following month and were told repeatedly that "the key to success of their plans would be the assassination of Trujillo."

The plotters numbered two dozen individuals, or more if those who played an indirect role were included. Espaillat said that the plotters included a tall United States consular official whom he designated "Mutt," and a short CIA agent he called "Jeff." In a written handout at the opening of a press conference, Espaillat said the CIA agent was using the unlikely name of Plato Cox. With Trujillo reportedly worth $800 million, with the mansions of his deputies studding the island, and with a number of major governmental figures involved in this last conspiracy against him, the preparations for his final demise had all the elements of a movie scenario.

Despite his great wealth Trujillo was accustomed to traveling in an unescorted car and armed only with a revolver. His driver was more heavily armed, but the assassins reasoned that in a gangland-style attack, the driver would be fully engaged in controlling the vehicle and that Trujillo would have no chance against automatic weapons, less politely called submachine guns, especially if there were enough of them. The dictator still seemed to be ten feet tall, and the attack was planned on the scale of a military saturation assault. Original talk was of at least three or four carloads of heavily armed men.

The plotters also included the head of the Dominican armed forces, but he must have been one of the most timid conspirators of all time. Although designated to form a provisional government once Trujillo was out of the way, the man insisted that he could not assume power until he had been shown the dictator's body, and he refused to use his position to obtain the needed automatic weapons. These, he said, would have to come "from outside."

The task of obtaining the weapons thus fell to the CIA. Unlike other CIA assassination attempts, which were independent operations conducted in dark secrecy, the one against Trujillo was comparatively open within the government. The CIA apparently was seeking to legitimize a practice it had already employed on a number of known occasions. To that end the agency came up with a document that has rarely been equalled for sheer impudence.

The document was submitted to the CIA itself and to the State Department for at least tacit concurrence on April 7, 1961, little more than a week before the Bay of Pigs, and was called "A Pouch Restriction Waiver Request and Certification." Its stated purpose was "to pouch to the Dominican Republic four M3 machine guns and 240 rounds of ammunition for issuance to a small action group for use in self-protection."

Worldwide regulations exempting diplomatic pouches from inspection by the host country stipulated that such pouches could not be used for shipping firearms. The CIA was actually taking the position that this provision could be waived unilaterally by the United States for a "worthy purpose"—such as the assassination of a chief of state. Someone made the mistake of asking Adolph Berle, chairman of the Inter-Agency Task Force on Latin America, what he thought the policy in this matter should be. Berle recorded the following in a memo to himself:

> On cross-examination it developed that the real purpose was to assassinate Trujillo. I told them that I could not care less for Trujillo and that this was the general sentiment, but

that we did not wish to have anything to do with assassination plots anywhere, anytime.

Nevertheless on April 10 the "Pouch Restriction Waiver Request and Certification" was approved by the CIA and the machine guns and ammunition it called for arrived in the Dominican Republic free of inspection on April 19. This was so soon after the Bay of Pigs, that the disaster had not yet been officially confirmed, but American policy with respect to Trujillo had already reversed itself. Under specific instructions from Washington, CIA and State Department representatives made urgent efforts to persuade the dissidents either to call off the assassination or to postpone it until a new assessment could be made. Also under instructions from Washington, delivery of the rapid-firing machine guns was withheld, and these never left the consulate. Nevertheless, the CIA had already passed three semiautomatic M–1 carbines and three .38 caliber Smith & Wesson revolvers to the dissidents, who had a small arsenal of weapons of their own. They politely told their American sponsors that the assassination was their affair, and that they could not change their plans to suit the convenience of the United States. Consul General Dearborn, in response to a request for guidance sent to the State Department, was told that he should keep in mind the president's view, expressed at a meeting of the National Security Council on May 5, that the United States should not initiate the overthrow of Trujillo before knowing what government would succeed him.

Dearborn responded in seeming frustration by pointing out that for more than a year the United States had been nurturing the effort to overthrow Trujillo and had assisted the dissidents in numerous ways, all of them known to the department. It was, he said, too late to consider whether the United States would *initiate* the overthrow of Trujillo. Despite his acerbic reply, Dearborn continued to receive more cables along the same line. One on May 24 urged him to "disassociate the United States from any obvious intervention in the Dominican Republic, and even more from any political assassination that might occur." Another on May 26 said he "must not run the risk of United States association with political assassination, since *the United States as a matter of general policy cannot condone assassination.*" According to former White House aide Richard Goodwin, the italicized portion of this latter cable was dictated by President Kennedy.

But nothing could be done to alter the relentless course of events, and plans for the assassination went ahead. Senate investigators were told that the carbines which the CIA had already passed to the dissidents had been left behind in the consulate by Navy personnel at the time the American embassy was closed. But since a scramble for just such weapons had been under way for months, some doubt could be cast on a version of the story that claimed the powerful carbines were available all this time. They may have been obtained by the spicier method described to Gall, who wrote:

> The key link between the assassins and the CIA in the arms shipments was a longtime civilian resident of Ciudad Trujillo, who operated a supermarket in a fashionable neighborhood where Trujillo also lived. The weapons were imported in small parts, to be assembled by the plotters, among the routine grocery shipments for the supermarket arriving regularly at the capital's port. The gun parts were in specially marked food cans, which were turned over to the conspirators.[3]

Though it played no visible part in the final operation against him, the CIA for years had been nourishing a grudge against Trujillo for having placed the agency in an embarrassing position in connection with the abduction and murder of Professor Jesus de Galindez of Columbia University. De Galindez was seized as he was entering a New York subway station on March 12, 1956, and was never heard from again. The pilot of a plane chartered to fly him to the Dominican Republic was also murdered, in what was called an automobile accident.

Trujillo's purpose was to silence the professor's anti-Trujillo lectures. With the eyes of his intelligence and security forces focused on this man, he may well have known that the CIA was financing de Galindez, but if so he chose to ignore the fact. At the time of his disappearance, the CIA had more than a million dollars invested in de Galindez.

The purpose of the CIA payments was to finance de Galindez in his role as representative in the Western hemisphere of the Spanish Basque government-in-exile, which was tirelessly engaged in trying to overthrow dictator Francisco Franco in Madrid. As soon as word of the abduction reached Washington, the CIA rushed an auditor to New York who successfully represented that he had authority to go through de Galindez's papers, and who succeeded in recovering the last of the agency's payments to him—a check for $7,240 which the professor had not cashed. Later investigation by the Justice Department showed that the CIA's monthly payments to him had varied from $4,845 to $26,039 and had totaled $1,016,000.

The embarrassing part was that Washington was now getting along famously with Franco. Under a three-year-old agreement signed in 1953, the United States was spending hundreds of millions of dollars to aid the Spanish people and build air and naval bases on their soil. Why the CIA would underwrite Franco's opposition in these circumstances was not easily explained to Madrid or to the American public. When all available facts were in his hands, columnist Drew Pearson wrote:

> The mystery still remains unsolved as to why the CIA was financing a Basque exile who was working against a government leader we were supporting with military and foreign aid. The taxpayers are put in the position of paying both to support Franco and to undermine Franco.

With his direct either-or approach, Pearson was unable to see the matter from a CIA point of view. From an ends-justify-the-means standpoint, it certainly could be desirable when negotiating with one side to have something going with the opposition at the same time. De Galindez, for example, had at his fingertips all kinds of information concerning Franco—much of it potentially damaging. Such information could conceivably be used as bargaining chips in future deals with the dictator. The CIA was not wont to pass up opportunities such as this.

Franco's days were numbered and succession uncertain. The Communist's underground opposition posed a possible threat to the future of Spain as a strategic base for the West. The CIA's involvement with Franco's opposition kept Washington informed and offered a chance to influence future events.

This wasn't the first time—nor would it be the last—that the CIA interfered in the conduct of foreign affairs by pursuing acts at odds with official U.S. policy. President Truman may have had this kind of double-dealing in mind when he commented:

> The CIA has become a symbol of sinister and mysterious foreign intrigue. . . . We have grown up as a nation respected for our free institutions and our ability to maintain a free and open society. There is something about the way the CIA is functioning that is casting a shadow over our historic position, and I feel we need to correct it.

When death in the form of two carloads of heavily armed men finally overtook Trujillo, he was in a two-year-old Chevrolet with his driver on a lonely coastal road near the capital, en route to a rendezvous with a twenty-year-old mistress. The assassins opened fire from the rear, and Trujillo was wounded in the back by one of the first shots. He sprang from the car and fired his revolver at his attackers.

In his book, Espaillat suggested that this act may have amounted to suicide since Trujillo might have been able to escape had he remained in his car. Contemporary dispatches, however, quoted the badly wounded driver as saying that when he heard firing behind him he "swerved the car to get away," but he was overtaken immediately and prevented from doing so. In either case once he left the car, Trujillo's fate was sealed.

His body, riddled with a total of six bullets (any single

one of three of them could have been fatal) and an un-counted number of shotgun pellets, was stuffed into the trunk of one of the cars. His own car, left by the roadside with his driver lying unconscious nearby, had been struck by fifty-two bullets, twelve of which penetrated the wind-shield.

The Secretary of the Armed Forces could not be lo-cated during the crucial period immediately following the slaying. Since it was therefore impossible to fulfill his stip-ulation that he be shown the body before taking power, that part of the conspiracy collapsed. In the confusion Trujillo's son, Ramfis—a playboy known in the United States chiefly for such exploits as bringing his horse into the family swimming pool while skinny-dipping with the likes of Kim Novak and Zsa Zsa Gabor—arrived by char-tered plane from Paris and took over the government.

The son may have received an assist in his seizure of power from circumstances that developed in which no one could anticipate what would happen from moment to mo-ment in the immediate wake of his father's demise. With a promptness based on previous knowledge, the Ameri-cans advised Washington immediately of Trujillo's death. Washington advised President Kennedy, who happened to be in Paris, and Pierre Salinger, his press secretary, in-formed the reporters in the president's entourage. The result was that the news was soon pouring out all over the world except at home, where the Trujillo government was suppressing it while taking six hours to prepare a cautious statement, attributing Trujillo's death to a conspiracy "in-volving a foreign government."

Ramfis proved to be effectively vengeful but ineffective in maintaining order. After seven riotous months he sailed back to Paris aboard a frigate, ordering his yacht the *Angelita* to follow. The yacht was later turned back by the Dominican navy, after it appeared that Ramfis had taken permanent leave, and was found to have a total of $4 million in cash aboard.

Tad Szulc visited Santo Domingo (formerly Ciudad Trujillo) for the *New York Times* nine months later, in September 1962. The country by this time was ruled by a seven-man council including two of the assassins. Unemployment was placed at between 250,000 and 600,000, an estimate remarkable for its size and its range. Szulc said in his dispatch to the *Times* that conditions could not be considered secure or stable.

The public conduct of the council members illustrates the point. Two—Luis Amiama Tio and Antonio Imbert, who fear reprisals from Trujillo supporters for having participated in the murder plot—travel the country under military escort. Their homes are guarded like fortresses by soldiers with submachine guns. . . . Nearby a group of United States Special Forces (Green Beret) officers and non-coms relax over a beer after a hot day of training Dominican troops in anti-guerrilla techniques—just in case Tovares Justo (leader of a Castro-admiring movement) sends his followers into the hills. At police headquarters an expert from Miami and two Los Angeles detectives are busy organizing riot-police squadrons and teaching the men to use truncheons instead of rifle bullets on disorderly crowds. A Chilean general imparts techniques to the Mounted Police Squadron. In the stable a visitor can admire the splendidly matched palomino horses, including a nineteen-hand-high stallion which cost the late dictator $35,000.

Concerning the unrest, and with tongue in cheek, Szulc quoted Foreign Minister José Antonio Bonilla Atiles as saying: "It is not easy to govern in a democracy."

Nothing specific had been published in Santo Domingo to link the United States with Trujillo's death. Though the official statement had said it was due to a plot "involving a foreign government," the press was under strict censorship and forbidden to speculate on *which* foreign government. When Che Guevara in Havana said the reference undoubtedly was to the United States, his remark was deleted from a wire service dispatch as it appeared in Santo Domingo, and it drew so little attention elsewhere that there was no reaction in Washington.

Seventeen days after Szulc's visit, Espaillat turned up in Canada. For reasons he described as "obscure" he had first been jailed and then had been released by the junior Trujillo's government. He had now worn out his welcome in both the Bahamas and Canada, was facing deportation, and was convinced he was being pursued by American agents who would kill him if they could.

Hoping to place himself in a spotlight which would deter would-be assassins, Espaillat drew up a list of charges against the United States, prepared an 800-word statement, and called a press conference. His charges mainly concerned payments made by the sugar-producing Dominican Republic to quota-influencing members of Congress, but the statement also included his accusation concerning the CIA's part in Trujillo's assassination.

Washington now felt obliged to react. Veteran State Department press officer Lincoln White said: "I've checked this out, and I'm told these charges are completely without foundation." It was possible to believe that White had received assurances, though he did not say where or from whom, and it was noted that he took no responsibility for the statement himself. Needless to say, Espaillat's charges were later found to be far from "without foundation."

According to Espaillat, the assassins were an oddly mixed lot. In describing them he named General José Roman Fernandez, Secretary of the Armed Forces, designated to head the new government in the original plot, and who Espaillat said "wanted money and power"; General Juan Tomas Diaz, who was "bitter because Trujillo had suddenly (and characteristically) retired him from the Army"; Antonio de la Maza, who "wanted revenge because Trujillo had murdered his brother"; and Amado Garcia, "a young, good-natured lieutenant formerly on Trujillo's personal staff, who wanted only to free his country from tyranny."

Espaillat continued:

A score of Dominicans participated directly or indirectly. All of the actual assassins—except Luis Amiama Tio and Antonio Imbert—are now dead. The Americans involved were less complex types doing their duty, obeying orders from Washington. With respect to the supermarket man he didn't seem to have any official status. He just didn't like Trujillo and never made any secret of the fact.

Trujillo at the last was an old man who in many ways resembled an old-time American machine political boss, trying to hold onto power as long as possible. When he was sixty-nine and American diplomat William Pauley urged him to retire, Trujillo replied grimly: "I'll retire when I'm dead." Espaillat wrote:

> He meant it, too. Power was the only reason for his existence. Trujillo had no intention of following the example of the parade of ousted strongmen who had passed through the Dominican Republic during their flights. The forlorn faces of Rojas Pinilla, Perez Jimenez, Peron and Batista were gruesome reminders of the fate of fallen dictators.

Espaillat speculated that in the last flash of consciousness, when he knew he was done for, Trujillo may have been well satisfied with his fate:

> A man who lived by the gun he died triggering one, shooting it out with his enemies. . . . Assassination is a traditional feature of the claw and fang of Caribbean politics. None knew this better than Trujillo. I have never heard even the Old Man's friends condemn his murder on moral grounds. But I have heard both his friends and his enemies denounce Mutt and Jeff for absenting themselves from the country (the CIA agent was in Washington at the time of the assassination and the consular official apparently left for Washington immediately afterward). By so doing they abandoned their co-conspirators to their fates—and those fates were not pleasant.

Since the Bay of Pigs was in mid-April and the assassination of Trujillo at the end of May, there were six weeks during which insiders at the CIA and State Department either spent weary nights contemplating further attempts to stop the shooting they had originally hoped for, or else waited resignedly for the other shoe to fall. One of those who waited with mixed feelings had to be Allen Dulles as he prepared to retire to his huge Wisconsin Avenue home, once a mecca for leading intelligence figures from all parts of the world and soon to become a lonely place.

Trujillo's death on May 31, 1961, ended the painful suspense. After a canvass in which no place seemed eager to receive his remains, and as though an ordinary plot of ground at home would be too mundane for a man who had defied time and tradition by surviving in absolutism so long, his body was flown to Paris. It was placed in a black marble mausoleum in Père Lachaise cemetery, not far from the tomb of Marcel Proust.

Nine years later, in 1970, Trujillo's remains were moved again, to a site near Madrid, Spain, where his son Ramfis had died at the age of 43 after a head-on automobile collision the previous year, and where his younger son Rhadames still lived. No reason other than family sentiment was given for the second removal.

The Great Rebel

5

Che Guevara, though from Argentina, was the military and literary hero of the Cuban revolution. He was barely thirty when he marched into Havana with his troops following the fall of the Batista government at the start of 1959. Every word that he wrote was treasured immediately, not only by his local admirers but by outside publishers as well. As Guevara explained in his *History of the Cuban Revolution*, Castro was the spiritual and political leader and had little time for the extremely grubby military operations which he so successfully delegated.

Although extremely well-educated (he held a medical degree), Guevara gloried in the hardships necessarily associated with guerrilla activity. In his *Guerrilla Warfare* (Random House, 1961), he wrote:

> The guerrilla goes on and on, hunting and being hunted, suffering cold and heat, sweating and drying out, without time for personal cleanliness. In Cuba it was literally a stinking life. Even individual hammocks could be identified by their smell.

When he was in Bolivia and so ill that he had to be carried through part of a march, he noted in his diary: "In an absence of water my stench preceded me by a league."

Since he was primarily a Latin hero, it was difficult for North Americans to visualize the extent of the mourning that followed Guevara's death in Bolivia in 1967. A paragraph from *Che Guevara on Revolution* (Delta, 1969), edited and with an introduction by Jay Mallin, and produced under a grant from the Ford Foundation at the University of Miami's Center for International Studies, suggested that this went far beyond anything that could be readily imagined by anyone living north of the Rio Grande. Mallin wrote in his introduction:

> Within weeks after the news of Guevara's death, placards proclaiming "Che is alive" and "Viva Che," together with appropriate portraits, became standard features of protest demonstrations everywhere. In Rimini, Italy, two priests presided over a mass for Guevara; a Brazilian Bishop asked for prayers for "Our brother Che Guevara" and a Brazilian Archbishop declared; "I find that Che Guevara was sincere." In Lima, Peru, grammar school children held hands, danced in a circle, and chanted, "*Con cuchillo y con cuchara, que viva el Che Guevara*" (With knife and with spoon, long live Che Guevara). In Santiago, Chile, a bookstore sold photographs of Guevara, mounted on a wooden base, at a rate of five hundred a month; and in Italy close to 15,000 copies of Guevara's *Guerrilla Warfare* were sold in a fortnight. A poll published in Spain showed Guevara to be "the most popular international figure of the year," and the student bulletin at the University of Salamanca declared: "There is a man of this century who has looked above and beyond his political party. From the point of view of dedication to the sick, to the weak and to his fellow men, this Ernesto Guevara . . . doctor by profession and guerrilla by necessity, can be a lesson to us all."

Whether or not Guevara deserved such praise was, for the United States, largely beside the point. Mallin elsewhere referred to the "Guevara myth" and to the "irony" of his worldwide adoption by peace groups after so much glorification of guerrilla war. Diplomacy, however, had to deal with the sentiment that existed.

America's CIA-directed intervention that brought about Guevara's death was a relatively small-scale operation. Aided by a serious miscalculation on Guevara's part, eliminating Guevara was, from the CIA's point of view, one of the most successful exploits the agency had ever conducted. Everyone knew that the CIA was the force behind Guevara's downfall, and yet the performance at every turn had been handed over to Bolivians so that no one could put a finger on the time and place where the CIA had done the deed. Only sixteen United States Army Green Berets were used to train the 800-man force of Bolivian Rangers that hunted Guevara down. And only two CIA agents, both of whom were conspicuous on the scene at the time of Guevara's execution without trial, became publicly identified with the operation.

Why Guevara left Cuba was never made entirely clear. As a minister of state in Havana, at a time when Cuba was vitally dependent on Soviet economic aid, he had been something of an embarrassment to the Castro government because of his outspoken criticism of Moscow for lack of generosity toward the underdeveloped countries; but he never lost Castro's public and private support. He turned up in Bolivia with a beautiful woman called Tania, presumed to be his mistress, who followed him to her death in his guerrilla band, but there was no evidence that this association affected his planning. The official explanation for his leaving Cuba was that he hoped to create "many Vietnams": as a contribution to the struggle against imperialism, for the relief of Ho Chi Minh's forces, and to thoroughly test his theories on guerrilla warfare.

Guevara dropped out of sight a few months after having been accorded the honor of addressing the United Nations Assembly on December 9, 1964. In his speech he said: "We morally support and feel as one with people everywhere who are struggling to make a reality of the right to full sovereignty."

After traveling incognito in Africa and Asia, and after sending advance agents to prepare a hidden campsite in the interior of Bolivia, he reached the Bolivian capital of La Paz, originally in disguise, late in 1966. With a band that at its peak numbered about seventy men—and Tania—he conducted eleven months of guerrilla warfare in the Bolivian hinterland. Sixteen of his men were battle-hardened Cubans, forty or more were Bolivians with similar ideological commitments, and the rest were from a scattering of countries, including Argentina and Peru.

By standard Marxist measurements there was no revolutionary situation in Bolivia, especially not for the kind of agricultural revolution Guevara had in mind. Most of the unrest was in the tin mines, to which he had no access. Bolivia had carried out a certain amount of agricultural reform, many small farmers had their own land, and the economy, although nothing to boast about, was slowly improving. But Guevara firmly believed—in impatient disagreement with all of the canonized saints of Marxist theory—that it was not always necessary to wait for a revolutionary situation to develop; such situations, he felt, could be *created*.

Guevara's beliefs, however, were not to be borne out in Bolivia. Not a single peasant joined his band; some of them even cooperated with the authorities by informing against him. Although in guerrilla terms he was well financed by Castro, he had no way in these circumstances to increase or even to maintain his strength. Meanwhile, with the aid of the CIA and its small contingent of Green Berets, the Bolivian government could deploy against him an unlimited number of Rangers who were trained by the Berets at a camp called Le Esperanz north of La Paz. Che's downfall was just a question of time; at the end he was down to fewer than twenty men.

Having in effect staked his career on the Bolivian operation Guevara was goaded by criticism into intransigence; he stuck to his guns longer than he should have. On September 8, 1967, a month before his capture, he wrote in his diary:

> A Budapest daily criticizes Che Guevara's political image and calls it irresponsible and pitiful and salutes the Marxist attitude of the Chilean Communist Party, which it says takes practical attitudes in the face of practice. How I would like to rise to power just to unmask cowards and lackeys of every sort, and squash their snouts in their own filth.

Another reason he remained in Bolivia when he still could have escaped was a belief that if captured he would be given a trial which would cause an international sensation. In various ambushes and skirmishes the Guevara guerrillas had killed approximately forty Rangers, but they had treated prisoners well, releasing them almost immediately and in good condition; enlisted men were released in their socks and shorts, while officers were permitted to keep their uniforms. Guevara had heard clear statements over the radio that he would be put to trial if he were captured, and he expected some reciprocity on the treatment of prisoners. On October 4, four days before his capture, he wrote in his diary:

> The radio broadcasts news of the transfer of the Army's Fourth Division forward headquarters from Laguna to Padilla, to cover the Serrano area where it is believed the guerrillas will try to escape. The radio commented that if I am captured by the Fourth Division they will try me at Camiri, but if I am captured by the Eighth Division I will be tried at Santa Cruz.

On October 8, when Guevara and a guerrilla called "Willy" (a Bolivian whose real name was Simon Cuba) stumbled into the arms of four Bolivian Rangers near the village of La Higuera, Guevara's first words were: "Don't kill us. I'm Che Guevara. I'm worth more to you alive than dead."

Guevara was unarmed and limping painfully at the time of his capture. A bullet had smashed his Garand rifle from his hands and had ricocheted into his right calf. A Bolivian guerrilla called "Inti" (Guido Paredo) and five companions were conducting a rear-guard action to distract the enemy while Willy helped Guevara to the other side of a steep rise, where he hoped to dress his wound. The maneuver failed when the Rangers on patrol appeared suddenly at the top of the rise just as Guevara and Willy reached its summit. A third guerrilla, Aniceto Reynaga Cordillo, was captured with them when he tried to come to their aid. Guevara was locked in one room of a two-room schoolhouse, and Willy and Aniceto were imprisoned in sheds nearby.

Luis J. Gonzalez and Gustavo A. Sanchez Salazar, experienced and competent Bolivian journalists, carefully investigated the events of the next twenty-four hours for their book, *The Great Rebel* (Grove, 1969). They said an order for the summary execution of the three prisoners, issued by President Rene Barrientos, reached La Higuera at ten A.M. the following day. The order was most extraordinary because of the publicly broadcast plans for a trial and repeated calls for Guevara's capture alive, and also because Bolivia had outlawed the death penalty. Guevara could not have known of the order immediately, but he soon had advance warning of his fate—he heard the shots that killed Willy and Aniceto.

At one P.M. a Bolivian sergeant shouldering an automatic weapon entered the schoolroom, having spent most of the noon hour drinking beer. Despite his wounded leg Guevara was standing, leaning against a wall.

The sergeant was disconcerted. "Sit down," he ordered.

"Why bother?" Guevara replied. "You are going to kill me."

"No. . . . Sit down," the sergeant insisted. He turned momentarily as though to go for help, then wheeled and fired a volley that killed Guevara instantly. The executioner was using a fully automatic M–2 carbine, a familiar weapon in the United States Army, and Guevara suffered six bullet wounds including one through the heart.

Gonzales and Sanchez Salazar wrote:

> Shot, executed, murdered or "finished off"—whatever particular personal interpretation is given to the facts—there is a human truth that rises above subjectivism. A man, a sick and wounded prisoner, was killed without any semblance of justice when he was in the hands of those whose duty it was to jealously guard his physical safety. Beyond any moral law and above any legal scruple, the truth was that an elementary

rule of war had been violated. . . . A feeling of guilty doubt spread through the Bolivian population and was even felt abroad.

Instead of retiring into. the background in these solemn last hours when its mission had been accomplished, the CIA suddenly seemed to be everywhere. In describing the activity before and after Guevara's execution, Gonzalez and Sanchez wrote:

> The night was long for the prisoner, for he was questioned several times. The man from the CIA—"Dr." Eduardo Gonzales—who had arrived by helicopter, took a special interest in these sessions. . . . Immediately after Guevara's death the CIA agent minutely examined his corpse, carefully photographing every feature of his anatomy. The fact that Guevara's eyes stayed open (known from universally distributed death photographs) was due to the fact that the agent kept forcing the eyelids back until rigor mortis set in. Several officers witnessed this thorough examination, including Lieutenant Tomas "Totty" Aguilera, who later described it to one of the authors. Gonzales devoted the following day to carefully and patiently photographing Che's campaign diary.

The same Gonzales and another CIA agent were on hand when Guevara's body, tied to a helicopter landing ski, was flown to Valle Grande, where it was positively identified and fingerprinted at Señor de Malta Hospital. Gonzales and the second CIA agent, identified as Felix Ramos, had reached Bolivia together the previous August 5. "They were extremely well dressed," according to Gonzales and Sanchez, "and kept repeating that they were going to invest money in Bolivian businesses." But apparently no one was fooled, and the two agents were soon seen in the company of Major Ralph "Pappy" Shelton, American commander of the Green Beret training unit.

Ramos was described as "a tall, heavyset man with sparse blond hair"; he was "the dominant figure." Gonzales and Sanchez wrote:

He supervised every phase of the Valle Grande operation. He was at the airport preparing the landing area for the helicopter, ordering the corpse to be taken to the hospital, keeping newsmen out and threatening to have two of them, Brian Moser and Richard Gott, expelled from the city. His power was so great that his orders could be revoked only by the Commander-in-Chief of the Armed Forces.

The guerrilla known as "Inti," of whom Guevara had often spoken highly in his campaign diary, and four others managed to fight their way out of the trap at La Higuera. Early in 1968 they reached Chilean soil. Though treated as heroes in the northern provinces, they were denied political asylum by the government at Santiago and were given only forty-eight hours in which to leave the country.

They were joined at this point by Salvador Allende, then president of the senate in the Chilean Congress. He advised them of their international rights and managed to get the original decision reviewed and modified. Instead of being expelled immediately, the guerrillas were flown to Santiago, where circuitous air travel to Cuba was arranged, and they were escorted out of the country at Chilean expense.

With Allende still accompanying them, the guerrillas were first flown to Pascua Island, 2,500 miles off the Chilean coast in the Pacific. Allende also accompanied them to French Papeete, the capital of Tahiti, where they were met by Cuba's ambassador to France. They were flown to Paris and, less than two weeks after entering Chile, from Paris to Havana.

Allende's election as president of Chile came two years later. Since his margin of victory over his nearest opponent was only 39,000 votes in a total of three million, any help he may have gotten from his association with the Guevara guerrillas could have made all the difference.

In the familiar role of trying to correct a situation that activities of the CIA had helped to create, the United States now set a course which eventually led to Allende's overthrow and assassination in a military coup in 1973.

The cost to the United States of "destabilizing" Allende was given as $11.5 million, which couldn't have been more than a small fraction of the total expenditure. But whatever the figure, it was dwarfed by the cost to the Chileans in terms of damage to their economy and loss of freedoms.

In the wake of Allende's downfall was a clear record that the United States, through the CIA, and this time under direct orders of President Nixon, had conspired with every resource at its command to create the iron-handed military dictatorship which emerged after forty-six years of democratic rule in Chile. The record also clearly indicates that this conspiracy was set in motion even before Allende took office.

Since Allende's election on September 4, 1970 was by a plurality of only 36.3 percent of the vote in a field of several candidates, under the terms of the Chilean Constitution his selection had to be ratified by the Chilean Congress when it met October 24. Although this provision had never been used to change or nullify an election result, there was speculation that the intervening six weeks would be a period of some uncertainty in which a coup might be staged.

Senate investigators later found that between October 5 and October 20 the CIA made twenty-one conspiratorial contacts with key Chilean military and police officials to urge them to stage a coup and to assure them of strong American support before and after the civilian government's overthrow.

The major obstacle to a coup was General Rene Schneider, commander-in-chief of the army, who insisted that the constitutional process must be observed. With time running out and Allende's confirmation only two days away, the CIA in the early morning hours of October 22 passed machine guns and ammunition to one of two groups that were sufficiently organized to stage coups: one of the coup leaders had been promised $50,000, and the other, perhaps wishing to put the matter on a more businesslike basis, was to have received $20,000 plus $200,000 in life insurance.

Later the same day, October 22, General Schneider was accosted on his way to work, by men brandishing machine guns and was shot dead. The CIA version was that the assassins had planned only to kidnap him, but were forced to fire when he drew a revolver to defend himself. The story also was—and this one was about as thin as gauze—that because there were two coup groups the CIA could not determine whether its weapons were the ones used in the slaying. The undeniable reality, however, was that General Schneider had put in a few good words for democracy, and that he was killed as a consequence.

A temporary result of the well-regarded Schneider's death was that the military united behind the civilian government. But with CIA-backed opposition constantly whittling away politically and economically at Allende's regime, the successful coup came three years later.

The debacle in Chile was one of a long succession of calamities for democratic government in Central and South America; Brazil had succumbed with CIA connivance to military rule in 1964; Panama and Peru in 1968; Bolivia in 1969; Ecuador in 1972; Uruguay as well as Chile in 1973, with Argentina soon to follow. Columnist Jack Anderson, reporting on the subject in October 1976, attributed the grim results to "seeing Communists under every hibiscus bush," and added:

> The heirs of George Washington and Thomas Jefferson actively have aided and abetted the rise of military dictatorship in the Western Hemisphere. In a few short years Latin America has become largely a Pax Americana with the Pentagon as its Vatican ... [and] this country, once regarded around the world as the bastion of freedom, now is thought no better than its Communist rivals.

The Sun Rises

6

The preparation of the president's daily intelligence report was considered to be the CIA's most important bureaucratic function from the agency's inception. For this task a sizable number of high-priced CIA employees were routed from their beds at unearthly hours so that the document could be on the president's desk at eight A.M. or whenever he chose to start his day.

President Truman stipulated that for his use the report had to be limited to a single page. The CIA later obtained permission to go to several pages by placing the equivalent of newspaper headlines opposite the lengthier material. A president could then run down through the summarizing statements and decide what he wanted to read. In this format the report became known as the president's "Book," or as PICKLE (for President's Intelligence Checklist). For many years only three copies were made in addition to the original—one for the director of Central Intelligence, another for the secretary of state, and a third for the secretary of defense.

From the ritualistic awe and high degree of secrecy with which the report was treated, it might have been supposed that its benefits in terms of information and wisdom were limitless. However, when the prestige of Defense Secretary Robert S. McNamara was at its height (he was frequently referred to as a computer on legs), it developed one day that McNamara had no use for his copy. Asked during a House hearing "Are you operating on intelligence that you receive from the CIA?", McNamara replied emphatically: "No, Sir! I receive information directly from the Defense Intelligence Agency, and that information is screened by no one outside the Pentagon." A full cycle had been described in which an agency set up to be impartial had become more biased in McNamara's judgment than one of the world's oldest and most prosperous military establishments.

McNamara wanted raw information and was contrasted in that respect to Charles E. Wilson, Eisenhower's first secretary of defense. Wilson—better remembered for saying of the first artificial earth satellite, "It's a neat trick but it has no significance"—once downgraded the importance of intelligence by saying, "We already know more about the Russians than we know what to do about." At a press conference in 1957 he commented resignedly:

> You see, what I get for my purposes is an agreed-upon intelligence estimate. . . . I have to take that or I would have to bore through an enormous amount of detail to try to say whether they were right or wrong. . . . I accept what they say, and I can't go back of that in my time available.

In retrospect and against the background of the Vietnamese War, the judgments of both Wilson and McNamara, actually about equal in spite of their differences, appeared to have been considerably inferior to those of Senator Fulbright who was operating without benefit of an intelligence service. When Fulbright said that the public press had been "generally more accurate than the official estimates" about Vietnam, it was accepted as another of his sly understatements. In fact, we now know that the record of "the media"—newspapers, magazines, radio and television—was far from distinguished as well.

An argument could be made that the less intelligence a man was provided, the better off he was, and that the best of all possible situations was to have none at all. When a great deal of other information was available and in the presence of many imponderables this might have been correct, partly because Intelligence operations tended to inflate the ego, discourage reliance on useful but unglamorous precedents, and to become an end in themselves (whether they produced anything or not).

On the other hand, in occasional closed situations, intelligence was the only source of information and the only means of approaching a problem. A quick recovery of the prestige of the intelligence community was made possible by the occurrence of one of those closed situations in the year following the Bay of Pigs. Perhaps because of a surge of overconfidence stimulated on the Communist side by their success in Cuba, the hardest of hard intelligence established eighteen months later that the Soviets were deploying nuclear missiles on Castro's island.

President Kennedy never wavered from an immediate decision that by one means or another the missiles must be removed, although he was fully aware that the issue could be interpreted as one of form rather than substance. Since the Soviets were already capable of dumping a great deal of nuclear explosives on the United States, and if this was taken as the equivalent of complete destruction, it could be argued that their acquiring the ability to do this from Cuban as well as Russian soil would not increase the already existing danger.

In the interpretations of the CIA and the Pentagon, however, the Cuban ploy if successful would have meant an enormous increase in Soviet power. Either 64 or 80 missiles capable of hitting targets over most of the United States and much of the rest of the Western Hemisphere were being installed in Cuba, and America's then highly valued superiority in intercontinental missiles would have been almost wiped out. At the time of the October crisis, America was about to deploy its 200th ICBM, whereas the Soviets were said to have "fewer" (though perhaps not significantly fewer) than one hundred.

Regardless of such statistics Kennedy was sure that for psychological reasons if no others, and especially in view of Castro's reputed unreliability, the Cuban deployment could not be tolerated. From his viewpoint the Soviet ability to destroy the United States had become a fact of life that had to be accepted, but their sharing the ability with anyone else or their flaunting the fact to gain political advantage had to be rejected.

Historical precedents for solving the crisis were difficult to derive and far from encouraging. If either the Germans or the Japanese had acquired nuclear weapons in big power quantities and had been challenged on the subject while operating inside or even outside the law, the only reasonable prediction that could have been made on the basis of precedent would have been that this meant almost immediate nuclear war. In the current context there was a possibility that the Soviets would prove somewhat easier to deal with.

For one thing Khrushchev, now in full power, was a phenomenon such as the world had not seen before nor was likely to see again. During his first year as Soviet premier he delivered nearly a hundred full-dress speeches and addressed more than a hundred messages to heads of government. He also traveled to far parts of the earth, expostulating extemporaneously, exposing all his prejudices, predilections, and basically good intentions. That the leader of the world's second greatest power could have crawled as far out on a limb as he did in the Cuban missile crisis, and then, with the entire population of the globe watching, could have perspiringly crawled all the way back, was a performance that even years afterward would seem almost incredible.

Although temporarily more subdued after Dulles's departure, the CIA was already back as "the mysterious gray presence" at all of the government's emergency sessions. New CIA Director McCone was a change for the agency in that he was purely an administrator with no special qualifications in intelligence. He was credited nevertheless with being among the first to predict correctly that Soviet antiaircraft missiles being moved with great speed into Cuba would be followed quickly by offensive types.

At the start of the crisis, the Air Force had taken over responsibility from the CIA for stepped-up U–2 reconnaissance over Cuba, with the CIA continuing to analyze the photographs obtained. The combination proved to be the means of establishing that an offensive buildup in Cuba was in progress. The switch in U-2 command amounted to a bureaucratic defeat of the first magnitude for the CIA, which until then had conducted Cuban U-2 flights at the rate of two a month. As many CIA men self-righteously contended, these flights, though conducted more or less openly, were still a flat violation of Cuban air space and international law, and therefore belonged in the agency's covert province. New CIA Director McCone, however, was showing little taste for bureaucratic infighting, and was persuaded to agree to the change in U-2 management.

A ground report from a CIA agent in Cuba, describing a missile much too large to be an antiaircraft type, which he spotted as it was being moved along a Cuban highway, might have been considered the first conclusive evidence except for an unexplained nine-day delay in the message's delivery to headquarters, which raised questions as to its authenticity.

The elite corps of the CIA's intelligence analysis section, the agency's Board of National Estimates, never managed a "direct hit" at this early stage of the crisis; the Board fired on both sides of the target, and demonstrated a remarkable ability to reverse itself when more information became available.

Another factor in the situation was the "defection in place" of Colonel Oleg Penkovsky, operating chief of Russia's military intelligence—the GRU—who would be executed as a traitor the following May. Possibly because he was already under suspicion, Penkovsky was not credited with disclosing the oncoming crisis itself, but the background information he had been supplying great Britain and the United States for months was important in analysis. F. H. Usher wrote in *The Great Spies* (Hart, 1967):

President Kennedy has always taken sole credit for calling Khrushchev's bluff in Cuba, a decision requiring judgment and steely nerves. But the decision was to a large extent based on Penkovsky's reports, which enabled American experts to judge precisely the extent and nature of the Soviet military threat in Cuba.

Among other things, Penkovsky was first to report that Gary Powers said he was shot down from 68,000 feet, and he furnished the size, range and explosive power of every missile in the Soviet arsenal. The verifiable authenticity of his information inspired confidence in reaching conclusions and made possible the correct evaluation of information that came from other sources.

The first Soviet surface-to-air (SAM) antiaircraft missiles reached Cuba in July 1962. In August, the CIA dispatched a report to the White House saying that these were being emplaced with exceptional speed and with more than 5,000 Soviet technicians on the scene.

The first offensive missile was off-loaded in Cuba on September 8. The ground report of its being spotted on a Cuban highway was written September 12 but did not reach headquarters until September 21. That was two days after the Board of National Estimates had submitted a conclusion that Khrushchev would not undertake such a "high risk" program as placing offensive nuclear missiles in Cuba.

Air Force Major Rudolph Anderson, Jr.—later killed in the only U–2 to be shot down over Cuba—returned on October 14 with clear photographs of an offensive missile base under construction. These, showing one missile ominously erected as though ready for firing, were accepted by Kennedy as proof that the unlikely project was under way. The Board of National Estimates, meanwhile, had submitted a "crash" report reversing itself and stating that Khrushchev was now prepared to risk nuclear war—another bit of "intelligence" which would prove not to be precisely the case.

Hard information by this time was overtaking CIA estimates before they could be completed. The United States soon had hard aerial proof of construction starts on 24 launching pads to be doubly armed with a total of 48 medium-range missiles capable of striking targets at distances of 1,000 miles, and of ground preparations for 16 launching pads for intermediate missiles with ranges of 2,200 miles. The only point not settled was whether the intermediate pads would be doubly or singly armed, which made the difference as to whether the overall total of offensive missiles in Cuba would be 80 or 64.

While Penkovsky's significance may have been slightly exaggerated by Usher in this particular instance, there was no question that he was one of the most important intelligence windfalls of the century. The manner of his acquisition by the West well exemplified the fact that in intelligence work, as in everything else, events rarely conform to a preconceived pattern.

It might have been supposed that British and American intelligence had somehow learned, as was the fact, that Penkovsky had become disaffected from the Soviet government after the death of Stalin, whom he admired. With his disaffection in mind as an entering wedge, it would then be expected that the two intelligence services would have vigorously pursued the man, offering him money and power, and trying to trap him with strong spirits, ladies of the evening, or whatever he preferred. But nothing of this kind occurred.

Actually it was the other way around, with Penkovsky vigorously pursuing British and American intelligence agents, offering his services and having them rejected. Penkovsky first offered his services to the CIA in 1955 when he was a military attaché in Turkey. It would have been logical to assume that his being outside his own country would provide an opportunity to learn what the man had to offer, but the decision of Counterintelligence Chief Angleton was that Penkovsky's offer was "too good to be true" and "more likely a trap."

After he had completed his tour of duty in Turkey, Penkovsky renewed his offer to the CIA through the American embassy in Moscow, but it was again rejected for the same reasons. Even after Penkovsky had produced thousands of pages of useful data for the West, Angleton was still insisting that he might be a "plant." British intelligence may have been initially wary of him, too, since when Penkovsky finally made his successful contact there, it was not with the intelligence service but with a British business representative named Greville Wynne, who then persuaded the intelligence people to accept him.

Wynne got into the picture because he was heading a trade delegation in Moscow. In Russia, especially after World War II when trained and educated people were extremely scarce, the intelligence services performed various unrelated chores, and Penkovsky was heading the reception committee for Wynne's trade delegation. Thus, while the suspicions and machinations of the intelligence services had long prevented this intelligence windfall, what started as straightforward economic intercourse readily produced it.

One of the more favorable aspects of the missile crisis was that the CIA was hewing to the administration's policy line instead of popping up on its own here and there in attempts to hamstring the potential enemy in connection with the main event, to make the White House more effective with dubious behind-the-scenes maneuvering and stage-setting, or to correct administration "errors" to conform with a philosophy heavily influenced by secrecy and extremism. With Great Britain in the handling of Penkovsky after he was finally "recruited," and with the Air Force in the Cuban aerial reconnaissance, the agency could even be said to have shown a capacity for teamwork, as foreign as that was to the CIA's usual way of doing things. While the gratifying change would be short-lived, it could be remembered as a goal to be sought in any civilian intelligence agency that might be set up to replace the CIA in the future.

In any case, in early 1962, the CIA's special purposes and independent tendencies were temporarily put aside because of the overpowering nature of the missile crisis, the agency's recent humiliation in Cuba, internal strains connected with its change in management, and setbacks in far parts of the world. As one CIA official later recalled:

"We were really a sick dog in those days. Anyone could kick us and be sure we wouldn't bite back"

McCone's arrival on the scene as CIA director was accompanied by some controversy because, from a small original investment sometimes placed at $100,000, he and his associates had made millions in West Coast shipbuilding during World War II. Senators argued that the government furnished the shipyards and built the ships, with McCone and his associates in effect providing management services, and that the take was much greater than could have been justified as a fee. This generated sixteen Senate votes against his confirmation, and he still may not have been speaking with the full authority of his office at the time of the missile crisis. Three telegrams renewing his apprehensions on that subject and sent by McCone from Paris—where he was on honeymoon with his second wife—were placed in the CIA's files without reaching the White House.

In Laos the CIA was losing out to the neutralist government of Prince Souvanna Phouma, which had been installed after the Geneva Accords in 1954 and included representatives of the pro-Communist Pathet Lao led by Prince Souphanouvong. The Pathet Lao's princely titular head was Souvanna Phouma's half brother and was the only Communist leader in history who had had to be addressed as "Your Highness." (This was no flippancy; while embracing Communist doctrine, Souphanouvong still insisted on receiving everything due him in accordance with his hereditary rights.)

The CIA had long backed right-wing General Phoumi Nosavan, who in 1960 had succeeded in overthrowing Souvanna Phouma. Lacking in popular support, General Phoumi's troops had proved so ineffective that the Pathet Lao had taken over large sections of the country on its own. In June of 1962, a month before the Soviets began moving missiles into Cuba, emergency American diplomatic measures succeeded in restoring the coalition government of Souvanna Phouma. The situation was thus partly righted, although the central government did not regain control of the eastern part of the country that became known as the Ho Chi Minh Trail.

No CIA reminders of the danger in Cuba were necessary. The halls of Congress and the Cuban exile community in Miami were alive with missile rumors. On August 31, nine days before the first offensive missile reached Cuba, Senator Kenneth B. Keating, Republican, of New York announced that he had received positive information that offensive types were on their way.

When the hard intelligence was finally available there was little difference of opinion in the councils of government and in Congress as to the policy that had to be pursued. Such widely incompatible figures as Senators Russell and Fulbright joined in urging immediate invasion of Cuba. Kennedy was fully prepared for that and ordered an impressive array of military force into Florida, but he decided to start with a more moderate approach.

First, following a tactic adopted by Khrushchev in 1960, Kennedy withheld for almost a full week the information that he knew there were offensive missiles in Cuba. The proof was brought to him after thorough analysis of the photographs on the morning of October 16, and he made the first public announcement of this turn of events on the evening of October 22. The catalogue of Soviet lies in the form of requested and readily supplied assurances contrary to the facts by that time equalled or exceeded those told by the United States in the Gary Powers incident before Khrushchev revealed that he had all the evidence including the pilot alive and well. Without credit to either country, the record concerning honesty in government was thus set in balance in a way that may eventually have been taken to heart by both Washington and Moscow. (Dr. Kissinger was able to say after his long diplomatic sojourn that the Soviets had never told him a direct lie.)

On the day that President Kennedy announced the missile crisis, a grim detachment of KGB agents arrived at Soviet military headquarters in Moscow to place Colonel

Penkovsky under arrest. Although the Soviet military and civilian intelligence agencies were bitter rivals, the KGB agents were thoroughly dumbfounded by the extensive evidence of treason against their formerly trusted military counterpart.

Possibly Kennedy or another American anxious to show how much this country knew, or someone in the British government with which Penkovsky was more closely associated, had inadvertently spilled the beans; or perhaps Penkovsky himself had recklessly betrayed himself in his eagerness to gain favor with the West. Certainly, as his observations later published as *The Penkovsky Papers* (Doubleday, 1965) would show, he was one of the hardest-working as well as one of the most highly placed traitors in history. (The book consisted mainly of his political musings from a pro-Stalin viewpoint, in addition to his intelligence reports. These were known to have been even more extensive, covering more than ten thousand pages.)

Many years later in a speech in April 1971, CIA Director Helms told the American Society of Newspaper Editors that America had been aided in the missile crisis by a "number of well-placed and courageous Russians." Talking to reporters afterward Helms confirmed that Penkovsky was one of the Russians he had in mind.

Helms did not elaborate and the specific motives of Penkovsky could not be spelled out, but that the GRU chief was self-centered to an extraordinary degree was beyond question. Throughout his dealings with American and British intelligence—some of which took place in London's Mount Royal Hotel—one of Penkovsky's most pressing concerns was directed toward obtaining assurances that when he defected physically to London or Washington he would be given a position as prestigious as the one he already held in Moscow.

This concern may have cost him his life, assuming his physical defection might otherwise have been arranged successfully. As it was, he remained in the Soviet Union long enough to be executed, because in the nature of things, even imported traitors not normally being considered suitable for high office, and also because he was so well-favored at home, such assurances could not be given him. He was told only that he would be given work in accordance with his training and abilities.

The Helms speech attracted attention and was inserted in the *Congressional Record* because it was the first he had ever made publicly. Like Dulles, and as a onetime United Press reporter who had interviewed Adolf Hitler, Helms expressed unqualified belief in objectivity, saying:

> This puts me on familiar ground as an old wire service hand. . . . Without objectivity there is no credibility, and an intelligence agency without credibility is of little use to those it serves. We not only have no stake in policy debates, we cannot and must not take sides. If I should take sides . . . the credibility of the CIA goes out the window.

If the newspaper editors were not listening too closely, they may have been under the impression that the CIA had adopted a new banner. Elsewhere in his speech, however, Helms made it clear that the CIA had in no way changed its ideological precepts, and a serious question could be raised as to how much objectivity would be possible under these circumstances.

Helms said that the CIA's campus employment recruiting had been discontinued where it stirred objections but would be resumed where possible and desirable. And in case anyone thought that old issue between personal and professional integrity and the CIA's brand of patriotism belonged to the dead past, he disabused them of the notion:

> If there is a chance that a private citizen traveling abroad has acquired information that can be useful to the American policymaker we are certainly going to try to interview him. And if there is a competent young graduate student interested in working for the United States government we may try to hire him.

Ironically, our efforts to obtain foreign intelligence in this country have generated some of the most virulent criticism of the Central Intelligence Agency. . . . The trouble is that to those who insist on seeing us as a pernicious and pervasive secret government, our words "interview" and "hire" translate into suborn, subvert, and seduce or something worse.

We use no compulsion. If a possible source of information does not want to talk to us we go away quietly. If some campus groups object to our recruiting on campus we fall back on the nearest Federal Office Building. Similarly we welcome the opportunity to place research contracts with universities; but again, these are strictly voluntary.

The principal significance that could be attached to these last remarks, especially the statement that "we use no compulsion," was that there was an occasion for making them. If the Department of Agriculture or even the Department of Defense had come out with statements that they did not use force in the collection of information no one would have been able to imagine what they could be talking about.

Helms on the other hand was speaking to a well-understood point, which was more than troubling to observers and students of government. In a front-page article April 25, 1966, the *New York Times* had had this to say:

In many ways public discussion has become too centered on the question of control [of the CIA]. A more disturbing matter may be whether the nation has allowed itself to go too far in the grim and sometimes deadly business of espionage and secret operations. One of the best-informed men on the subject in Washington described the business as "ugly, mean, and cruel." "The agency loses men and no one ever hears from them again," he said. "And when we catch one of them it becomes necessary to get everything out of him, and we do it with no holds barred."

The *Times* article was one of a series of five based on interviews with 50 present and former government officials, and on reports from 20 foreign correspondents with experience in 35 countries. According to Gay Talese's *The Kingdom and the Power* (Doubleday, 1969), either the CIA director or recently retired Director McCone was permitted to read and criticize the articles in advance of publication. No doubt changes were made where warranted, but it would have been difficult to challenge the passages on brutality because Secretary of State Rusk had said almost the same thing in a public speech.

Rusk, a fast friend of the CIA at this time—although he later complained of not having been told of the assassination plotting that went on while he was in office—could well have been the person referred to in the article as "one of the best-informed men on the subject in Washington." In his public speech he said:

> A tough struggle is going on in the back alleys of the world. It's a tough one, it's unpleasant and no one likes it, but that is not a field that can be left entirely to the other side. The back-alley struggle is a never-ending war, and there is no quarter asked and none given.

That the necessity for such tactics was as great as Rusk believed could be doubted on the basis of other evidence. Allen Dulles, the master spy of them all—urbane, convivial and much more gregarious than his stiff and unbending older brother—was certainly a familiar and, even though he traveled in an armored car, an often unguarded target around Washington for many years, but he said in an interview that he had never been shot at and knew of no attempt to abduct him. While not ruling out the possibility of an attack, this did not suggest that his occupation was especially more hazardous than many others.[4]

Even Khrushchev turned out to be harmless as a person, although the Soviet leader was something of a roughneck compared to the gentlemanly Zhou Enlai. Khrushchev demonstrated his rough-and-tumble tendency by taking off a shoe and banging it on his desk to get the attention he thought he deserved at a meeting of the United Nations Assembly in 1960. In some circumstances he could, like Zhou, have become a target for assassination.

An argument could be made that the United States

would have benefited considerably more if instead of a hardfisted spy network the country had produced a man comparable to the frail British philosopher Bertrand Russell, who was destined to figure in the Cuban missile crisis. Assuming that Dulles and the British Russell were equally patriotic as well as equally secure as they appeared to be in their positions of prominence, their ideas as to where their national interests lay had to be poles apart.

The key statement in the Helms speech as far as it concerned objectivity was one likely to go unnoticed in a day when anti-Communism was taken almost as much for granted as breathing the air. There were, however, *degrees* of anti-Communism, and a person or organization had to be pretty far down the line to acquire an admiration for another country's traitors. Certainly, such admiration would rarely be found in the regular military services. In an organizational sense a fervent reference such as Helms's to Penkovsky as "a courageous Russian" could have come only from an outfit with the special and extreme anti-Communist cast of the CIA or the John Birch Society.

By contrast the aged Bertrand Russell was a scientist and a mathematician as well as a philosopher, who had watched Hitler and Mussolini lead basically proletarian movements to positions far to the right of anything business, professional, aristocratic or politically conservative groups had ever expected or wanted to see. That kind of background, and the gruesome events that followed, as well as the new life-destroying nuclear possibilities for which these events had set the stage, caused him to be much more alarmed than most people were when the Cuban missile crisis broke out. And it would be Russell, not the CIA nor any of the other official guardians of our security, who would pounce on the situation and bring the first break for the better in the missile crisis.

President Kennedy was at his best on that somber evening of October 22 when, with everyone prepared by rumors and the scheduling of the broadcast for an extraordinary revelation, he announced over the networks the gravity of the Cuban missile crisis.

He began:

> This government as promised has maintained the closest surveillance of the Soviet military buildup on the island of Cuba. Within the past week unmistakable evidence has established that a series of offensive missile sites is now in preparation on that imprisoned island. The purpose of these bases can be none other than to provide a nuclear strike capability against the Western Hemisphere.

After describing the buildup in "fullest detail" Kennedy continued:

> This urgent transformation of Cuba into an important strategic base constitutes an explicit threat to the peace and security of all the Americas in flagrant and deliberate violation of the Rio Pact of 1947, the traditions of this nation and hemisphere, the Joint Resolution of the 87th Congress, the Charter of the United Nations and my own public warnings to the Soviets on September 4 and 13.

In the manner of a tongue-lashing he then detailed the catalogue of Soviet lies:

> The size of the undertaking makes clear that it has been planned for some months. Yet only last month when I had made clear the distinction between the introduction of ground-to-ground missiles and the existence of defensive antiaircraft missiles, the Soviet government publicly stated on September 11 that, and I quote "The armaments and military equipment sent to Cuba are designed exclusively for defensive purposes," unquote. That statement was false. Only last Thursday, as evidence of this rapid offensive buildup was already in my hand, Soviet Foreign Minister Gromyko told me in my office that he had been instructed to make it quote "quite clear" unquote, as he said his government had already done, that the Soviet assistance to Cuba, and I quote, "pur-

sued solely the purpose of contributing to the defense capability of Cuba," unquote; that, and I quote him, "training by Soviet specialists of Cuban nationals was by no means offensive," unquote; and that if it were otherwise, Mr. Gromyko went on, "the Soviet government would never have become involved in rendering such assistance." That statement was also false.

Kennedy continued by expounding America's overt foreign policy, as distinct from the covert version that the CIA had espoused for so many years and in so many different ways:

> Neither the United States of America nor the world community of nations can tolerate deliberate deception and offensive threats on the part of any nation, large or small. We no longer live in a world where only the actual firing of weapons represents a sufficient challenge to a nation's security to constitute maximum peril. Nuclear weapons are so destructive and ballistic missiles are so swift that any substantial increase in the possibility of their use, or any sudden change in their deployment, may well be regarded as a definite threat to peace. For many years the Soviet Union and the United States, recognizing that fact, have deployed strategic nuclear weapons with great care, never upsetting the precarious status quo which assured that these weapons would not be used in the absence of some vital challenge. . . . American citizens have become accustomed to living in the bull's-eye of missiles located in the USSR and in submarines. In that sense missiles in Cuba only add to an already clear and present danger. . . . But this secret, swift, extraordinary buildup of Communist missiles—this sudden, extraordinary decision to station strategic weapons for the first time outside Soviet soil—is a deliberately provocative and unjustified change in the status quo which cannot be accepted by this country if our courage and our commitments are ever to be trusted again, by friend or foe.

The president wound up his Monday night speech by declaring "a strict naval quarantine on all offensive military equipment under shipment to Cuba," effective at 10 A.M. Wednesday, October 24. The word "blockade" was officially avoided because that had been defined in international law as an act of war, whereas "quarantine," a word used by President Roosevelt in an anti-Axis speech in Chicago in 1937, had no specific legal meaning.

The Soviets meanwhile were deploying missiles with a speed that an expert in large-scale construction said amounted to a scientific breakthrough. Twenty-five Soviet and Soviet-chartered freighters were simultaneously at sea en route to Castro's domain at the time of Kennedy's speech. Most of them were carrying auxiliary equipment, but five were lumber ships with large open hatches built for carrying logs as great as the cedars of Lebanon and suitable for hiding well-covered offensive missiles.

Russian submarines began prowling around the more important freighters soon after the blockade was announced. The United States dispatched 180 warships to the Caribbean area, with twenty-six of them assigned initially to a blockade line stretching from the Florida coast around Cuba to Puerto Rico and beyond. An invasion force of 250,000 army troops and 90,000 Marines was rushed to Florida; half of the country's then 600-plane fleet of B–52 bombers was airborne with nuclear weapons aboard; and enough conventional bombing strength to strike 2,000 targets in Cuba without reloading was on or near Florida runways. All intercontinental missile bases, in both the United States and the Soviet Union, were brought to the firing stage by maximum alerts.

With so much power poised or in motion, both Kennedy and Khrushchev recognized that time was of the essence. Somehow, somewhere, someone would go berserk if a solution was not reached immediately. Assuming that war would have been avoided, there was a possibility that Khrushchev could have come off better than he did if he had pulled back his ships, declared a retaliatory blockade of Berlin, and appealed to the United Nations. He could have contended that he was violating no law. But the risk involved in such a delay was entirely too great.

Suddenly, before the blockade could go into effect, a conciliatory note was struck by Khrushchev in a message to Bertrand Russell, together with an equally conciliatory suggestion for an immediate summit meeting which the Soviet leader sent to United Nations Secretary-General U Thant. These welcome signals sparked a late buying spree and the largest daily gain since June 28 on the New York Stock Exchange.

Many Americans as well as British had the impression that despite his blustering, Khrushchev was not a bad fellow, or at least was a big improvement over Joseph Stalin. To his credit, when he said "the living would envy the dead," the Soviet leader had portrayed both more horribly and more accurately than any other government leader the result to be expected from nuclear war. Bertrand Russell, with no official involvement but with a lifelong record of concern for the human race, had sent him a message asking "continued forbearance."

Khrushchev replied:

> I beg of you, Mr. Russell, to meet with understanding our position, our actions. If we encourage banditry in international relations [the blockade] . . . the United States will crudely trample upon and violate international rights. . . . If the American government will be carrying out the program of piratic actions outlined by it we shall have to defend our rights and international rights which are written down in international agreements and the United Nations Charter. We have no other way out.

But Khrushchev was in fact searching desperately for a way out.

In a manner even more informal and unofficial than the exchange with Russell, an American news reporter and a Soviet intelligence agent collaborated to provide the necessary quick solution. The Soviet intelligence agent was Aleksander Fomin, who under the "loose cover" title of "Counselor of Embassy," was the KGB chief in Washington—a fact well-known to the United States but ignored on a quid pro quo basis because the Soviets were tolerating a CIA station chief in Moscow.

Fomin was likable and gregarious, not at all resembling a back-alley assassin. Among the Washingtonians he had met was John Scali, later United States ambassador to the United Nations, a former Associated Press man who at this time was a television reporter for the American Broadcasting Company. On Friday, the fourth day of the crisis, Fomin asked Scali to determine whether or not the United States would be interested in pledging not to invade Cuba in exchange for withdrawal of all offensive missiles and bombers from the island.

Since in an absence of nuclear weapons Kennedy had already given an unqualified pledge not to invade Cuba—a promise tested excruciatingly under fire—the offer in effect was to withdraw missiles and bombers in exchange for a return to the situation that obtained before they were introduced. After relaying the inquiry to the White House through the State Department and receiving a favorable reply, Scali reported back to Fomin that the United States saw "real possibilities" in his proposal.

Agreement in principle thus was reached in a few oral sentences, although an attempt by Khrushchev's foreign office to raise the less critical issue of American missiles in Turkey had yet to be fended off, and a procession of difficulties at every stage would accompany the execution of the agreement. In view of the many Soviet ships en route to Cuba and all the possibilities that fighting could have broken out at sea, it looked afterward as though a last-minute decision to extend the blockade line only 500 miles out from the island—instead of 800 miles as originally planned—might have made the difference between peace and war.

The initial Fomin-Scali exchange took place in midday on Friday and a lengthy personal message from Khrushchev making the same offer arrived at the White House that evening at 9 P.M. (4 A.M. Moscow time). Khrushchev, who wrote in his memoirs that he was sleeping in his clothes during this period "in order not to be caught literally with my pants down," must have sent his message without informing other branches of his government.

Before Kennedy could reply to the first one, a second teletyped message, signed "Khrushchev" but written in his foreign office, arrived on Saturday. The second message offered to withdraw missiles from Cuba in exchange for withdrawal of American missiles from Turkey.

The 1,500-mile Jupiter army missiles in Turkey were old, fully-exposed, liquid-fueled types reminiscent of the eight-hour countdowns at Cape Canaveral and were already obsolete and scheduled for withdrawal. Such medium-range Army and Air Force Missiles in Turkey, Italy, and originally England had been deployed only to serve an interim deterrent purpose until a sufficient number of intercontinental types were in place.

The second offer thus might have been as acceptable as the first except that a public carving up of power, exchanging missile for missile under threat and on a quid pro quo basis with all the human lives potentially involved, apparently was too gruesome for Kennedy's taste.[5] He replied to the first message and ignored the second.

Since the second message had gone through channels and had been broadcast by Radio Moscow whereas the first had not, the text of the message which Kennedy ignored became public, whereas the one to which he replied did not. (It was considered inappropriate to release a personal message when the person could do that himself if he wished.) The omission was still a glaring discrepancy, and it fueled further reports that Khrushchev was overwrought and perhaps not in control of himself or his government at the end of the crisis.

Six years later in the November 1968, issue of *McCall's* magazine, in a posthumous article excerpted from *Thirteen Days* (W.W. Norton, 1969), Robert F. Kennedy sought to set the record straight:

> A great deal has been written about this [withheld] message, including the allegation that at the time of its preparation Khrushchev had become so unstable or emotional that

he had become incoherent. It was very long and emotional. But it was not incoherent, and the emotion was directed at the death, destruction and anarchy that nuclear war would bring to his people and to all mankind. That, he said again and again and in many different ways, must be avoided.

We must not succumb to "petty passions" or to "transient things," he wrote, but should realize that "if indeed war should break out it would not be in our power to stop it, for such is the logic of war. I have participated in two wars and know that war ends when it has rolled through cities and villages, everywhere sowing death and destruction."

The United States, he went on to say, should not be concerned about the missiles in Cuba; they would never be used to attack the United States and were there for defensive purposes only. "You can be calm in this regard: that we are of sound mind and understand perfectly well that if we attack you, you will respond in the same way. But you too will receive the same as you hurl against us. And I think you understand . . . that we are normal people, that we correctly evaluate the situation.

"Consequently, how can we permit the incorrect actions which you ascribe to us? Only lunatics or suicides, who themselves want to perish and to destroy the whole world before they die, could do this." But, he went on: "We want something quite different. . . . Not to destroy your country . . . but despite our ideological differences to compete peacefully, not by military means."

Khrushchev's lengthy Friday message was vague on details. On Sunday morning, after a clarifying exchange, Kennedy sent this eloquent reply:

Mr. Chairman, both our countries have unfinished tasks, and I know that your people as well as the United States can ask nothing better than to pursue them free from the fear of war. Modern science and technology have given us the possibility of making labor fruitful beyond anything that could have been dreamed of a few decades ago.

I agree with you that we must devote urgent attention to the problem of disarmament, as it relates to the whole world and also to critical areas. Perhaps now, as we step back from danger, we can make real progress in this vital field. I think we should give priority to questions relating to the proliferation of nuclear weapons, on earth and in outer space, and to the great effort for a nuclear test ban. But we should also work hard to see if wider measures of disarmament can be agreed to and put into operation at an early date.

The week-long crisis in which survival had hung in the balance ended on this cordial and high-minded note. On Friday the naval blockade had intercepted an American-made freighter which was registered in Lebanon, owned in Panama, and operated by Greeks under Soviet charter. But the boarding was without resistance and the vessel was allowed to proceed when found to be carrying only trucks and truck parts.

All other Soviet and Soviet-chartered vessels had either turned back or were lying dead in the water at a safe distance from the blockade line. Progress toward a settlement was so apparent on Saturday that despite the death of Major Anderson when his U–2 was shot down—by Soviet-trained Cubans, according to statements by Khrushchev and Castro—a retaliatory bombing raid scheduled for such an event was canceled.

In the midst of the historic weekend, Kennedy had to send Khrushchev a quick apology when a U–2 from Alaska strayed—this time really strayed—deep inside Siberia. Schlesinger's judgment was that the nonviolent settlement could not have come much later than it did. "If work had continued on the bases," he wrote, "the United States would have had no real choice but to take action against Cuba the following week."

Kennedy issued a statement praising Khrushchev for his "statesmanlike decision" but the phrase, with its implication in the circumstances of a sacrificing defeat, apparently was not to the Soviet leader's liking. In his memoirs, *Khrushchev Remembers* (Little, Brown, 1970), he ignored both the praise and the sharp penalties he had accepted among his followers.[6]

Though this was after the Sino-Soviet split, there was

some evidence that Khrushchev would have brought Communist China with him for whatever that might have been worth, if he had chosen to plunge ahead into war. When the blockade was declared the publication *Jemin Jih Pao*, representing the Central Committee of the Chinese Communist Party, had called upon the socialist countries to close ranks against "this flagrant piracy." When Khrushchev reversed his field, however, the infuriated Chinese invented a new word to accuse him of "capitulationism" as well as other Communist crimes. According to Che Guevara, who was with Castro listening to a radio broadcast when they learned of the Kennedy-Khrushchev bargain, the Cuban dictator became so enraged that he kicked a wall and broke a mirror.

The still-seething Castro was able to cause a thirty-day delay in the removal of old and not yet operational IL–28 jet bombers because these, along with MIG fighter planes and at least some of the SAM antiaircraft missiles, had been sold to the Cubans. The offensive missiles still belonged to the Russians and were removed almost immediately.

Castro also refused to accept the agreed-upon United Nations inspection of the removal operation. This was overlooked because there was plenty of inspection by American reconnaissance planes which maneuvered at altitudes as low as fifty feet above the departing Soviet vessels. Equally low passes at speeds as slow as could be considered reasonably safe were made by planes carrying Pentagon reporters. (I was aboard one of these press planes, representing United Press International.)

The missiles removed were sixty feet long, more than twice the length and several times the weight of the SAM antiaircraft types. Though they had arrived concealed in the capacious holds of those lumber ships, they left above decks and on every kind of vessel, in full view except for canvas coverings. The canvas covers were supported by circular or semicircular staves which made the missiles look from the air like huge sectional caterpillars.

Soviet crews looking skyward from the missile ships

took their bloodless defeat in stride, often waving in friendly fashion at the low-flying American planes. On some of the low passes Soviet crewmen, pointing and waving, pulled back the canvas coverings so that airborne observers could see the missiles themselves.

Moscow said forty-two of the medium range missiles had reached Cuba, and that was the number the United States was able to count going out. Apparently six more of this type and some or all of the intermediate range missiles—none of which actually reached Cuba—were at sea when the blockade was declared. Khrushchev said ruefully in his memoirs: "We had almost completed our shipments."

Elsewhere in his memoirs, back in blustering form, Khrushchev wrote of the crisis as though he had scored a victory. He quoted Robert Kennedy as saying to his ambassador in Washington, in a way signaling the close approach of war, "I don't know how much longer we can hold out against our generals."[7] Khrushchev added:

> We could see that we had to reorient our position swiftly. We sent the Americans a note saying that we agreed to remove our missiles and bombers on condition that the President give us his assurance that there would be no invasion of Cuba. . . . Finally Kennedy gave in and agreed to make a statement giving us such assurance.

Undoubtedly the Soviet leader would have given almost anything to have gotten away with the Cuban deployment without war.[8] As it was he had to settle for his "de-Stalinization" speech and his de-Stalinization of Russia as the major achievement of his career. (The role of the CIA in the de-Stalinization episode—see Chapter 15—was an inglorious example of how petty a great nation can be made to appear when foreign relations are left to a troublemaking agency of this kind.)

In several instances the CIA would have deserved high marks if the issue had been one of efficiency rather than of morality and fairness. In a day when the stacks at the

Library of Congress had been so rifled by congressional and other peculations that a person requesting a significant volume could be about half sure of eventually receiving a slip marked "not on shelf" (with no information available as to when if ever the item could be expected to be "on shelf"), the CIA claimed to be able to supply promptly almost any foreign information a president could require.

There were reasons to believe that the claim was not idle. The information files were known to be extensive and served by a retrieval system that was nearly instantaneous at the CIA's spacious Langley headquarters—which with its tall highway-type street lights looked from a distance like a thriving community and certainly an easily identifiable bombing target. Sometimes called "Allen's folly" for the latter reason, the headquarters finally did receive correct highway identification markers reading "Central Intelligence Agency" on the argument that there was no secrecy left to be lost.

In addition to military, scientific, economic, and political data, the CIA kept on hand all sorts of odd information that might be useful to its agents abroad. An example that happened to get published consisted of separate-volume studies of personal names in thirty-one languages, and illustrated the lengths to which CIA research could go. The volumes began with "Amharic Personal Names" and ran through Arabic, Armenian, Albanian, Bulgarian, Burmese, Chinese, Czechoslovak, Estonian, Finnish, German, Greek, Gujerati, Hausa, Hindi, Hungarian, Latvian, Korean, Lithuanian, Mongolian, Polish, Rumanian, Russian, Serbo-Croatian, Slovak, Slovene, Swahili, Tegulu, Thai, Turkish, and Vietnamese.

Every so often this sort of thing paid off. After Soviet missiles had been withdrawn from Cuba, with more than 300 competing Cuban exile groups in the United States to generate rumors, and with prominent figures such as Senator Barry Goldwater ready to voice their information and apprehensions, there were frequent reports that some of the missiles had been left behind in the removal operation.

Castro had been persuaded to permit unmolested U-2 inspection of his island, partly on the argument that spy satellites would soon be doing the same thing; so it could be established that there were no missiles on the surface in Cuba. Artificial underground launchers could also be ruled out because large-scale excavation with its long lines of dump trucks was one of the easiest activities to spot from the air. The only possibility remaining was that there might be some missiles deployed in natural caves, and the CIA had the answer for this one, too: a complete speleological survey of Cuba.

Speleologists, nicknamed spelunkers, were ardent professionals and hobbyists preoccupied with exploring caves. Back before the Castro takeover when Ernest Hemingway was living in Cuba and Havana was one of the world's favorite vacation spots, they had recorded the dimensions and other characteristics of every cave of any size on the island. A quick comparison of their measurements with the requirements for launchers showed there were none that could be accommodating nuclear missiles.

Kennedy and Castro

7

On September 7, 1963, Premier Fidel Castro showed up with no advance notice at a reception at the Brazilian embassy in Havana, a highly unusual thing for him to do. After a brief participation in the festivities, he harangued reporters attending the reception for three hours on the evils of the United States—this marathon attack being the apparent purpose of his visit.

Among other things, he said he knew of the CIA's many attempts to assassinate him and other Cuban leaders, and warned that two could play at the assassination game. "We are prepared to fight them and to answer in kind," Castro said, according to the Associated Press account of his discourse. "United States leaders should think that if they are aiding terrorist plans to eliminate Cuban leaders, they themselves will not be safe."

Castro's words would be interpreted by Senate investigators many years later as a sinister threat, but their impact at the time was close to zero. The AP story did make the top of the front page of the *Miami Herald* and received more or less conspicuous display in other newspapers, but some papers carrying the Associated Press account deleted its references to assassination attempts, and there was no mention of that subject in the United Press International version as it appeared on page 9 of the *New York Times*.

UPI led off instead with a Castro quote accusing President Kennedy of being "the Batista of his time"—Fulgencio Batista being fresh in Cuban memories as the dictator whom the Castro forces triumphantly overthrew after a long struggle and drove into exile on New Year's Day in 1959.

"Kennedy is a cretin," Castro continued, in a statement that must have caused even some readers of the *Times* to consult a dictionary. "He is a member of the oligarchic family that controls several important posts in the government. For example, one brother is a Senator and the other, Attorney General. And there are no more Kennedy officials because there are no more brothers." The UPI account continued:

> Puffing on a cigar, Dr. Castro leaned back in an easy chair. "Kennedy is thinking more about re-election than about the American people," he said. "He thinks only Kennedy and nothing else."
>
> Dr. Castro said he was not interested in United States domestic politics but that it seemed to him that "Eisenhower was less demagogic than Kennedy."
>
> Recent sea and air raids by exiles on Cuban industry have done no damage to speak of, he said, and added that Cubans knew "the hand of the United States and its Latin American puppet governments, particularly Guatemala, Costa Rica and Nicaragua, is behind these attacks.
>
> "Every day we grow stronger and stronger, and the United States' paramilitary operations against the revolution have done no harm," Dr. Castro said. "We have more militiamen than ever before."

At his next news conference Kennedy, presumably referring only to the UPI version, took a light view of Castro's remarks. "I've had so many things said about me lately that I thought what Castro said was not particularly bad," the president smiled. "He's attempting to demonstrate that he's an independent figure."

Five days after Castro's warning the National Security Council's "Special Group," chaired by McGeorge Bundy representing the president, called a "brainstorming" session of its Cuban Coordinating Committee, consisting of representatives of the CIA and of the State, Defense, and

Justice Departments. By the time Senate investigators looked into the matter the record did not show whether the meeting was triggered by Castro's remarks or whether the committeemen had either or both of the AP and UPI accounts before them. In the absence of any positive evidence to that effect, and since during the previous June the Special Group had ordered a sharp step-up in covert and paramilitary activity in Cuba (Operation Mongoose), it seemed probable that the session was merely part of an ongoing program.

Nevertheless, by coincidence or otherwise, the committeemen reached a written conclusion that there was "a strong likelihood that Castro would retaliate in some way against the rash of covert activity in Cuba." Among the possible retaliatory steps were "increased attempts at kidnapping or attempts at assassination of American officials and citizens." Here they were close to seizing history by the hair, but their next decision was that assassination attempts were "unlikely," and no special measures were ordered to guard against them. The only Castro retaliatory steps labeled "likely" were the jamming of American radio broadcasts and attacks through front organizations on American targets in Latin America.

Castro was hurting far more than he had cared to admit. A succession of rebel and government communiqués had recently pictured Cuba as in turmoil and perhaps close to civil war. In addition to sounding off at the Brazilian embassy, Castro, through the United Nations and various journalists, had made known to the American government his desire for talks between himself and Kennedy, and had appealed to the Soviet Union for help.

The response to the latter appeal came on September 11 when Havana Radio boldly announced that Moscow had warned the United States that further exile raids on Cuba "will push the world to the brink of thermonuclear war" and "will not be tolerated." However, nothing of this nature was received by the United States, and news of the "warning" was not included in any of Moscow's broadcasts except one beamed toward Cuba.

The Cuban exiles were nothing if not fanatical and aggressive whenever Washington gave them a go-ahead. The same September 11 barrage of dispatches included news of a one-plane bombing attack on Cuba's largest sugar mill, a report of 100 casualties including seventy dead in a clash between rebel guerrillas and Castro militiamen in Oriente Province, another report of 200 casualties in central Cuba, and a rebel communiqué claiming that eighty militiamen and eighteen guerrillas had been killed in an encounter with 1,500 Castro troops in Las Villas Province. "Exile sources including the usually reliable Sentinels of Liberty Movement reported continuing clashes between guerrillas and militiamen, with heavy casualties on both sides, in the area of Sierra de Escambray," a communiqué said.

Even allowing for a great deal of exaggeration, it still appeared to many American observers that some U.S.-backed operations against Castro's Cuba might be going on.

Despite his offhand comment at the news conference, Kennedy must have been stung a little by Castro's calling him "the Batista of his time." After reacting favorably to Castro's proposal for talks, the president was at pains to disassociate himself emphatically from the Batistianos two months later in an interview with Jean Daniel of the Paris *Express*, and later *L'Observateur*. As chronicled by Daniel, Kennedy said:

> I believe there is no country in the world, including the African regions, including any and all of the countries under colonial domination, where economic colonization, humiliation and exploitation were worse than in Cuba, in part because of my country's policies during the Batista regime. I believe that we created, built and manufactured the Cuban movement, without realizing it. The great aim of the Alliance for Progress is to reverse the policy. . . . The United States now has the possibility of doing as much good in Latin America as it has done wrong in the past.

After Kennedy had gotten in a few more plugs for his pet Alliance for Progress project, designed to rejuvenate Latin America, he and Daniel turned to the discussion of more immediate though not unrelated matters. Castro Cuba was a thorn in the side for the Alliance project. Any accommodation that could have been reached there would have been a boost for the effort.

Daniel agreed to see Castro in Kennedy's behalf. He was authorized to assure the Cuban leader of all the good relations anyone could wish with the United States if he would agree to discontinue subversive activities. Daniel was further authorized to cite excellent American-Yugoslav relations as proof that the United States could coexist with a socialist society. Who could have imagined that in only a few short weeks, with the whistle of a bullet fired from six stories up, all this would become academic?

The arrangement with Daniel led to one of the strangest historical coincidences of all time. Simultaneously, at the moment Kennedy died, Daniel was conducting peace and progress negotiations with Castro and the CIA in another meeting was equipping a high Cuban official with a poisoned pen and other weapons with which to attempt to assassinate Castro. The situation was reminiscent of the simultaneous attempts to protect and to assassinate Lumumba, and of Gary Powers's foray into Russia when Eisenhower was preparing for a cordial summit meeting with Khrushchev.

That a great and cherished country could have been allowed to appear to be so gruesomely two-faced, not just once but on repeated occasions, was a phenomenon that passed all understanding. But the thing had happened, again, in the worst possible way, and there was nothing bitter tears or bitter recriminations could do to help. If there was any consolation at all to be extracted from the situation, it may have been that Kennedy would never have to face up to this one.

The French Jean Daniel later demonstrated that, as was the case with many Americans, every detail connected with Kennedy's death—the time of day, what he himself was doing, and how the news came through—afterward stood out clearly in his mind. In an article for the *New Republic*, he began:

It was around 1:30 in the afternoon. We were having lunch in the living room of the modest summer residence which Fidel Castro owns on magnificent Veradero Beach, 120 kilometers from Havana. For at least the tenth time I was questioning him on details of negotiations with Russia, before the missile installations of last year. The telephone rang and a secretary in guerrilla garb announced that Mr. Dorticos, President of the Cuban Republic, had an urgent message for the Prime Minister. Fidel picked up the telephone and I heard him say: "*Como? Un Atentado?*" ("What's that? An attempted assassination?") He turned to me to say that Kennedy had just been struck down in Dallas, and then turned back to the telephone and exclaimed in a loud voice: "*Herido? Muy gravemente?*" ("Wounded? Very seriously?")

He came back, sat down and repeated three times the words: "*Es una mala noticia.*" ("This is bad news.") He remained silent for a moment, awaiting another call with further news. He remarked while he waited that there was an alarmingly sizable lunatic fringe in American society and that this deed could equally well have been the work of a terrorist or a madman. Perhaps a Vietnamese? Or a member of the Ku Klux Klan? The second call came through: It was hoped they would be able to announce that the United States president was still alive, that there was hope of saving him. Fidel's immediate reaction was: "If this is true he is already reelected." He pronounced these words with satisfaction.

Daniel reverted to a session he had had with Castro the previous night, which he said lasted from ten in the evening to four in the morning and revolved around the interview President Kennedy had granted him October 24. He had delivered the president's messages, including the one about capitalist-socialist coexistence, and Castro had responded with "a relentless indictment" of American policy, claiming that Washington had had ample opportunity to normalize relations with Cuba but instead had tolerated "a CIA program of training, equipping and organizing counterrevolution." Castro said he was not in the least fearful for his life, since if he were to become a victim of the United States "this would simply enhance the radius of his (posthumous) influence in Latin America and throughout the Socialist world." He said a leader would have to arise in the United States who would be "capable of understanding the explosive realities of Latin America and of meeting them halfway."

Daniel, still referring to the previous night, continued:

Then, suddenly, Castro had taken a less hostile tack: "Kennedy could still be this man," he said. "He still has the possibility of becoming, in the eyes of history, the greatest president of the United States, the leader who may at last understand that there can be coexistence between capitalists and socialists. He would then be an even greater president than Lincoln."

The midnight session had apparently wound up on a lighter note, with Castro emphasizing his newfound support for Kennedy, and declaring: "In the last analysis I'm convinced that anyone else would be worse." He also told Daniel "with a broad grin" that if he saw Kennedy again to "tell him I am willing to declare Goldwater my friend if that will assure Kennedy's re-election."

Returning to the grim realities of the present Daniel said:

We were easily able to get NBC in Miami. The news came through: wounded in the head, pursuit of the assassin, murder of a policeman. Finally the fatal announcement that Kennedy is dead.

Fidel stood up and said to me: "Everything is changed. Everything is going to change. The United States occupies such a position in world affairs that the death of a president of that country affects millions of people in every corner of the globe. The Cold War, relations with Russia, Latin America, Cuba, the Negro question . . . all will have to be rethought. At least Kennedy was an enemy to whom we had become accustomed. This is a serious matter; an extremely serious matter."

The CIA's simultaneous meeting designed to accomplish Castro's demise was held in Paris with a Cuban official code-named AM/LASH, who was plotting an attempted coup in which the murder of Castro would be the first step. Musty records examined by Senate investigators twelve years later showed that AM/LASH was in France on November 19, 1963, and was asked by the CIA to delay his return to Cuba for the November 22 meeting at which arrangements would be made to supply him with rifles, telescopic lenses, explosives, and the poisoned pen. The poisoned pen was described in testimony as "a ball point pen mounting a needle," with the latter said to be "so fine a victim would not feel its insertion." Though it was difficult to visualize how such an instrument could have been effective, evidence could be cited that the CIA probably knew what it was doing in this area: when the Russians tried out the tiny "curare" carried by Gary Powers on a dog, the animal died within ninety seconds.

Like the assassins with whom the CIA had dealt in the Dominican Republic, AM/LASH turned out to be quite demanding. In the fall of 1963 he had been insisting for some time that he must have a face-to-face meeting with Attorney General Kennedy to assure himself of United States support in the projected coup. But Robert Kennedy, in a top-level CIA briefing in May 1962, had been told that the CIA's assassination program had been discontinued, so granting that request was out of the question.

Finally, on October 29, 1963, a high CIA official—Desmond FitzGerald, chief of the Special Affairs Staff—met with AM/LASH and by describing himself as the "personal representative" of Robert Kennedy (though he had never consulted Kennedy on the subject), managed to satisfy the would-be assassin on that point. On one occasion FitzGerald asked Director Helms whether he should consult Robert Kennedy, but Helms testified he told him that wouldn't be necessary.

The November 22 meeting was between AM/LASH and a case officer and was concerned only with weapons. Strangely enough, years later when FitzGerald had died and the matter was under Senate investigation, the case officer could not remember what became of the poisoned pen. The witness recalled that AM/LASH was not well impressed with the pen, which he regarded as amateurish, and showed much more interest in the telescopic sights and explosives with which Castro might be killed from a distance or even by remote control. But he could not remember for sure whether or not AM/LASH had taken the pen with him when he left the meeting. He thought not. Things were more than a little unsettling at that moment, since AM/LASH and the case officer learned of Kennedy's death just as their meeting broke up.

The chilling thought that Kennedy's murder might have been accomplished in retaliation for the dealings with AM/LASH must have occurred to someone at the CIA almost immediately. The record showed that the next day the case officer was ordered to break off contact with AM/LASH and return to headquarters at once. Typically for the CIA, however, this sudden attack of conscience—if it could be called that—had the ultimate effect only of adding another devious twist to the plot.

AM/LASH was told by the CIA that for moral reasons the United States could not participate in his "first step"—the murder of Castro. Arrangements were then made to transfer on a top secret basis that part of the support to an exile leader (Manuel Artime) with whom the CIA was already dealing in paramilitary operations against Cuba. Direct negotiations with AM/LASH were then resumed on the extremely thin pretense that they concerned only support after the "first step" had been accomplished. Artime was among the most famed of the exile leaders, and how anyone could have supposed that AM/LASH wouldn't have known of him was a question to which no answer suggested itself—perhaps his link with the CIA could have been unknown to AM/LASH.

The tortuous negotiations with AM/LASH—involving other European capitals in addition to Paris, two air drops of weapons into Cuba early in 1964, and big outlays of cash whenever he was met—continued for another eighteen months before they were finally broken off on June 23, 1965. By that time there was ample evidence that the AM/LASH plot was known to a number of sources outside the CIA, including the FBI, exile leaders, underworld figures used in the earlier assassination attempts, and Soviet and Cuban intelligence. The CIA's final message to its stations on this subject said:

> Convincing proof that entire AM/LASH group insecure and that further contact with key members of group constitutes a menace to CIA operations. . . . Under no circumstances are newly assigned staff personnel or newly recruited agents to be exposed to operation.

Secrecy within the CIA may have reached a maximum in connection with the assassination plots. Two days after the Dallas tragedy, newly installed President Johnson was briefed by CIA Director McCone concerning the agency's operations against Cuba, but this could not have been very instructive since the only assassination plots McCone knew about were the earlier ones against Castro, in a program he understood had been discontinued. Even the earlier plots he had learned about only three months before when, after twenty-two months in office, he spotted an article in the *Chicago Sun-Times* revealing that the CIA had been trafficking with Mafia mobsters.

Nevertheless, Johnson became convinced of Cuban involvement in his predecessor's death. The new president, no friend of the Kennedys after he entered the White House, told a number of visitors including Howard K. Smith of the American Broadcasting Company that "Kennedy tried to get Castro but Castro got him first." His conclusion could not have had anything to do with AM/LASH, however, since the Senate committee found "no evidence whatever" that Johnson ever learned of the AM/LASH negotiations which continued for another eighteen months after he took office.

Another person who did not know of the assassination plots was the CIA analyst who was the "point of record" for the agency's research on behalf of the Warren Commission which found that Lee Harvey Oswald had acted alone in Kennedy's death. In a memorandum for Senate investigators, the analyst said he did not learn of the plots until 1975, although if he had been a reader of Drew Pearson's and Jack Anderson's columns he could have started getting details of them many years earlier.

Even where the information concerning assassination plots was available, there was a strong tendency to discount or ignore it. For example, the book *Cuba: The Pursuit of Freedom*, by Hugh Thomas, which was brought out by Harper & Row in 1971 and which must have been one of the longest and most thoroughly researched single-volume works ever published (1,696 pages), contained brief and passing references to only one assassination attempt (AM/LASH) against Castro. Even that one probably made it into the book only because Castro and other prominent figures were involved in the AM/LASH case's final disposition.

Unless his angry words at the Brazilian embassy were counted as such, no evidence was ever found of Castro or Cuban involvement in Kennedy's death. However, the dictator and his cohorts spent some anxious months fearing Cuba would be blamed. In a series of 1974 sessions with Frank Mankiewicz and Kirby Jones, who were preparing for a CBS documentary on Cuba, Castro admitted that it would have "looked terrible" if Oswald's request had been granted when he applied at the Cuban embassy in Mexico City two months before the Dallas slaying for permission to visit Cuba. "Luckily," said Castro, "the bureaucratic process prevailed and our consular official routinely denied Oswald's request for a visa. We had never heard of him."

Over a period of four days, Mankiewicz and Jones conducted thirteen hours of formal interviews with Castro. He told them:

> We have never believed in carrying out the type of activity of assassination of adversaries. It would have been easier to have killed Batista than to have fought the Moncada [the early attack on one of Batista's major military encampments, in which the Castro forces were beaten back] . . . but it went against our political ideas to organize any type of personal assault. . . . We understood what the implications were [at the time of Kennedy's death] and we were concerned that an attempt would be made to blame Cuba, but this was not what concerned us most. In reality we were disgusted because, although we were in conflict with Kennedy politically we had nothing against him personally. We would have been foolish to have harmed Kennedy, because Kennedy was thinking of changing his policy toward Cuba, and his negotiators were in Cuba at the time of the assassination.

Kirby Jones was inclined to take Castro's words at face value. He wrote:

> At no time during Castro's rule has Cuba been accused of plotting the assassination of its adversaries. During the fighting in the mountains there was never a reported attempt on Batista's life. And lastly, why would a small country like Cuba try to assassinate a president of the United States when discovery and proof of the act would have meant certain and clear military action and probably the destruction of Castro's Cuba?

Even though the Senate committee withheld AM/LASH's identity, exile leaders spotted his case immediately as that of Rolando Cubela, a hero of the revolution, a former president of the student federation at the University of Havana, and a major in the Cuban Army when major was Cuba's highest military rank.

During Cubela's plotting with the CIA, he was the number-two man in the Interior Ministry (which oversaw the National Police), and was a privileged character permitted to travel abroad and lead a wastrel's life because of his revolutionary background. He was arrested six months after the CIA broke contact with him, and he escaped death only because Castro chose to send a personal appeal for clemency to a five-member military tribunal which then sentenced Cubela to twenty-five years in prison.

Castro contended in his appeal that the death penalty was "not necessary," and said:

> The aim of the revolution is not to eliminate men but to eliminate the vices that give rise to crimes. . . . We must be hard without vacillation when needed but never unnecessarily.

Since Cubela pleaded guilty ("To the wall," he cried tearfully. "To be executed, that is what I want. It is justified."), not many details of the plotting came to light in the limited evidence presented against him. However, his trial was open, with 500 spectators attending, and the CIA involvement was fully exposed as far as Cubans were concerned. In the United States, however, influential publications as well as sane individuals were more than reluctant to believe that America could have become its own worst enemy. "President Castro blames the United States Central Intelligence Agency but that is a stock charge," said the *New York Times*. *Time* magazine commented: "As usual in Castroland the prosecutor explained that the CIA was behind it all."

For the same reason no visible attention was paid in the United States to the Cuban government's claim that two officials of its embassy in Madrid, Spain, had received $100,000 in CIA money for arranging a contact for Cubela. Actually the payment was made after the CIA's attack of conscience, when the agency with the aid of the American embassy in Madrid was arranging a contact between Cubela and Artime, with Cubela supposedly unaware that the CIA was pulling the strings for that part of the conspiracy.

This unlikely but expensive piece of fiction must have

given Cubela and Artime some good laughs when and if they were sober enough to stand the strain. Nothing came out in the trial or later in Cuba concerning the conspiracy activities that were under way at the time of Kennedy's death, and in view of Castro's expressed apprehensions there may well have been a studied avoidance throughout the prosecution of anything that could be connected with the Dallas tragedy.

After Castro's appeal for clemency the theme of Cubela's trial was that he had been led astray by drink, drugs, and other vices into becoming easy prey for the enemies of the revolution. An incidental outgrowth was that twenty or more Cuban officials—including the highest ranking officer in the military establishment, Major Efigenio Almeijeiras—were unseated on charges such as "high living," "showing the same instability of character and lack of seriousness as Cubela," and "having close relations with antisocial elements, vagabonds, bums and corrupt people." The charges against Cubela did specify that he tried to kill Castro with a rifle equipped with a telescopic lens, from a house near Castro's residence on Veradero Beach, thus verifying the case officer's recollection that Cubela was unimpressed by the poisoned pen.

That Castro survived the CIA's many attempts on his life seemed to be quite miraculous. In four other assassination attempts against foreign leaders detailed by the Senate committee, the targets were dead, and this without a CIA agent's ever having pulled a trigger. Herbert L. Matthews, an old Cuba hand in the sense that there used to be old China hands, concluded that in the Cuban case the CIA and its minions were so ill-informed and inept that Castro was never in real danger.

On the other hand, the CIA was anything but inefficient in macabre matters generally, and the Mafia mobsters were certainly well schooled in an environment of homicide. (Both Giancana and Roselli themselves later were the victims of unsolved gangland slayings: Giancana was rubbed out before he could testify for Senate investigators and Roselli met the same fate afterward. Traffi-cante was the only mobster to survive publicly known participation in the CIA's plots.) Above all, on the patriotic side, the Cuban exile community (where the CIA organized what became known as its "Secret Army") was heavily salted with derring-do types willing to run high risks to kill Castro; while on the criminal side, the CIA's $150,000 reward offer should have been enough to whet the appetite of the least venturesome hit man.

So it was a puzzling situation. One possibility was that Cuban intelligence and security, without fanfare, had done a superb job of foiling the CIA's many moves. For example, although Cubela (AM/LASH) was not a decoy or provocation as some had suggested, he may have served the same purposes if he was under suspicion and safe surveillance for months or years before his arrest— the purposes of keeping Cuban intelligence informed and the CIA's assassination experts busy without danger.

For whatever reasons, an act which would have poisoned Cuban-American relations for generations, perhaps forever, was avoided; and the rift between the United States and Cuba prevented from becoming as deep or unbridgeable as that between Great Britain and Ireland, for example, or the one between the Russians and the Polish patriots. Jean Daniel noticed this when he was in Cuba, and he described the hours immediately following Kennedy's assassination in this way:

> The Cubans have lived with the United States in that cruel intimacy so familiar to me of the colonized with the colonizers. Nevertheless it was an intimacy. In that very seductive city of Havana to which we returned in the evening, where the luminous signboards with Marxist slogans have replaced the Coca-Cola billboards, in the midst of Soviet exhibits and Czechoslovak trucks, a certain American emotion vibrated in the atmosphere, compounded of resentment, of concern, of anxiety, and yet also, in spite of everything, of a mysterious and almost imperceptible rapprochement. After all, the American president was able to reach accord with our friends the Russians during his lifetime, said a young Cuban intellectual as I was taking my leave. It was almost as though he were apologizing for not rejoicing in the assassination.

Saga of the Orient

8

As American attention shifted to the Far East in the mid-1960s, a number of incidents came to light that had escaped notice during the events in Cuba.

In 1965 Premier Lee Kuan Yew of Singapore, which had become an independent city-state after its separation from the British-supported Malayan Federation, was talking to an American reporter about an incident of five years before, saying: "In 1960 an American CIA agent was arrested after an apparent attempt to bribe and subvert Singapore intelligence authorities." Lee implied that there was more to the story than he cared to repeat, but that he had been willing to forget the whole matter:

> I told them [the Americans], "All right, we will keep quiet. You take this man away and provide $33 million to the Singapore government for economic development."

Someone on the American side, badly underestimating his man, tried to reduce the economic aid to a tenth of the stipulated amount by suggesting in effect that everybody would be looking in the opposite direction if Lee took some of the money for his own use.

Now the premier was really angry:

> Through an intermediary they offered me and my party $3.3 million. I mean, the insult! I told them they could keep it!

The premier was mollified to some extent in the course of several months of negotiations, but he still resented the implication that he could be corrupted personally, and he insisted on a letter of apology. This was supplied under date of April 15, 1961, over the signature of Secretary of State Rusk.

Lee was unaware that his remarks on the five-year-old subject would be of journalistic interest in faraway America. A dispatch based on them caught a late edition of the *New York Times*, but this first story contained no mention of the Rusk letter of apology.

The State Department too hastily issued one of its "completely without foundation" denials, and the hot-tempered Lee reacted violently: "If he was going to be called a liar by the American State Department, the deal was off!"

He produced his letter from Rusk, and waved it in the faces of reporters. The contrite and humbled State Department was obliged to issue another apology, which said that in the first instance the matter had not been checked out all the way to the top.

New York Times correspondent Seymour Topping, in commenting from Hong Kong for the Sunday edition, summarized the peripheral situation in an area of the world where the Vietnam War was now giving the United States its greatest concern:

> Lee Kuan Yew, prime minister of Singapore, this week joined the array of Southeast Asian leaders, once good friends of the United States, who are now bitter critics. Others are President Sukarno of Indonesia, Prince Norodom Sihanouk, the Cambodian Chief of State, and General Ne Win, the ruler of Burma. There is a remarkable similarity in the complaints that were lodged by these leaders as they drifted away from the United States. For example, all have charged that the CIA conducted hostile operations against their governments during periods of ostensibly correct relations with the United States.

In concluding his weekend article Topping went on to say:

In practical terms Prime Minister Lee's remarks mean that the United States can no longer count on Singapore, the hub of the Commonwealth defenses in Southeast Asia, as an extension of its own in the area. Possibly the most aggrieved officials are those who had looked hopefully to Mr. Lee, a 40-year-old Cambridge-educated lawyer, as an exemplary friend of the West. His dynamic social reform program and his earlier articulate denunciations of Communists had suggested that eventually he might attract a large pro-Western following in Southeast Asia.

The trouble in Burma dated back to the Chinese Nationalist guerrillas on whom the CIA had lavished so much aid before 1954, some of whom were still in Burma. Seeing visions that would come to pass years later, Sihanouk had interpreted CIA aid to Cambodian rebels as an attempt to overthrow him. Sukarno was engaged in trying to put down army revolts in Sumatra and the Celebes and had protested the CIA's sending his opposition a number of old bombing planes, one of which was flown by an American pilot named Allen Pope.

Pope was charged with killing twenty-eight Indonesians in the course of six bombing raids and was sentenced to death. With diplomatic pressure working for him he was released after several months and went to work for an outfit called Southern Air Transport, which eventually would turn up on the CIA's list of wholly-owned proprietaries.[9] When questions were asked at the time, the Pentagon described Southern Air Transport as "a civilian operation holding a $3.7 million contract to move mixed cargo and passenger loads on Far Eastern routes." Further reporting developed that its headquarters was a post office box in Taipei, Formosa, and that its president was Alexander E. Carlson of Miami, Florida, the man who hired the American pilots killed at the Bay of Pigs. The English-language newspaper *Dawn* at Karachi, Pakistan, commented: "This CIA operator, then, presumably is on the loose somewhere in Asia."

At the start of the Kennedy administration another peripheral country, mysterious Laos, was still considered the most critical area in the Far East. For once, liberal, conservative, and middle-of-the-road observers were agreed on the cause of the trouble there.

Senator Eugene McCarthy wrote:

> In Laos the CIA pursued policies that conflicted with the official and public policies of the State Department. In 1958 a highly volatile Laos was governed by a coalition. . . . The situation was hardly ideal but to Ambassador Horace Smith and the State Department this coalition seemed to offer the best hope for a stable Laos. According to Smith, who is not the only ambassador to complain about CIA "spooks" who flit through American embassies pursuing their own brand of foreign policy, the CIA with the backing of the Pentagon threw its support behind right-wing General Phoumi Nosavan. . . . Millions of dollars worth of United States aid were wasted.

The hard-line version as enunciated by Stewart Alsop in the *Saturday Evening Post* came to the same conclusion:

> Little Laos fairly crawled with CIA agents. These gentry, in late 1960, in another of their famous coups, overthrew the neutralist government and installed a militarist regime headed by General Phoumi Nosavan. The Phoumi army clique had just one quality to recommend it, but it was a quality dear to the heart of the CIA: it was militantly anti-Communist. Unfortunately this attitude did not recommend itself so heartily to the Laotian people as it did to the CIA; General Phoumi had almost no popular support, and when the Communist Pathet Lao began to gobble up vast chunks of the country there was almost no resistance. The United States was placed in the humiliating position of practically begging to get the very type of neutralist government its CIA had conspired to overthrow.

Walter Lippmann, near the end of a fifty-year career, wrote:

> I venture to argue that the reason we are on the defensive in so many places is that for some ten years we have used

money and arms in a long, losing attempt to stabilize native governments which, in the name of anti-Communism, are opposed to all important social change. This has been exactly what Mr. Khrushchev's dogma calls for—that Communism should be the only alternative to the status quo with its immemorial poverty and privilege.

When the Laos situation quieted down, American attention shifted to South Vietnam, but with no original thought or intention of becoming involved in war. Throughout most of 1963 and until President Johnson took office in November, an impression backed by statistics remained that the United States was getting *out* of Vietnam.

That year President Diem had asked for a reduction in the American contingent of twelve thousand military advisers stationed in the country. American aid had been cut back drastically, to $93 million from $267 million the previous year. And the Communist Vietcong, with its obsolete arms—no AK-47 submachine guns, no mortars, and no rocket launchers during these days—had considerably reduced its activity.

With his erratic brother Nhu still obscure and after nine solid years in office, President Diem gave an appearance of great stability until the beginning of social turmoil for reasons unrelated to the Vietcong. Many observers then and later thought that if Diem could have been left alone he might have continued to govern indefinitely.

Once again, however, the CIA's operatives had been active behind the scenes from which vantage they succeeded in undermining Diem's authority. The agency was found to be providing $3 million a year ($250,000 a month) to finance a private military force—a sort of vestpocket army which was not under Diem's or regular military command. This force was assigned to the brother, Nhu.

A more destabilizing factor, poised in a more destabilizing way, would have been difficult to contrive. To top it all Diem and his brother represented a Catholic minority in a largely Buddhist country, and the brother could not resist launching slaughtering attacks on Buddhist pagodas.

In July, 60,000 Buddhists demonstrated against the government. In August, 15,000 announced they were fasting in protest against the government's repressive policies. By the time of Diem's overthrow on November 1, 1963—twenty-one days before the assassination of President Kennedy—five Buddhists had publicly soaked themselves with gasoline and burned themselves to death in the streets.

The overthrow of Diem left a vacuum which no effort was made to fill. With the White House in the wake of Kennedy's death refusing to accept any government that could be called neutralist, strictly military rule which proved ineffective had to be set up. Instead of aiding a local administration, the United States soon found itself more in the position of actually running the government; and when that didn't work either, the U.S. virtually took over the country itself, economically speaking.

South Vietnam, normally one of the great rice-exporting areas of the world, soon was importing from the United States a quantity of rice per year that exceeded the annual crop of the state of Mississippi. And from there with seeming inexorability the situation went from bad to very bad, and from worse to much worse.

The brothers Ngo Dinh Diem and Ngo Dinh Nhu also had an official relationship, with the latter designated as "Political Counselor" to the president. The vague title could have meant almost nothing but grew phenomenally in importance in 1963 after the CIA began providing Nhu with his own military force. The 1,500-man army, called Special Forces, was modeled after the American Green Berets who trained these troops under CIA supervision.

A third though greatly subordinate member of the ruling triumvirate, who answered to the brother Nhu, was Colonel Le Quang Tung, commander of the Special Forces and head of the "Presidential Survey Office," sometimes called a "Vietnamese CIA." When the government was finally overthrown by unanimous decision of the regular military leaders, they moved first with grim determination against Colonel Tung before hunting down the Ngos.

The CIA's policies for once stirred a revolt in the agency's own ranks, which was described by Roger Hilsman in *To Move a Nation* (Doubleday, 1967). Hilsman was a former chief of the State Department's Bureau of Intelligence and Research and was assistant secretary of state for far eastern affairs during the crucial year of 1963.

He wrote:

> The head of the CIA mission to Vietnam [John Richardson] argued persistently that the United States should continue to support Diem and Nhu. But most of his staff disagreed with him, and emotion reached such a pitch that some members of the staff felt the only way their views could reach Washington was through leaks to the press. The disagreement became such common knowledge that *The Times of Vietnam* had a story in it—headlined "CIA, Your Split Is Showing." . . . Every faction became so convinced of the rightness of its cause that leaking to the press became a patriotic act. . . . The CIA took a particular beating in the United States press over payments to the notorious Colonel Tung, Nhu's hatchet man who headed the Special Forces.

Because of the plethora of leaks, United Press International on September 9, three weeks after the "pocket" army had taken part in the most widespread of the 1963 pagoda raids, was able to provide a full account of the undercover imbroglio. Colonel Tung was "now considered the most powerful military official in South Vietnam," said UPI, quoting "informed sources."

> The sources said there was bitter opposition from most CIA men in South Vietnam to continuing the monthly payments to Tung. They pointed out that Tung's Special Forces units were created, trained and armed by the CIA for work with Montagnard tribesmen and clandestine operations into North Vietnam. . . . The Special Forces were armed with CIA funds, and were given the best training in jungle fighting and

guerrilla operations available, under CIA supervision, by officers of the United States Special Forces. Some squadrons were also especially trained in assassination and sabotage, the sources said.

UPI's reference to the CIA's including assassination in its training program attracted no unusual attention, but having a colonel described as "the most powerful military official" in a country with a surplus of generals struck like a thunderclap and produced cries of wounded outrage as well as flushed faces and gnashing of teeth at the regular command headquarters. Fortunately Tung was already the most hated man in South Vietnam, so UPI had only contributed to an already existing state of affairs.

The truth was that a program that might have looked all right on paper in Washington had turned out to be a typical CIA effort to strengthen a government by enabling it to murder, incinerate, flagellate, humiliate, and/or emasculate its political and—in this case, because of the Buddhists—religious opposition. And worse still, this was to be accompanied by a little effective destabilization of the government under the auspices of the wildly extreme Nhu.

On the basis of a short visit to Saigon and a little collateral reading, Hilsman made the following observations:

> Nhu, able and vigorous though he clearly was, seemed to be an influence leading to disaster. He had a paranoiac suspiciousness in his makeup and a grandiose, even apocalyptic view of himself and his family that hinted at madness. . . . I was reminded that Nhu had visited Algeria for a few days at the height of the Algerian crisis and then had gone on to Paris to offer his services to de Gaulle—assuring him that he, Nhu, could solve the Algerian problem in a week or two at most. Now (at a dinner) Nhu was telling us that he had conceived a grand strategy to defeat world Communism once and for all—by having the United States lure Communist China into a war in Laos, which he said was "an ideal theater and battleground." It made me shudder.

None of these psychotic characteristics so obvious to Hilsman deterred Saigon Station Chief Richardson of the CIA from cultivating Nhu. This would have been incredible except that in choosing the more radical of two anti-Communists, Richardson was adhering to well-established CIA policy. Because of the agency's backing, Nhu claimed to have the real support of the United States long after other appearances and reality itself were much to the contrary. Meanwhile Nhu was emboldened to describe President Diem as "inept" and "weak" for backing into compromises with the Buddhists. (Diem backed into them by claiming that whatever agreement was reached had been his position all along.)

When the generals plotting the government's overthrow met in a crucial session at the end of August they decided Nhu's claim was valid—American words had favored Diem but American actions had been calculated to benefit Nhu. This was a key factor in preserving the Diem government for another two months.

From his vantage point in the Kennedy administration Hilsman also closely observed the results of a belated Washington decision to withdraw Richardson, an action which Hilsman said caused the CIA much pain. Involved was the question of whether the administration did or did not desire the overthrow of Diem. (It would have liked to have kept him without his brother, but since there was no way to separate them this preference could be called academic.)

Hilsman interpreted the withdrawal order as follows:

> Richardson was close to Nhu personally. Nhu himself would interpret Richardson's recall as a signal that the United States really did mean business and that CIA views no longer were predominant in the councils of the United States. . . . It would help to signal our determination not to cooperate with a government having Nhu in a position of predominance.

The generals were doing their own interpreting, and they decided Richardson's recall meant that both Diem and Nhu were open to attack. The CIA station chief left

Saigon October 5, seven weeks before Kennedy's assassination.

The close timing and the CIA's obvious anger over Richardson's withdrawal caused speculation that the agency might have been involved in Kennedy's death. Since Lee Harvey Oswald purported to favor Castro, who was still fending off agency attempts to assassinate him in Cuba, this involvement might have created bedfellows even stranger than those usually found in politics if there had been any way of proving such a supposition.

The Buddhist crisis had a curious beginning. President Diem attempted to de-emphasize his family's minority status in a country about ten percent Catholic and up to eighty percent Buddhist. Although the flying of flags other than the national emblem was a common feature of ceremonial proceedings throughout the world, he decided to enforce an old ordinance against flying anything except the Vietnamese flag. He felt that there had been too great a display of Catholic banners in ceremonies celebrating the installation of another of his brothers as a Roman Catholic bishop.

To Diem's surprise the Buddhists, who were understandably a bit sensitive after the way some of their pagodas had been treated by the government, interpreted his order as directed against them. Since he was firmly convinced that a ruler never should admit a mistake, Diem could reverse himself only with the most painful face-saving maneuvers. During the interval before any action toward a reversal could be taken, at ceremonies celebrating the 2,527th anniversary of the birth of Gautama Buddha, the Buddhists massed with their banners in the ancient former capital of Hue and refused either to furl their colors or disperse.

Government troops were called. A trigger-happy major, who said he thought he heard an explosion and whose unit was operating from armored cars supplied by the United States, ordered his men to open fire. Nine Buddhists were killed and some of the bodies were crushed under the wheels of the armored cars.

In a manner not unknown to its larger counterparts,

the government at Saigon issued a false cover story that a Vietcong grenade had been thrown into a crowd at Hue, and that a number of persons had been killed in the ensuing panic. This outrageous fabrication, which infuriated Buddhists who were on the scene, soon had to be replaced with something nearer the truth. But when several thousand Buddhists massed at the same location the following day, government troops again were called and this time attacked and dispersed them.

A number of prominent Buddhists responded to that incident by signing an open letter declaring their readiness to "march down the road to martyrdom." The letter presented five demands: (1) the right to fly religious flags; (2) equal status for Buddhism and Catholicism, meaning nullification of an old French law defining the former as an "association"; (3) the right to preach Buddhism as a religion, apparently nailing down demand No. 2; (4) compensation for the relatives of those who died in the original mass killing at Hue; and (5) punishment for those responsible for the deaths.

Although Diem eventually would get around to saying that the first three of the conditions laid down were in effect already and that the last two would be granted, each of his obscure and ambiguous statements came too late to ward off further trouble. On June 10, with reporters and photographers present and 350 monks and nuns chanting in a circle around him in downtown Saigon, a 70-year-old Buddhist priest named Quang Duc poured a large bucket of gasoline over his head and burned himself to death in the first of the self-immolations. The horror of this incident and those that followed shocked the world and stirred patriotic and religious fervor among the country's twelve million Buddhists, less than half of whom normally bothered to practice the rites.

The mostly poverty-ridden Buddhists had some outdated equipment and had learned a little about public relations. They began grinding out antigovernment propaganda on mimeograph machines in their ramshackle pagodas. A long series of skirmishes ensued in which pagodas were raided, equipment was broken up, and monks and priests were beaten with police clubs.

Then in a military sweep organized on a national scale, hundreds of pagodas were attacked with tear gas, gunfire, and hand grenades on the morning of August 21. More than 1,400 priests and monks were thrown in jail, at least thirty were killed or wounded, and many others were driven into hiding.

Martial law was declared the same day and no death toll was given, though it was clear that most of the monks and priests were in custody or had gotten away. Within forty-eight hours many of the pagodas were reopened and turned over to monks more friendly to the government—some of them police and intelligence agents entirely new to the cloth. These latter must have fooled almost no one, although they may have had a slightly better chance of doing so than would have been the case in the West, since Buddhist monks had less training and no life-long commitment—they could resume life as laymen and then don robes again if they chose.

The pagoda raids could be regarded as a slaughter or as a national desecration. From either point of view, they were an unacceptable insult. In Saigon Defense Minister Vu Van Mau, a Buddhist, resigned his office, shaved his head and applied for a permit to go on a pilgrimage to India. The permit was denied and he was placed under temporary arrest. In Washington South Vietnamese Ambassador Tran Van Chuong, a Buddhist and father of Madame Nhu but no admirer of his son-in-law (Madame Nhu was a converted Catholic) resigned in protest against "this bad regime." When Madame Nhu later went on a speaking tour of the United States attempting to explain the pagoda raids her father followed her on many of the same platforms to give the opposite view.

A spontaneous wave of protest and rage in South Vietnam forced the closing of the country's two universities at Saigon and Hue, and of the elementary and secondary schools in Saigon. More than four thousand student demonstrators, many of them children, were jailed. On August 23, two days after the pagoda raids and with many key facts concerning them still unknown, the *New York Times* commented:

> A provoked Vietnamese people may turn against the Ngos in increasing strength. If, as appears possible, significant elements of the armed forces turn with them the Ngo family will be ousted.

What the *Times* could not know was that the use of Colonel Tung's Special Forces in the pagoda raids had already assured fulfillment of the second of the two conditions mentioned in the newspaper's prediction. Since the basic training of Tung's forces had begun only sixteen months before, and the formation and training of his units had been carried out with usual CIA secrecy, existence of the "pocket" army and especially its peculiar status free of regular command were not generally known.

The first news dispatches concerning the pagoda raids said that "troops" or in some cases "airborne troops" had been used in their desecration. These brought indignant denials from the Saigon Military Command Headquarters, but the denials offered no explanation as to what did happen. As long as four days later the Voice of America, which was the principal source of accurate news in Saigon because its programs used regular American wire service copy, was still broadcasting erroneously that some of the police in the raids were "disguised as army troops."

The leaders of the armed forces remained silent except for their angry denials, but they were under no illusion as to where the trouble lay. Many of them thought Tung had made a deliberate attempt to saddle them with the blame for the inflammatory conduct of himself and his troops. Not a single word was spoken on behalf of the government during the rapid formation of a blood-oath commission including fourteen generals and ten senior colonels to prepare for the coup.

As previously mentioned, the action did not come at this juncture, because Nhu and the CIA still seemed to be packing enough wallop to give the leaders pause; but the decision was unanimous, and everything was in place and ready to go when the time came two months later.

Troops were first seen moving silently through Saigon at 1:30 P.M. on November 1. At 1:45 P.M. General Tran Van Don, acting chief of the South Vietnamese armed forces, telephoned General Joseph Stilwell, deputy United States commander, to say that the coup was underway—a warning Hilsman said had been promised.

Several of the generals telephoned Diem and Nhu, speaking alternately into the telephone to show they were together. The brothers, isolated in Gia Long Palace and guarded by a thousand troops, refused to surrender when given an opportunity to do so. Diem later called repeatedly over the palace radio, as he had done successfully during an attempted coup in 1960, for outlying forces to come to his aid. In other broadcasts Nhu urged action in support of the government by youth groups he and Madame Nhu had organized.

This time there was no response to their pleas.

At 4:30 P.M. Diem telephoned United States Ambassador Henry Cabot Lodge and asked him if he knew what was going on. Lodge replied in the affirmative, agreed that Diem was entitled to consideration from the United States, and mentioned a possibility that Diem's safe conduct out of the country might be arranged.

Diem neither accepted nor rejected the implied offer of safe conduct, and in his last words to an American said only that he was trying to restore order.

At 4:45 P.M. the brothers received a brief call from Colonel Tung, who had been seized at an airport trying to escape. He was allowed to remain alive only long enough to tell the brothers that there was no hope of resistance and then was taken outside and shot.

In a sense Tung fared better than the brothers, since he received a quick death and decent burial with his ancestors. The fates of Diem and Nhu, however, remained obscure for some time. Little was known about how they spent their last desperate hours, and the location of their graves was originally kept secret. One fact did come out: Almost to the end, with the government tottering crazily, Nhu was said to have boasted that he had "taught the Buddhists and the Americans a lesson."

At 5:15 P.M. the generals gave the brothers another chance to surrender. When they again refused, an attack on the palace by four Vietnamese fighter-bombers was ordered. The bombs did moderate damage and one of the planes was shot down by Vietnamese naval forces which were stationed in the Saigon River and had failed to get the word.

At 3:30 A.M. (still November 1 by American time) a full-scale infantry attack on the palace began. The defenders surrendered but the brothers were found to have escaped to the home of a wealthy Chinese friend in suburban Cholon. Their hideaway was quickly discovered by means not stated, possibly because they had had rush telephone lines installed at the Chinese home and the information could have been obtained from the telephone company.

At 6:30 A.M. Diem offered to surrender if he and his brother were granted safe conduct. The CIA, which had a man (Lucien Conein) in the coup headquarters, transmitted to the American embassy a request for a plane to fly them out of the country. Hasty arrangements were attempted but eventually, because it would have taken twenty-four hours to obtain from Guam a plane with sufficient range to fly them to a country willing to receive them, and no doubt with more than a suspicion this was going to be too late, the effort was abandoned even though the possibility of such a request had been foreseen.

As the rebel forces advanced upon them the brothers made one more attempt to escape, fleeing from the Chinese home to a small Catholic church in Cholon. There they were captured—an announcement said they surrendered—and were bound and placed face down on the floor of an armored car, ostensibly for transfer to command headquarters. They were killed en route. The rebel government issued an announcement that they had committed suicide, but when fellow members of their religion pointed out that for Catholics this would be a mortal sin, the announcement was amended to say they were victims of "accidental suicide"—a contradiction in terms which the *New York Times* said "strains credulity."

John Mechlin, in *Mission in Torment* (Doubleday, 1965), said:

> What counted was that the armed forces turned against Diem almost to a man. . . . Except for the resistance of the presidential guard not a weapon was raised in the regime's defense.

The death toll in the coup was placed at thirty-three—nine rebel soldiers, four palace guards, and twenty civilians including the official victims and innocent bystanders. Tung was included as a civilian despite his rank because his position as chief of the "Presidential Survey Office"—the so-called "Vietnamese CIA"—was considered to have been nonmilitary.

As for the brothers, the new government announced that they had been buried "with appropriate religious ceremonies" but refused for a year to say where. This led many to believe that examination of the bodies would have shown that they were shot or stabbed, or shot and stabbed, in the back.

The creation of two Vietnams was itself a violation of the Geneva Accords, which divided Vietnam at the 17th parallel only for the purpose of "regrouping." This process was to have taken a maximum of three hundred days, during which period the French colonial forces would withdraw from the country. Internationally supervised elections were then to have been held to reunify the country.

Premier and later President Diem (he became president after a year by ousting Paris-residing Emperor Bao Dai and holding a so-called election in which he received 98 percent of the vote) refused to take part in the planned reunifying elections. He was urged to go through the motions of negotiating unsuccessfully with Hanoi regarding the elections, but with the North more populous and the South divided, he would take no chances. "We have not signed the Geneva Accords," he said. "We are not bound in any way by these arrangements, signed against the will of the Vietnamese people."

When Diem's adamant stand cost him the support of the British and French governments, financially flush America stepped into their places. Many universities were being considered for government contracts at this time, and Michigan State University happened to have a unique "School of Police Administration." The East Lansing institution was awarded a multi-million-dollar contract to equip and train a 50,000-man "Civil Guard" to strengthen the Diem regime.

This was another demonstration of the CIA's unshakable dedication to the idea of government by force. According to professors who served on the project, the unusual university program included target practice and riot drill, with guns and live ammunition considered part of the classroom equipment. Providing cover for CIA agents was incidental to the main work.

The *London Daily Telegraph* thought that with or without CIA involvement the Michigan State contract was to be deplored. Commenting later, the *Telegraph* said:

> The project illustrates the decay of traditional academic principles in the modern university. . . . The university neglected scholarship and became the obedient servant of American policy in Vietnam; Diem in turn helped bring the university twenty-five million in American dollars. . . . When asked about the propriety of the project Professor Ralph Smuckler, acting head of international programs at Michigan State, hinted that the university had tried to sever its links with the CIA as early as 1956. "It may not have been right to get into it," Professor Smuckler said, "but we were caught and had to follow through."[10]

Though hundreds of thousands of tons of armaments sent to fight Communism in China had wound up in the hands of the Communists, and the same fate awaited a still larger quantity to be sent to Vietnam, the policy of trying to govern by force continued to be unremittingly pursued. There were vigorous and repeated criticisms of the policy but, partly because of attempts to be fair, these always tapered off into ineffectuality.

When the existence of the "pocket" army and its use against the pagodas were first revealed, for example, the *Washington Post* commented:

> The United States has been understandably embarrassed by the disclosure that the CIA has been secretly aiding the South Vietnamese Special Forces. . . . Yet this is unfortunately not the first time the government has been made to look foolish by the misnamed Central Intelligence Agency. . . . One might have supposed that the Bay of Pigs debacle would have alerted the White House to the risks of allowing an intelligence agency to sit in judgment over its own operations.

Lest these words and those that followed sound too harsh, however, the *Post* added farther down in its editorial:

> Let it be said that the CIA contains men of undoubted skill and patriotism. Let it be said that much of the American problem in Saigon springs from circumstances that not even the wisest of men could easily meet. But some self-inflicted wounds form a part of the heartbreaking calamity. . . . It would be heartening if the present embarrassment were turned to a useful purpose by effecting a real reorganization of the CIA.

The *Post* did not appear to be giving its readers much news by informing them that any fairly large group would be bound to include "men of undoubted skill and patriotism." And since the CIA had already successfully eluded hundreds of attempts to reform it, the hope expressed sixteen years after the agency's creation for "a real reorganization" of no specified origin seemed to be carrying optimism too far.

Roger Hilsman, no doubt having in mind the CIA employees who bucked their superior in Saigon, also felt constrained to soften critical passages:

> The CIA is not a threat to our liberties and never has been. It is composed of dedicated officers of extremely high standards of integrity and patriotism. Should anyone attempt to subvert the agency to purposes that would threaten our society it would be the members of the CIA who would be first to sound the alarm.

Without getting into those "extremely high standards of integrity and patriotism" which were never illustrated in CIA programs even though present in its personnel, such well-intended comments amounted to leaning on a badly bruised reed. Their underlying assumption was that there was something special about the United States which automatically delivered us from evils detected in other countries. There were plenty of splendid people in pre-Hitler Germany, too, and everyone saw how helpless they were made by an extremist, hard-knuckled, ends-justify-the-means organization.

A few weeks after Kennedy's death President Johnson addressed to the South Vietnamese government a New Year's Day message in which he said:

> Neutralization of South Vietnam would be only another name for a Communist take-over. . . . The United States will continue to furnish you and your people with the fullest means of support in this bitter fight. We shall maintain in Vietnam American personnel and matériel as needed to assist you in achieving victory.

Forty-seven volumes of Pentagon papers were not needed in order to perceive from this highly combative and scarcely felicitous New Year's Day greeting that American policy had gone into reverse. Johnson's message was addressed to General Duong Van "Big" Minh, chairman of the Council of Generals which overthrew Diem. Even Minh was considerably less warlike than the American president and himself was unseated a month later by General Nguyen Kahn for being too soft with the "neutralists"—meaning those live-and-let-live people who were always around when the high-spirited types wished to plunge humanity into a morass of misery.

Defense Secretary McNamara, straining to accommodate himself to the new situation, had clearly and publicly recognized the policy reversal even earlier, just before Christmas on December 21. On that date McNamara refused to discuss a program he had announced eleven weeks earlier which would have ended major American military activity in South Vietnam during 1965.

The Johnson administration's exclusion of all forms of neutralism meant that the only acceptable alternative to fighting the war would be an agreement to commit political suicide on the part of everyone except the United States and its allies. Since such an agreement was impossible, the logic for fighting the war became inexorable.

On August 4, 1964, on the basis of a Tonkin Gulf incident in which it could not be determined whether or not anything had happened (as Senator Fulbright said, one United States destroyer may have been struck by one bullet but even that could not be verified), Johnson ordered retaliatory bombing raids against North Vietnam. The raids were already underway by the time Congress was notified.

The bombing raids proved popular at the time. In conjunction with his call for "The Great Society," Johnson's aggressively hawkish Vietnam policy enabled him to win a landslide election victory to a full term. After the post-election holiday was over, with hearts sinking in those who correctly foresaw the consequences, the United States began the sustained bombing of North Vietnam in February of 1965. The big military buildup began the following month with the landing of the first ground combat units (Marines).

Bernard B. Fall, the Howard University professor who was one of those who correctly foresaw the consequences and who wrote *Hell in a Very Small Place* (Lippincott, 1967) and other early Vietnam stories—and who was later killed while on a Marine patrol—reminded readers as 1965 ended that on Oriental calendars this had been "the Year of the Snake." Others could make their own interpretations of that, but Fall was a gentle soul; he said history should record it as "The Year of the Hawks," and added:

> The hawks have beaten not only the doves but even the mere questioners of their seemingly unerring truths into vocal ineffectualness. This leaves the chance for an accommodation—on the basis of other than five years of all-out war and ten years of "pacification"—on shaky ground.

When its grand palace strategy collapsed into deepening war the CIA returned to its original responsibility for arming mountain tribes numbering close to 700,000 individuals in South Vietnam's central highlands. Whereas lowland Vietnamese were Mongoloid like the Chinese, the Montagnards were of much less warlike Polynesian descent and spoke thirty different Malayo-Polynesian dialects. There had been Vietnamese of the Mongoloid type in North Vietnam as early as the second century B.C., but their southward movement which drove these mountain people from the fertile lowlands had occurred only in the last three centuries.

In 1964 when approximately nine thousand of the tribesmen had been armed, the Montagnards staged a revolt in five CIA training camps. The basis of their complaint was that this was not their war. They shrewdly kept American officers with them so that their lowland compatriots could not attack them with artillery or by other indiscriminate means, and the revolt had to be put down with a combination of threats, promises of tribal autonomy, and other concessions. Perhaps because their later operations involved highly secret incursions into neighboring countries to obtain targeting information, this was the last time the Montagnards would figure prominently in the news.

An offshoot of the mountain training, however, was persistently in the news up to the time of America's withdrawal from the war. The Montagnards for the most part were organized into twenty-member teams called CCNs (for Command and Control, North). These became prototypes for teams later recruited and trained among lowland Vietnamese in the CIA's infamous Phoenix assassination program.

The Phoenix operations, always justified on the ground that similar atrocities were being committed by the Communists throughout the countryside, were credited in one account with the assassination of 16,400 members of the Communist "infrastructure" over a twelve-month period. Another tally said 27,000 members of the Communist apparatus had been "neutralized" in one year. Officially, 20,587 victims died during the two-and-one-half years of the program's operations.

Former CIA Director Colby, in his book *Honorable Men* (Simon and Schuster, 1978), protested that he did not testify that more than twenty thousand individuals were "assassinated" in the Phoenix program; he only said they were "killed," eighty-five percent of them by "Vietnamese and American military and paramilitary troops." However, the victims in this case were ostensibly civilians, perhaps guerrillas or part-time guerrillas, but mainly petty officials, hardly of combat age, and difficult to identify as battle casualties.

Also, the military units to which Colby referred presumably included outfits similar to the CCNs, carried on the books as Provincial Reconnaissance Units and otherwise known as assassination teams. Colby said "only" about twelve percent—approximately 2,500 individuals—had been killed "by police or other security forces." His book did not say how the remaining three percent died, although this would be more than six hundred individuals—approximately one per working day for the two-and-a-half-year period.

The Montagnards, unsuited for war and with little or nothing to gain from the present conflict, never became involved in anything as bloodthirsty as the Phoenix program, and no similar tally of their activities was kept. Undoubtedly their over-the-border targeting information was important from time to time, although in the course of hundreds of briefings and press conferences at the Pentagon I cannot remember their ever having been mentioned as a factor in the continually worsening infiltration problem in South Vietnam.

If America's participation in the war was considered to have started with the landing of Marines and the all-out bombing of the infiltration routes lumped together as the Ho Chi Minh Trail (not a trail at all, but rather a couple of big areas sliced from Laos and North Vietnam), the impossibility of the task undertaken could be said to have become apparent almost immediately.

Instead of decreasing the infiltration into South Vietnam, the all-out bombing begun in February of 1965 somehow permitted the influx to rise dramatically to 4,500 men a month for the year, as compared to 1,000 a month in 1964. A further increase, to 5,000 a month, was recorded for 1966.

These official estimates, compiled on a daily and weekly as well as a monthly basis in the field, created such a bleak impression of progressive defeat that an order went out from Washington to discontinue their release. Amazingly, at least for those unfamiliar with the thick Laotian jungle that hid the traffic from the sky, even those figures did not include 30,000 regular North Vietnamese troops that moved into South Vietnam during the same period, nor did they take into account the southward movement of huge quantities of modern weapons and ammunition which, as much as manpower, were the Communist answer to the arrival of American forces in strength.

Only after the war would it be revealed that defense and military sensitivity concerning the infiltration statistics had been carried to the point of misleading the White House on the subject from time to time. This was a recognized crime, although misleading reporters, even by the most scrupulous government sources when there was occasion for it, was considered a normal and justifiable procedure.

In a way that could not be swept under the rug, the Tet offensive of 1968 finally demonstrated the failure of the Johnson policy. In spite of thirty billion dollars, half a million men, and enormous quantities of commodities moving annually from the United States to South Vietnam, the situation had worsened. The military command at Saigon methodically drew up an estimate that 206,000 additional troops in the American force level in South Vietnam would be needed to restore a winning posture, but little or no consideration was given to the possibility of providing such an increase. The more general conclusion in Washington was that the outcome would not have been especially different if a million or two million instead of only a half million American troops had been on the scene.

In the face of such futility the United States never again mounted an offensive in terms of the victory which President Johnson had envisioned almost as though it were an accomplished fact when he took office. What could not possibly have been foreseen was that even with the final outcome apparent and in fact accepted, it would still take five years to wind down American participation in the war. Another unforeseeable circumstance was that the last dismal stages of the winding down, including the Christmas bombing of 1972, would be accompanied by something called Watergate, which would duplicate at home many of the practices pursued so persistently by the CIA abroad.

Long Live the Shah

9

Although Watergate and the energy crisis would dominate the American scene during most of 1973, the importance of neither was at all understood at the start of the year. This could seem more than strange since as of mid-January it was a full seven months since the well-publicized Watergate break-in. But the proof was unquestionable, for one reason because neither Watergate nor the energy crisis figured in the speculation as to why CIA Director Helms was appointed as the year opened to become United States ambassador to Iran.

In an absence of such understanding the unusual and in fact unprecedented appointment could not be explained. Speculation veered crazily from one subject to another. One of the country's leading commentators, Joseph Alsop, in an article given a two-column display next to the editorial page in Washington's leading daily, theorized that in pursuing his daily intelligence reports President Nixon had become convinced Helms was permitting his analysts to become too stereotyped in their thinking, and therefore he had to go. Another columnist speculated that Helms was being punished belatedly for having refused to go along with some of the Pentagon's far-out estimates of the Anti-Ballistic Missile (ABM) threat. A third conjectured that Helms had failed dismally in another unpublicized attempt to coordinate the activities of the intelligence community.

The truth was that Helms, with more foresight than most, had refused to become involved personally and had limited the involvement of the CIA in the Watergate cover-up; and that advance rumblings of the energy crisis had provided an excuse to get rid of him. Iran was considered something of a CIA province, and Shah Mohammed Reza Pahlavi, whom the CIA had so generously helped back into power at the expense of Premier Mossadegh in 1953, was still high in the saddle. One laudatory account at this time had it that the shah was regarded by his people as "not so much an accepted institution as he is the embodiment of all that is best in the country's cultural and political tradition."

Although the extent to which the CIA was actually responsible for the demise of Mossadegh's regime remains debatable, the CIA itself counted the shah's return to power as one of its proudest achievements. In an extraordinary series of articles published just a year after the fall of Mossadegh in the *Saturday Evening Post*, an "informed source in the intelligence community" (undoubtedly a CIA officer, and perhaps then-Director Allen Dulles himself) was quoted as saying:

> In Egypt the Communists were making capital of the lascivious regime of King Farouk until skilled American operatives became available to advise the leaders of a pro-American junta (headed by Nasser) when the time seemed right for a palace coup ... Another CIA-influenced triumph was the successful overthrow, in the summer of 1953, of old dictatorial Premier Mohammed Mossadegh and the return to power of this country's friend, Shah Mohammed Reza Pahlavi.

The CIA source proceeded with a detailed account of the Iranian overthrow. A more dispassionate version will be offered below, but here is how the agency itself viewed the operation:

> On May 28, 1953, President Eisenhower received a letter from Mossadegh amounting to a bare-faced attempt at international blackmail: the United States would fill his bankrupt treasury with American dollars—or else. The "or else," Mos-

sadegh hinted darkly, would be an economic agreement and mutual defense pact with Russia. Mossadegh was conspiring with the Communist Tudeh Party as it operated in the back alleyways of the ancient Iranian capital of Teheran. He had only one asset to pledge to Russia in exchange for aid—the resources of the rich Iranian oilfields and the refinery at Abadan, which Mossadegh had seized from the Anglo-Iranian Oil Company under the guise of nationalization. With that economic stroke accomplished Moscow would be in a position to achieve the prime objective of Russian foreign policy since the days of the Czars—access to a warm water outlet on the Persian Gulf, the Free World's lifeline to the Far East. A Russian score there would mean the crumbling of the democracies' position in the Middle East from Cairo to Baluchistan.

With the problem thus set up in giant proportions, the CIA said its solution had required more than a little doing. First the White House stalled Mossadegh for one month and then turned him down with a blunt "No!" This was described as a calculated risk and as a daring gamble that Mossadegh would not remain in office long enough to carry out his "threat." "The doing began in short order through a chain of stranger-than-fiction events involving Dulles, a diplomat, a princess, and a policeman," the CIA said.

The events would never be revealed in full because of security, the CIA implied, while hinting at them as best it could:

On August 10 Dulles packed his bags to join his wife for a vacation in the Swiss Alps. The political situation in Iran was becoming more conspiratorial by the hour. Mossadegh was consorting with a Russian economic mission. Loy Henderson, United States ambassador to Iran, felt he could leave his post for a short "holiday" in Switzerland. Princess Ashraf, the attractive and strong-willed twin sister of the shah, chose the same week to fly to a Swiss Alpine resort. It was reported that she had a stormy session with her brother in his pink marble palace because of his vacillation in facing up to Mossadegh. The fourth of the assorted characters in this drama,

Brigadier General H. Norman Schwarzkopf, at this time took a flying vacation across the Middle East. His itinerary included apparently aimless and leisurely stops to see old friends in Pakistan, Syria, Lebanon—and Iran.

Schwarzkopf, who was head of the New Jersey State Police at the time of the Lindbergh baby kidnapping, had been in Iran before on an assignment to reorganize the Iranian National Police. The CIA said he would deny any connection with the events but that after his arrival things happened in one-two-three order. The conference in Switzerland presumably developed his instructions and helped pave the way for him. Concerning Mossadegh's final overthrow, the CIA said:

> On Wednesday August 19th, with the army standing close guard in an uneasy capital, a grotesque procession made its way through the street leading to the heart of Teheran. There were tumblers turning handsprings, weight lifters twirling iron bars, and wrestlers flexing their biceps. As the spectators grew in number the bizarre assortment of performers began shouting pro-shah slogans in unison. The crowd took up the chant; and there, after a precarious moment, the balance of public sentiment swung against Mossadegh. On signal, it seemed, the army forces on the side of the shah began an attack. By nightfall, following American-style strategy and logistics, the loyalist troops had driven Mossadegh's elements into a tight cordon around Mossadegh's palace. They surrendered, and Mossadegh was captured as he lay weeping on his bed, clad in striped silk pajamas. Thus it was that the strategic little nation of Iran was rescued from the closing clutch of Moscow.

Such was the CIA's proud account of how the shah returned to power. From a more tolerant and objective point of view, however, Mossadegh could be considered a man worse than some but a good deal better than many. Called "the weeping premier" because he frequently burst into tears while addressing street crowds from balconies in historic Teheran, Mossadegh also enlivened the news from time to time by appearing in his pajamas for some of the balcony sessions, and by collapsing and being carried off on a stretcher during fainting spells in which he was overcome by emotion.

In the early 1950s, Iran, with fifteen percent of the world's petroleum reserves, was still far from the comparative affluence it achieved by the time of the energy crisis two decades later. Literacy in the towns and cities was estimated at seven percent, with something close to zero prevailing in the countryside. Since eighty-five percent of the country's twenty million people were scratching a bare subsistence from primitive agriculture or leading a nomadic tribal life, there was plenty to weep about.

Even though in his seventies and prone to emotional upheavals, Mossadegh proved to be a tough old man. He held power for twenty-eight months, a long period considering that, through an international arrangement that might with reason have been called a conspiracy, he was cut off from both oil revenues and—an equally large figure in these days—American aid.

After becoming head of the National Front Party and then premier, Mossadegh had broken diplomatic relations with Great Britain in 1952 and had rebuffed American efforts to heal the breach. Although his Front Party received Communist support, he also canceled a Caspian Sea fisheries agreement with Moscow and announced a foreign policy of dealing impartially with East and West.

The Iranian oil industry, until then a British monopoly, was nationalized but operated at a snail's pace because its product was prevented by boycott from reaching markets. Describing this situation later the *New York Times* said Iranian oil "was barred from world markets for more than two years by a successful British commercial blockade backed by world oil interests." These questions arise: Where, when, and how does one get the backing of "world oil interests?"

American aid was discontinued because Mossadegh was "flirting with the Kremlin" and "threatening" to sell oil to the Soviet Union. This was before the Soviets were found to have produced more oil at home than they knew what to do with for the time being, after which they were accused of "dumping" petroleum and its products at ruinous prices in all parts of the world. (So brilliant a strategist as General MacArthur was said to have been trapped by the misconception involved here. He gravely miscalculated in Korea because he could not imagine that the potential enemy would move into poverty-stricken South Korea when the oil of Iran, enough to power a military sweep across western Europe, was right on his Caspian Sea doorstep.)

Although himself a large landholder, Mossadegh continued in his economic isolation to accept aid from the officially outlawed Communist Tudeh Party. By so doing he alienated a large part of his army, although he retained the loyalty of his chief of staff. Despite the loss of 100,000 jobs in the oil industry, he was able to show slight improvements in employment, overall economic production, and the balance of trade.

Meanwhile he conducted a running feud with Shah Pahlavi. At one point a committee of eight from the majlis, the lower house of the Iranian parliament, was appointed to attempt to settle the differences between the shah and the premier. Then Mossadegh was accused of planning to dissolve the parliament and to make himself a dictator. On August 15, 1953, with "considerable reluctance," the shah signed an order dismissing Mossadegh and appointing Major General Fazollah Zahedi to serve as premier.

Certain that trouble would result, the shah and his queen Soraya left immediately for a vacation in Rome. The commander of the Royal Guards was left behind to deliver the dismissal order. When he attempted to do so, Mossadegh had him arrested, claiming the dismissal order was illegal and forbidding communication between members of the government and the shah. Premier-designate Zahedi went into hiding, and street demonstrations were organized in Mossadegh's behalf.

The pro-Mossadegh demonstrators went too far. They smashed statues of the shah and his father, Shah Reza Khan Pahlavi, who claimed descent from Darius I and had established the current dynasty in 1925. Destruction and desecration were widespread. After forty-eight hours a counterdemonstration was organized and pro-Royalist army units were brought into the city. An estimated three hundred people were killed on August 19 during nine hours of street fighting that involved both military and civilian partisans. With or without the aid of circus performers the pro-Royalists got the upper hand. General Zahedi then emerged from hiding, dispatched tank battalions to surround the palaces of Mossadegh and the shah, and placed Mossadegh under arrest.

The part played by the CIA in these events was unknown to the public at the time. The agency had not yet gained the reputation that would have made it suspect. According to later accounts, the counterdemonstration was directed from a Teheran basement by Kermit "Kim" Roosevelt, grandson of President Theodore Roosevelt and seventh cousin of President Franklin D. Roosevelt. Others including Schwarzkopf were said to have been above ground paying out money with a lavish hand to strong-arm squads shouting "Long Live the Shah" and "Death to Mossadegh." One report was that the CIA had spent $10 million on the counterdemonstration.

The only official statement on the subject was made by Dulles, who said: "I can say that the report we spent many dollars on that [the counterdemonstration] is utterly false." The word "many" was subject to interpretation, however, and at the prodigious rate soon established for American aid to Iran, several million dollars to overthrow a government might not have seemed much. During the first ten years after the shah's return to power, American grant aid to Iran amounted to $1.3 billion; and at the end of the decade a House committee reported: "It is now utterly impossible to determine, with any accuracy, what became of these funds."

With the shah and Zahedi in office, the oil dispute was speedily resolved. American aid, including long-term loans not in the above total, was resumed immediately with a spot payment of $45 million which was delivered in a few days. The British lost about half of their former

Iranian oil monopoly, but on a dignified and highly re-
munerative basis.

Under a twenty-five-year agreement signed with the
shah, the British directly retained forty percent of the oil
rights. Another forty percent went to a six-company
American group including Standard of New Jersey (later
Exxon) and Standard of California. Fourteen percent was
assigned to Royal Dutch Shell, and six percent to a French
firm. Since Royal Dutch Shell was half or more British-
owned, the British could be said to have retained forty-
seven percent of the rights, or fifty-four percent in terms
of control. In addition they were guaranteed a $75 million
payment for the loss of the rest, and because of the great
expansion in Iranian oil, forty-seven percent yielded considerably more than could have been anticipated from
100 percent at the previous rate of growth.

The *Nation* disclosed a possible conflict of interest,
pointing out that the New York law firm of Sullivan and
Cromwell, in which both of the Dulles brothers had been
prominent partners, was the long-standing legal counsel
for the Anglo-Iranian Oil Company. But although the
British did fare well in the 25-year agreement, none of the
other participating companies had anything to complain
about, and the disclosure attracted little attention. There
was no suggestion at the time that here and in Saudi Ara-
bia the United States and its partners had walked into a
trap which two decades later would snap shut with earth-
shaking effects on Western economies.

How much the CIA contributed to Mossadegh's overthrow was anybody's guess. Warren L. Nelson, who
worked as a newspaperman in Teheran before becoming
Middle East editor and later a defense correspondent for
United Press International, looked into the matter and
concluded that the agency's role had been exaggerated.
Certainly there was no reason to believe that fanciful bit
about the circus performers; and there were major economic, political, and traditional factors making the duration of Mossadegh's regime more surprising than its termination. In the much later skyrocketing of Mideast oil

prices in the 1970s, there was certainly no reason to think that the shah felt in any way indebted to the United States for his restoration to power and subsequent aid.

In the twenty years since Mossadegh's overthrow the population of Iran had increased by fifty percent, from 20 to 30 million. There were 3.7 million schoolchildren in the country, as compared with only 250,000 in 1953, with many other modernizing advances in the same proportion. However, with his secret police (Savak) and his American-equipped military forces, and with his CIA advisers frequently at his elbow, the shah had considerably overdone the matter of government by force. It was like having a Kent State affair every few days.

After two decades of this, at the time of Helms' appointment as ambassador, Iran was a country about to explode. Possibly because he was much more aware of the situation than were the CIA's analysts, the shah decided to take drastic measures. Even before Helms' Senate confirmation and arrival in Teheran, in what the *Washington Post* called "a dramatic reversal," he announced in militant fashion before the Iranian parliament on January 22, 1973, that he would refuse to renew his 25-year Western oil concessions when they expired in 1979. He also threatened to nationalize the oil industry immediately if the Western companies did not take prompt steps to double his production and increase Iran's royalty rates.

The speech had sounded a clarion call for an entirely new order of things in the Middle East. The *Post* said sources in the industry were bitter because of the shah's militancy, and that they foresaw difficult days ahead. At the time the shah spoke, Iran was receiving $2.1 billion a year from oil. In a matter of several months the figure would balloon to $20 billion a year, with another $40 billion going to Saudi Arabia, the largest oil exporter, with Iran second.

The shah seemed well aware from the first that he had a tiger by the tail, and told the parliament:

> The industrial world will have to realize that the era of their terrific progress and even more terrific income and wealth based on cheap oil is finished.

On one level the events in Iran served to bring out the ideological change that had gradually taken place since 1953. Although no distinction could now be made between the shah's stated foreign policy and the one enunciated by Mossadegh, and despite the fact that the shah was embarked on a stupendous campaign of commercial-type highway robbery, no one was resorting to accusing him of subversion. Compared to the days when anyone obnoxious was automatically a Red, this was a shift of a kind almost imperceptible except over long periods of time.

But the CIA had undoubtedly played a part in the course of events in Iran. Whatever the exact extent of that role may have been, it can certainly be said that CIA involvement in Iranian affairs did nothing to avert the oil crisis, the rise of Khomeini, or the taking of American hostages. Indeed, CIA intervention can be said to have abetted those disastrous events.

PART II

The CIA at Home

Bureaucracy Unlimited 10

The Central Intelligence Agency was originally mandated under provisions of a vast and confusing piece of legislation enacted in 1947. Although known as "The military Unification Act" this measure created an Air Force and a Defense Department, thus establishing four separate entities where before there had been only the War Department and Navy. The only way to reconcile the purpose and content of the bill was to suppose that of the four entities—Army, Navy, Air Force and Defense Department—the last would be so firmly in control of the other three that in effect they would be one unit.

But the strongest of the secretaries of defense subsequently proved unable to prevent the military services from going their separate ways in many respects. In a technological age they were especially unable to prevent the expansion and proliferation of the services' highly specialized intelligence branches. Eventually, as in the original legislation, additional agencies and services were created to perform some new task or to aid, supply or coordinate those already in existence.

Thus, the true character of the CIA was largely hidden at its inception. Major attention was on the omnibus reorganization bill's creation of a separate air force and its replacement of the time-honored War Department with the Department of Defense. Few saw the importance of the CIA section or realized that in the name of secrecy Congress was abdicating a large chunk of its authority, including to some extent the power to raise armies and make war.

In 1952 the National Security Agency (NSA), accountable to the Defense Department, was set up at Fort
Meade, Maryland. With an annual budget of well over a
billion dollars, it was for many years the largest intelligence branch of the government. NSA's grandiose assignment was to crack the codes of potential enemies, neutralists and, just to be on the safe side, close allies as well; to
monitor their communications by land, sea, and air on a
worldwide basis; and to computerize all this information
for current and future use. Whole trainloads of tapes and
other data were shipped to the once sleepy military res-
ervation at Fort Meade, and the computers were kept so
busy that the contents of some of the freight cars had to
be scrapped without being processed. The only intelligence agency with a bigger budget was the Air Force's
later National Reconnaissance Office (NRO), responsible
for managing the spy satellite program. (By the 1980s
NSA and NRO together were spending more than $4 bil-
lion a year, or approximately as much as the budgets for
the entire intelligence community before the spy satellites
hove onto the horizon. Apparently around two-thirds of
the amount went for construction and operation of the
satellites whose photographs provide round-the-clock intelligence data and, in many respects, turned into reality
President Eisenhower's "Open Skies" proposal of 1955.)

In 1961 after the Bay of Pigs, the Pentagon created
the Defense Intelligence Agency (DIA), which was assigned to all the legitimate functions of the CIA. Behind
this move was the Pentagon's embarrassment when the invasion failed, for the Joint Chiefs of Staff had approved
the plans for the Bay of Pigs provided that "the assumptions were correct." In effect the military establishment
was saying that never again would it be dependent on an
outside agency for its intelligence and analyses.

The Federal Bureau of Investigation had retained a
responsibility for counterintelligence activities within the
United States. The bureau continued to maintain offices
in all the major capitals of the world, claiming that infor-

mation concerning intelligence activities within the United States often originated abroad. The CIA could scarcely object, since it was maintaining offices all over the United States and approaching tourists and other travelers in efforts to obtain foreign intelligence at home. The State Department was still in the intelligence business, and the then Atomic Energy Commission, another creature of the unification act, had to have a separate agency for its kind of intelligence.

On charts of organization the United States Intelligence Board was for many years at the top of all this activity. The director of the CIA, given a second title as Director of Central Intelligence (DCI), was chairman of the board and his deputy was one of its members. The Defense Department was also doubly represented by NSA and DIA—as big as they were, the Army, Navy and Air Force were crowded out of this picture—while the State Department, the FBI and the AEC furnished one member each. In 1976 USIB was renamed the "Committee on Foreign Intelligence" and was shrunk to three members— DCI, the president's Special Assistant for National Security Affairs, and the Deputy Secretary of Defense—in an effort to increase the DCI's authority. But as will be seen, neither this gambit nor President Carter's giving the DCI control over the "preparation" of all intelligence budgets was getting at the main problem.

Except for the CIA, and the FBI after J. Edgar Hoover's death, the intelligence operations were largely non-controversial. The NSA, engaged in global eavesdropping, often recalled that in 1929 Secretary of State Henry L. Stimson closed down the department's code-breaking office with the remark that "gentlemen do not read each other's mail," but a generation or so later this statement represented a ludicrously unrealistic standard of international ethics. Despite major incidents such as the Israeli attack on the *Liberty* in 1967 and the North Korean capture of the *Pueblo* in 1968—both of them intelligence ships under NSA command—communication-monitoring in some form was generally accepted as necessary.

There was one glaring, fatal flaw in the setup as far as unification of the intelligence community was concerned: the CIA was nominally at its head but the Defense Department was getting most of the money. Before inflation began in the 1970s, the intelligence community as a whole was spending in excess of $5 billion a year and the CIA was receiving an estimated fifteen percent of that, or around $750 million annually. Regardless of how lines of authority were drawn on charts, bureaucratic loyalties unerringly went to and firmly remained with wherever the paychecks were issued. The CIA, further handicapped by its unsavory reputation, could not establish effective coordinating supervision in these circumstances, and soon gave up the attempt.

Many congressmen who supported the original legislation had thought that the CIA would be intimately familiar with all intelligence activities and would parcel out assignments and lay down restrictions to avoid duplication and other wasted motion. That nothing of the kind had ever been achieved was revealed in connection with the North Korean capture of the *Pueblo* and its intelligence-gathering crew, when CIA Director Helms issued one of the agency's rare above-the-table statements:

> Neither this agency nor I personally have had anything to do with the mission of the *USS Pueblo*, the ship itself nor any of its crew.

There were no reporters and there was no press room at the CIA. Without further elaboration the Helms statement had a sphinx-like finality. After much cudgeling of journalistic brains a conclusion was reached and proved to be correct: that the various intelligence agencies operated with such autonomy that Helms did not even know of the *Pueblo*'s ill-fated mission for NSA.

Such coordination as existed was at a thin layer at the top, engaging only in a final phase of activities, usually in connection with submissions to the White House. Far from being in the day-to-day confidence of other agencies the CIA received merely an occasional fill-in on their activities, usually in the form of a processed final report. The word "processed" here was likely to mean that the real information had been processed out and a possibly erroneous conclusion that was above all safe from criticism had been substituted. FBI Director Hoover with usual foresight had persuaded a congressional contact to slip into the original legislation a provision that his agency was obliged to furnish the CIA with information "only upon request." In other words the CIA would have to know enough of a secret to be able to ask for it before its delivery from the FBI was in order.

The CIA was always and everywhere militantly anti-Communist. The agency would accept the most savage and corrupt right-wing dictatorship in preference to a Communist or Communist-influenced government. On the other hand, to the confusion of some of its followers, and as a balancing factor thought to be in the interests of enlarging the forces against Communism, the CIA leadership from the beginning preferred to deal with the non-Communist or anti-Communist left when it was safely possible to do so.

A host of seeming contradictions resulted. For example, when official American diplomacy was supporting the Dominican Republic's dictator Rafael Trujillo, an avowed anti-Communist, the CIA was financially aiding his arch enemy, Dr. Juan D. Bosch. Most of the subsequently exposed financial largesse which the CIA distributed on an ideological basis went to student groups and to liberal publications and organizations, including labor unions, for which Congress would not have appropriated a penny if the members had had any way of knowing what they were voting on.

And while firmly identified with what Barry Goldwater defined as conservatism, otherwise called radical conservatism, the CIA boasted that its staff included more liberal intellectuals than could be found in any other agency. The implication was that no side of a question involving security could escape thorough dissection by the CIA's analysts. More than half of the analysts had advanced degrees—thirty percent had PhDs—and another boast was that there were enough of them to provide a qualified staff for any college or university.

CIA headquarters was divided into four sections, or directorates: "Science and Technology," "Support," "Intelligence," and "Plans." The first was an elaborately equipped area for analyzing U–2 and other reconnaissance photographs as well as all kinds of military test data; the second was a logistic establishment designed to furnish military equipment and supplies; and the third dealt with information and analysis—military, political, scientific, economic, and industrial—for every part of the world. "Plans," later called "Operations," was a cover name for the clandestine section, which was otherwise known as "the Department of Dirty Tricks." All four divisions had their main offices in the same gleaming white building that towered seven stories above others in the tree-covered, 140-acre CIA compound at Langley.

Total employment at the Langley headquarters at the start of the 1970s was just over eight thousand men and women. United Press International reporter Al Spivak scored a scoop by arriving at the precise figure when in a forgetful moment the CIA reported to Congress the amount of office space available at Langley and also how much this provided per employee. If other estimates were correct, Spivak's exclusive meant that about half of the CIA's total employment was at headquarters, with the rest either elsewhere in the Washington area or spread around the globe. And despite long years of rigid secrecy on the subject, Senate investigators were finally able to report that more than half of the CIA's total appropriations through 1970 had gone to the "Department of Dirty Tricks." For 1975 that proportion was given as still more than thirty-seven percent. "Dirty Tricks," with its playful connotation, was a decided euphemism for operations that went as far as murder, and even mass murder.

Former CIA Director William Colby, in his book *Honorable Men* (Simon and Schuster, 1978) and in lectures all across the country, has stated repeatedly that when he was in office the allocation of the agency's budget for covert activities had been reduced from more than fifty percent in the 1950s to less than five percent.

His statement was highly suspect on its face, since no corresponding reduction in budget or insertion of new functions was known to have occurred, and it flatly contradicted the finding by the Senate committee that the allocation was still more than thirty-seven percent in 1975.

When the latter was pointed out to him, Colby's only reply was that the committee figure included "a portion of the total overhead" which the senators considered assignable to such activities. He thus revealed that he had made no provision for this extremely large consideration in his figures, although such consideration was of course included in the data for the 1950s.

A more misleading treatment of statistics could hardly have been imagined. Moreover, going unmentioned in Colby's presentation was a footnote stating that even the thirty-seven percent figure did not include "DDA [Deputy Directorate for Administration] budgetary allocations in support of" such activities.

These allocations could easily have doubled the figure, and that without setting any new records. The committee found that in some years covert or clandestine activities— the terms were used interchangeably—had absorbed *as much as eighty percent of the CIA's budget*.

In other words, Colby's startling statement was completely misleading. Thorough analysis revealed just what a person would have suspected on the basis of common sense—that there had been no significant change.

The CIA liked to trace its history to the Office of Strategic Services (OSS), set up by President Roosevelt and Major General William J. "Wild Bill" Donovan at the start of World War II. Except for the absence of the life and death struggle that justified the OSS there were many similarities.[11] Allen Dulles was one of Donovan's top lieutenants in that war, and many other CIA officials were veterans of that service. One of the major anomalies of the CIA was its essentially wartime character in a mainly peacetime environment—a posture made possible by the long continuation of the Cold War.

President Truman discontinued the OSS a few weeks after the Japanese surrender in 1945. Three months later he established the Central Intelligence Group (CIG) with Admiral Sidney Souers as its first director. Souers was succeeded by Air Force General Hoyt Vandenberg, who was succeeded by Admiral Roscoe Hillenkoetter, who was in office when the CIG was converted into the CIA. Hillenkoetter stayed on until 1950, and Army General Walter Bedell Smith headed the agency until 1953.

The subsequent CIA directors were Dulles, who reigned for eight years; McCone, a West Coast shipbuilder and former chairman of the Atomic Energy Commission; Admiral William F. Raborn, who directed the development of the Polaris missile submarine; Helms, the first government career man to get the job; James Schlesinger, another former AEC chairman; Colby, an OSS veteran with experience in law and the State Department; and George Bush, the volatile former Republican National Chairman and future vice president whose political connections stirred objections in Congress. After the withdrawal under fire of Ted Sorensen, nominated by President Carter as a reform candidate but rejected by leading Senators, Admiral Turner took over the agency for the Carter administration, to be succeeded by William J. Casey when President Reagan took office.

CIA men abroad were called case officers within the organization. As individuals they were generally efficient, dedicated, highly motivated and incorruptible.[12] The trouble in the CIA was likely to be that, for anything short of the meanest of all-out wars, they were *too* highly motivated. A severe beating administered to a reluctant informant, or the assassination of a would-be left-wing dictator, could seem trivial to them in the light of their goal of outscoring the nation's potential enemies. And naturally, until one happened, they could not imagine a nationwide furor over actions which to them seemed unimportant.

Many CIA operations overseas were carried out under

"loose" cover. At each of the American embassies, in a mirror image of what the Russians were doing at theirs, a CIA station chief was given a "loose cover" title such as "Special Assistant to the Ambassador." Everyone familiar with the operations of the embassy would be aware that the well-financed special assistant, living on a scale equal to the ambassador's and often spending money more freely, represented the CIA. His staff members might be listed as economists, agronomists, accountants, or representatives of the Agency for International Development or the Treasury Department—anything except what they were—but again with no real secret as to the source of their paychecks.

By contrast a "deep" cover agent, masquerading as a tourist, businessman, scholar, or consultant, or perhaps running a shop of some kind or working under false pretenses for the local government, would never go near an American embassy. The true identity of this type of agent might be withheld even from the Chief of Intelligence at Langley. His reports would then be signed with a code word and he would receive compensation through a variety of ruses—third person contact or a post office box, for example.

In addition to seeking information such an agent might be inciting revolution or sabotage, or supporting paramilitary operations against the local government or one in a neighboring country. Long-standing deep cover agents would usually be or would become citizens of the country in which they operated. They might be in positions of high military or civilian trust, in which case they would be called "agents in place." One of the CIA's most highly touted achievements, accomplished in cooperation with Great Britain, was to have an "agent in place" behind the Kremlin walls during the period immediately preceding the Cuban missile crisis. (See Chapter 6.)

Unlike FBI agents CIA men had no power to arrest or to investigate ordinary crime. Questions sometimes arose as to how they spent their routine working days. A member of the pre–1960 Michigan State University technical assistance program in South Vietnam recalled that the five

CIA agents attached to that project always reported to their offices at eight A.M. sharp. They were courteous, intelligent, well-informed, and willing to be helpful. But after only one hour at their desks, they always locked their offices and disappeared for the rest of the day. The supposition was that they were out making information contacts or deliveries, or were carrying out assignments that might range from placing a tap on a telephone line to blowing up an important bridge.

Despite what seemed to be the most rigid security procedures, the CIA was infiltrated throughout its first three formative years by a "deep cover" agent for the Soviet Union—and this was not out in the field but right inside headquarters. The agent's name was Harold Adrian Russell Philby, nicknamed "Kim," and he was masquerading as an intelligence agent for a country other than the one he was serving. In 1947 the British Embassy assigned him to the CIA as an adviser. In 1950 he fell under CIA suspicion when fellow agents David MacLean and Guy Burgess, with both of whom he was known to have been closely associated, defected to the Soviet Union. Like MacLean and Burgess, Philby was a member of the espionage cabal which was revealed many years later, in 1979, to include Sir Anthony Blunt, the former curator of Britain's royal art collection.

In 1951, after the United States had protested his presence, Philby was withdrawn from Washington. In other parts of the world he continued for another twelve years to enjoy the confidence of many Britons in both intelligence assignments and as a news correspondent. He even resigned from intelligence and was later rehired. In 1963 he also defected to the Soviet Union and held a news conference to reveal that he had been serving Moscow since the 1930s.

The one early occasion on which the CIA cast secrecy completely to the winds occurred in 1964. Gradually since 1958, when soaring Soviet steel production compared to sagging Western statistics made it appear that the Communists might win the economic race, a significant reversal had taken place. Communist countries everywhere were now showing a slower rate of economic growth than their non-Communist neighbors. The brainy analysts at the CIA were convinced that with the exception of the Sino-Soviet ideological split this was the most important global development since World War II. Breaking with seventeen years of precedent they called a press conference to emphasize the gratifying economic trend.

The press conference was held deep among the trees at Langley. All fourteen members of the CIA's Board of National Estimates appeared with other officials for the session. However, the economic statistics were not new to the reporters, whereas the novelty of being received in style at the spy agency seemed well worth committing to type. Their dispatches added little to an understanding of the economic growth trends, and instead raised disturbing questions as to why the United States government, with more appropriate agencies dedicated to the purpose, would choose a spy organization as the source from which to reach fundamental economic conclusions.

Undaunted by criticism, the CIA continued its operations in global economics, and as time passed, seemed to find more and more spy-related roles in that field. During the American wheat sales to Russia, for example, mysterious estimates at first unattributed and later traced to the CIA challenged the harvest and marketing assessments on which the negotiations were based. At times there were two American estimates of Russian grain requirements, one from the regular government and the other from the CIA. The latter, almost invariably proving to have been overly-pessimistic from the Russian point of view, were presumably based on satellite photographs also available to other agencies. In the energy crisis, the CIA was at least as bad as most of the rest of us in predicting early on that the Soviets along with the West would become drastically short of petroleum by 1985, when in truth as 1985 neared both we and the Russians sometimes had trouble determining whether we were speaking of the oil shortage or the oil glut.

Brothers in Misery

Allen Dulles walked into retirement from a record that, except for the Cuban missile crisis—a highly special case—would continue to leave its brand on every major American involvement in the foreign field for another decade—on down through the Vietnamese War, until a turnabout was effected by the shuttle diplomacy of Dr. Kissinger.

Of Dulles himself it could be said that no man had ever more clearly foreseen a pitfall into which he later fell. In one of his policy recommendations concerning the CIA before its creation, he had written with heavy emphasis:

> For the proper evaluation of the situation in any foreign country it is important that the information be processed by an agency whose duty it is to weigh the facts, without having the facts or the conclusions warped by the inevitable and even proper prejudices of the men whose duty it is to determine policy and who, having determined a policy, are likely to be blind to any facts which might prove the policy to be faulty.

Even years later he told an interviewer:

> We've got to keep our absolute integrity. Keep out of politics. Be absolutely fearless. Report the facts as we see them regardless of whether or not they are palatable to the policymakers. If we ever lose our objectivity then we are finished.

Could these be the words of a man who had wet-nursed and brought to maturity an agency generally regarded as the most flagrantly biased ever to put down roots on the shores of the Potomac? The only explanation offering itself was that Dulles was caught between the professional requirements of intelligence and the more glamorous possibilities of reshaping the world with a hidden hand. While he paid tribute to both aspects of his job, the latter eventually took precedence over everything else.

His beginning year as CIA director was impressive, both because of his own performance and because anything he accomplished after assuming command in 1953 was bound to look good against the background of the CIA's bleak record for its first six years. Like other government organizations the CIA had been caught napping by the Soviet achievement of the atomic bomb in 1949, and along with General MacArthur had been equally surprised by the outbreak of the Korean War in 1950.

Worse, and this time with the evidence filling the airwaves and available on every hand, the CIA and MacArthur guessed wrong on whether the Chinese Communists would enter the war if allied forces swept across the thirty-eighth parallel and into North Korea headed for the Yalu River and the Chinese border. On that subject President Truman wrote in his memoirs:

> On October 20 [1950] the CIA delivered to me a memorandum which said they had reports that the Chinese Communists would move in only far enough to protect the Suiho electric plant and other installations along the Yalu River. Actually the Chinese had begun crossing the Yalu four days earlier with the apparent intention of throwing the United Nations forces out of Korea.

Truman was charitable in his phraseology, since the memorandum indicated that the Chinese "at most" would try to protect the Yalu plants, and there was later evidence that they had begun crossing the river even before Truman and MacArthur met on Wake Island, October 15. Yet

MacArthur did not know the Chinese were in Korea in force until November 1, and he had no idea of their real strength until late November when he was attacked *from his rear* by a "Chicom" force of 180,000 men.

The Chinese attack coincided with MacArthur's declaration of an "end the war" offensive. Before the offensive could get under way he was obliged to order a retreat, declaring the country had become involved in "an entirely new war." No doubt his skill in extricating his troops prevented the debacle from being even more costly; but it was a bitter defeat and a baffling, prolonged intelligence failure by any standard.

In reversing this trend for the time being at least, Dulles demonstrated that he thoroughly enjoyed the conspiratorial atmosphere of intelligence work and took a personal interest in CIA operations ranging through seventy countries. In the wake of Stalin's death he easily predicted the rise of Khrushchev. In the Suez crisis of 1956, no doubt with a helping hand across the sea from Great Britain, twenty-four hours before the event, he provided Eisenhower with the information that the Israelis would invade Egypt while the British and French in concert attacked Suez. Performances like this compared more than favorably with what had gone on before, and also with what would transpire in the future.

For example, as was pointed out by the House Intelligence Committee in the report smuggled to the *Village Voice* by Daniel Schorr, the CIA guessed wrong or failed to predict the Tet offensive in Vietnam and the Soviet invasion of Czechoslovakia, both in 1968; the Mideast War of 1973; and the first nuclear explosion in India, the coup in Portugal, and the overthrow of Archbishop Makarios in Cyprus, all in 1974. To these might be added the CIA's dangerously placating underestimates of the political unrest in Iran under the shah, far worse than those of many well-informed newspaper readers, and its failure to obtain advance word of any kind concerning the Communist takeover in Afghanistan in 1978, as well as the 1979 intelligence mess over when, where, and whether there had been Soviet combat troops in Cuba. Yet this was the organization that would like us to believe that it would have prevented Pearl Harbor had it been in existence at the time, and that our pre-CIA intelligence evaluations were vastly inferior to those we were receiving today. Perhaps it should also be pointed out that both the CIA and the DIA did correctly predict the short duration of the six-day Arab-Israeli war of 1967—both agencies said it would be over in a week or ten days. This was a comparative piece of cake, since the Israelis were dedicated, efficient, and in Mideast terms armed to the teeth, whereas the Arabs were confused, disorganized, and armed only with defensive-type weapons (such as interceptors).

As an administrator, meanwhile, Dulles scored a solid victory over Senator Joseph R. McCarthy, Republican, of Wisconsin. When one of McCarthy's aides let it be known that the CIA was considered a "juicy" subject for future investigation, Dulles wrote to McCarthy on October 23, 1953, saying that if there were Communists in the CIA he would like to deal with the matter immediately. Months later when McCarthy charged that Communists in the CIA had "created a situation even more dangerous than Red penetration of the Army Signal Corps," Dulles produced his earlier letter and revealed that McCarthy had not even bothered to acknowledge its receipt.

Dulles and Eisenhower then arranged for an investigation of the CIA by a Hoover Commission Task Force headed by General Mark W. Clark, for whom McCarthy had expressed admiration in a dispute over whether Clark had mishandled the Italian campaign in World War II. Being thus headed off from claiming that the Hoover Commission investigation was whitewash and also unable to explain the long time lag in his apprehension of the danger within the CIA, the Wisconsin senator for once was effectively silenced.

Dulles's standing was so high and his position as a person of prominence and as a government figure so well recognized that there was sometimes speculation as to what could have propelled him so far and so mistakenly from the intelligence field in which he excelled.

A foretaste of the type of foreign policy to be expected from Foster and Allen Dulles was provided in Eisenhower's first inaugural address immediately following their selection as secretary of state and CIA director, respectively. At the policy's root was the assumption that a type of deception which no self-respecting individual would think of practicing was nevertheless either beneficial or actually essential for the existence of the nation.

After stating that "we certainly have no obligation to protect a nation that is fighting us in Korea," Eisenhower said he was issuing instructions that "the Seventh Fleet no longer be employed to shield Communist China." This policy, known as "unleashing Chiang Kai-shek," was formulated by Foster Dulles, and though it must have come as a surprise to mainland Chinese that they had been protected, the policy was made to stick for a time.

Through its cover organization known as Western Enterprises, Inc., on Formosa, and through surviving connections with Chinese Nationalists who had settled in Burma, the CIA organized a series of sharp and sometimes bloody guerrilla raids onto the mainland. These were designed to make it appear that the way was being prepared for an invasion of the mainland by the reconstituted and reequipped Nationalist forces that had taken refuge on Formosa in 1949.

When an armistice had been signed in Korea, however, it developed that the brothers had never thought that unleashing Chiang Kai-shek was a practical proposition, but had merely favored the policy as a threatening posture in the hope of obtaining better armistice terms. With the armistice negotiations completed, the "unleashing" pretense was abandoned, with the Seventh Fleet still on patrol in the Formosan strait.

Naturally the Dulles brothers felt no embarrassment at having perpetrated this deception, because it was in the interest of the country. The only trouble was that the benefit to the United States here was difficult to perceive. It seemed equally likely that, if anything, the armistice negotiations had been damaged somewhat by the guerrilla raids.

As though to overemphasize its supposed reversal of policy after the armistice was signed, the CIA closed down Western Enterprises, Inc., in 1954. The agency also resettled to Formosa 7,000 of the 10,000 Nationalist guerrillas who had taken refuge in Burma. Most of the contingent remaining in Burma had become involved in opium cultivation or traffic, using money and planes supplied by the CIA. They were able to find a ready market in General Phas Syrinod, the police chief of Thailand, who was a dealer in narcotics and also strangely or perhaps naturally enough the CIA's regional agent in the distribution of free arms and ammunition for guerrilla warfare.

One reason for closing down Western Enterprises, Inc., may have been that the CIA was heavily engaged elsewhere in Asia and also in Europe in 1954. Major events in this vintage year for the agency included the Geneva Accords ending the French Indo-China War, and with them the first American involvement in South Vietnam; and, on the other side of the world, the defection to the Communists of West Germany's security chief, Dr. Otto John, to be succeeded by a CIA-sponsored ex-Nazi, Lieutenant General Reinhard Gehlen.

The Pentagon papers eventually would show that the ink was scarcely dry on the Geneva Accords when a CIA team headed by Colonel Edward G. Lansdale arrived in Vietnam to prepare for possible paramilitary operations. One of the weird disclosures in the papers was that as an incidental action on the trip, the Lansdale team had contaminated the fuel supply of the Hanoi bus system with a kind of grit that would make motors wear out quickly. As in the case of hundreds of other dirty tricks perpetrated by the CIA, the provocation for and purpose of this operation were nowhere apparent.

At the same time the CIA was subsidizing General Gehlen's private intelligence apparatus in West Germany at the rate of $6 million a year. When Major General Arthur Trudeau, the United States Army's Chief of Intelligence, publicly objected to giving such support to an ex-Nazi, Trudeau was summarily transferred to the Far East. Gehlen had been the German chief of counterintelligence on the eastern front in World War II and afterward had become noted for promoting uprisings, slowdowns, assassinations, and sabotage in the same area. With his CIA money, operating from fortress-like headquarters outside Munich, he succeeded in undermining Dr. John's authority.

On July 20, 1954, after visiting Dulles in Washington in an effort to straighten things out, Dr. John defected to East Germany. Exactly one year later, on July 20, 1955, Gehlen succeeded him as West Germany's Chief of Security.

Dulles remained unscathed through all this, as he did later in the U–2 episode. As far as public recognition was concerned he was at a peak just before his fall, having received a total of nine laudatory citations including the Freedom Award during the twelve months preceding the Cuban invasion.

And yet all that would count for nothing compared to the Bay of Pigs, which was not one of the government's more expensive ventures but was so close to home and such a classic of its kind that it would be remembered long after other exploits had been forgotten. The Senate Foreign Relations Committee, poorly served as it was, produced the estimate that the Bay of Pigs had cost $62 million, and this compared with hundreds of millions poured into distant and militarily impotent lands such as Laos. But for every American who understood the fuzzy business that went on between Souvanna Phouma and Phoumi Nosavan in Laos, there were hundreds if not thousands for whom the Cuban affair was a vibrant part of life.

President Kennedy did not have to request Dulles's resignation. He merely let it be known that he was looking for a new CIA director. Dulles left office in November 1961, after his participation in the investigation of the invasion. His guarded language in his book, *The Craft of In-*

telligence (Harper, 1963), and his refusal to discuss any of the vital issues, made it impossible to determine from that work how he felt about the climax to his career.

Privately he was said to have felt that he was let down, especially by President Kennedy's cancellation of the second air strike which was to have coincided with the Cuban landing. The second strike was later reinstated, but the damage had been done and cloud cover further limited its effectiveness. Dulles remained publicly silent on the subject throughout the eight years he lived in retirement.

Foster Dulles, the more intellectual and forceful of the two brothers, now is remembered chiefly as the author of the two discredited policies of "massive retaliation, at times and places of our own choosing" and "brinkmanship." "The ability to get to the verge without getting into war is the necessary art," he said. "If you are scared to go to the brink you are lost."

Within a year after Allen Dulles left office, the intelligence community along with the rest of the Kennedy administration enjoyed a great resurgence of prestige during the facing-down of the Russians in the Cuban missile crisis. If the favorable momentum of that incident could have been carried forward a new formula for living together, saving hundreds of billions of dollars and tens of thousands of American lives, might have emerged. Unfortunately the Dulles pattern and concept had already been thoroughly established, and because of a lack of fresh vision in the White House after Kennedy's death, events following the brilliantly successful crisis were able to proceed on a dismal course leading from one national calamity to another.

Cold War Magic

12

As the nature of the CIA's involvement in domestic and foreign affairs came to light over the years, several attempts to gain some control over the agency were made by Congress. How such attempts could balk, sputter, and fizzle away into nothingness was well illustrated in 1966 when Senator Fulbright almost literally moved heaven and earth in that direction with a final result of zero.

At that time in the Senate there was a so-called watchdog panel, sometimes called a joint subcommittee though there was no provision for such a thing in the body's organizational charter,[13] which theoretically exercised some surveillance and control over the CIA. The extent to which this was an utter sham could be gathered from the fact that Senator Richard B. Russell, Democrat, of Georgia, the leading progenitor and protector of the CIA in the Senate, was the watchdog group's permanent chairman, serving as such by tacit agreement. Russell was also chairman of the Armed Services committee, and any proposal involving the CIA would automatically be referred to the Armed Services committee, from which, if it was found to be objectionable, such proposal would never emerge.

Despite its glaring limitations, the watchdog panel was the only game in town as far as congressional supervision of the CIA was concerned. Fulbright, as chairman of Foreign Relations, sought representation on it for his committee.

The panel, in addition to its permanent chairman, consisted of three appointees each from the Appropriations and Armed Services committees, and was commonly referred to as "the secret seven." Fulbright's proposal would have provided for the addition of three from Foreign Relations and, significantly, that the chairman would be elected.

Also, for some reason senators in foreign relations were generally of quite a different turn of mind from their colleagues in armed forces and appropriations. They included a number of senators who were dubbed "militant doves" by the press. If Fulbright's move were successful, some of these senators would sit on the watchdog panel, with the obvious result that CIA executives would be questioned more closely and persistently.

The first giant hurdle was to bring the matter to a vote. Backed by a nearly bi-partisan vote of 14 to 5 in his committee, and with the cooperation of both the majority and minority leadership in the Senate, Fulbright devised a unique plan to bring this about. The plan called for an agreed-upon agenda to which both sides of the aisle would adhere, and with debate to be conducted behind closed doors in the Senate's first executive session in more than three years.

The showdown came on July 14, 1966, which apparently by pure coincidence although some thought it an appropriate one, was the 177th anniversary of Bastille Day.[4] Vice President Hubert H. Humphrey, as president of the Senate, rapped the body to order at 11 A.M. When the routine business consigned to the "morning hour" with no quorum yet available had been completed and there were no further requests for the floor, Senator Mike Mansfield, Democrat, of Montana, as majority leader, rose to end that part of the session:

> Mr. President, I ask unanimous consent that the distinguished chairman of the Committee on Foreign Relations now be recognized concerning a resolution he will offer.

In accordance with the agreement, there were no objections. Fulbright sent to the desk a four-paragraph resolution, which the clerk read aloud, calling for the creation of a committee as previously indicated. The proposal was presented in an unprecedented way as the offering of Fulbright's full committee.

The agenda now permitted Russell to make his first move:

> I raise a point of order, Mr. President, that before the resolution goes on the calendar it must be referred to the Armed Services committee.

Humphrey was well prepared. He began by seeming to agree with Russell, that in normal circumstances the resolution would have to be referred to his committee—because the CIA was a creature of the National Security Act of 1947, which also created the Defense Department, and was therefore in Russell's legislative province. Since, however, the resolution had been introduced in an unprecedented manner by a full committee, Humphrey decided that there was no precedent for referring it to another committee. He then resurrected a parliamentary rule that, where no precedent existed for resolving a point of order, the question should be submitted to a vote of the Senate as a whole.

This was the same as ruling against Russell, since a poll of the Senate on the point of order would in effect be a vote on the resolution. The vote and the closed-door debate that went with it were thus assured, and the ruling had to be chalked up as a first round victory for Fulbright.

Most probably, though, Russell had foreseen from the beginning a strong possibility that the matter would have to be settled by a vote of the Senate as a whole, and while chafing at the delay was feeling renewed confidence that the final victory would be his. With even the most vicious cloak-and-dagger methods for combating Communism still widely considered essential, and with the CIA as the only instrument for providing them, he had no reason to feel discouraged concerning the ultimate result. He would need only to wave an imaginary wand and the magic of the cold war would be there to succor, sustain and support him.

Mansfield had more than good reason to fear that, despite his own and other impressive backing, the Fulbright foray was bound to founder. Twelve years before, in 1954, the future majority leader himself had drafted a resolution to create a joint congressional committee to monitor the CIA. Mansfield had worked patiently for two years until he had thirty-four co-signers on his proposal. But when the matter finally came to a vote in 1956 the Mansfield resolution was defeated 59 to 27, with fourteen of the co-signers voting in the negative. Congressional actions with respect to the CIA could more often than not be described as unprecedented, and the spectacle of fourteen of its registered sponsors voting against a measure certainly fell into the "unprecedented" category.

On the earlier occasion, with the cold war still at maximum intensity, the opposition to the Mansfield resolution had summoned big oratorical guns to voice dire predictions concerning the effect that making the CIA accountable to Congress would have on the fight with Communism. The small-framed Mansfield had said he felt like a David facing a battery of Goliaths. The Senate appeared to have been frightened into killing the measure, although with the CIA involved there was no telling what had gone on behind the scenes. No investigation of the matter seemed possible, since by law the CIA could not be required to account for the funds it spent, and no one would know how or where to begin.

In fact, the extent to which usual procedures and precautions had been by-passed in the case of the CIA was sometimes difficult even for hardened observers to believe.

One example was the outrage expressed by Senator Willis Robertson, Democrat, of Virginia, because he did not even know the agency owned and operated planes of any kind at the time the CIA's U–2 spy plane flights over

Russia finally came to light in 1960. Robertson was a member of the defense appropriations subcommittee, an outfit charged with part of the responsibility for hiding the CIA's money in the budgets of other agencies, and moreover a rock-ribbed conservative high on the agency's preferred list as far as voting policies were concerned; yet even he had never been vouchsafed one word regarding the U–2s. Robertson said at the time:

> I had been hearing testimony presented by the Central Intelligence Agency before the Committee of Appropriations for thirteen years. Never during that time were we told what the money would be used for. It was a deep, dark secret. I asked a number of members of the defense appropriations subcommittee if they knew the CIA owned and operated planes, and they said they did not.

Another example was President Kennedy's belated discovery in 1962 that the CIA, at an eventual cost of around half a million dollars, had chemically contaminated part of a cargo of Cuban sugar that was bound for the Soviet Union. This was at a time when Kennedy was trying to inject a spirit of high-minded decency into the government, and a mere mention of the contamination to almost any of his aides would have been enough to nip that operation in the bud. Instead Kennedy learned of it only by accident, and only after the deed had been done, although fortunately before the sugar had been transported to Russia. When called on the carpet the CIA claimed that the chemical was non-poisonous and merely spoiled the taste of the sugar. Why a U.S. agency would conduct such an operation—apparently intended to merely annoy a potentially powerful enemy and bearing an eventual cost of around half a million dollars—was a question no one could answer.[15]

By the time of the Fulbright venture in mid–1966 the cold war was considerably less intense than it was when Mansfield suffered his humiliating defeat. Cold war stalwarts still manned the same ramparts but held their ground less securely. Senator McCarthy earlier in the year had introduced a resolution calling for $150,000 to attempt an investigation of the CIA, but had now withdrawn his proposal in favor of Fulbright's more moderate entry. The committee proposal, for the time at least, involved no money.

Since a moderately expurgated transcript was later published, and a few discreet inquiries from the press were permitted, a fairly good summation of the closed door session could be pieced together.

Russell, at the height of his power, was impatient throughout the proceedings. He saw no reason for debate, open or closed. Four years before, during the confirmation of John C. McCone to head the CIA, the senator from Georgia had startled a hearing room audience by referring to the CIA directorship as "a position of importance second only to the presidency." Today, however, his stand was that despite this importance the machinations of the CIA, supposedly restricted to overseas operations, were no legitimate concern of the Foreign Relations committee. He regarded the resolution as an attempt by Fulbright and Senator Eugene McCarthy, Democrat, of Minnesota, to "muscle in" on a part of his jurisdiction.

Fulbright attempted a balanced presentation which would offend no potential support. He conceded that many capable and dedicated individuals were employed by the CIA, and complimented the agency on its efficiency. But as the three-and-one-half hours of debate wore on he became a bit more explicit, and in an exchange with Russell revealed the underlying reason he was seeking information about the CIA wherever he could find it. After Russell had chided him for not seeking the information through his own committee, he asked the gentleman from Georgia to yield.

Russell: I yield.

Fulbright: We had the director of the CIA before our committee on two occasions. His testimony was restricted to very superficial aspects of their activity. I do not know of any further witness. In effect the resolution is an outgrowth of the failure of the committee to receive what it believed to be significant information from the director of the CIA. As a body with jurisdiction over foreign affairs the Committee on Foreign Relations has a basic constitutional responsibility to be informed on CIA operations.

Russell: I am not trying to muscle in on the Senator's committee. I am trying to keep him from muscling in on mine.

Fulbright: It is a very peculiar situation. Actually there is no precedent in the entire history of the Senate for dealing with a body like the CIA. It is a very peculiar agency.

Russell: Mr. President, I do not yield further.

Fulbright: Very well; but the Senator himself has said that.

Russell: I do not deny it at all. It is a very peculiar agency.

Fulbright: The formal supervision we are seeking has never been voted on. I think that is very peculiar.

Russell: Mr. President, I do not yield further and I do not accept the Senator's statement. There is nothing here that would justify the statement that the CIA will not give the Committee on Foreign Relations any information.

Fulbright: "Significant," I said.

Fulbright, with a sly grin, also released a small bombshell by revealing that the National Security Council had not met for nearly a year:

It has been stated that the CIA functions within the National Security Council, a White House organization, and that it initiates no activity that has not been ordered by the council. This seeks to imply close, continuous supervision by an organized mechanism. In this connection I noted with great interest a recent report that the National Security Council met on May 8 of this year for the first time since July 1965. Furthermore, the NSC staff machinery of earlier years has atrophied to the point of non-existence.

The disclosure came as a shock to some who knew that all of the members of the National Security Council entered the White House frequently and could certainly have sat down together if there had been an occasion for them to do so. The underlying truth was that the period was one in which President Johnson was keeping his own counsel in a single-minded policy on Vietnam, and with the CIA going its own way as usual, the NSC as such had nothing to do. To put the matter differently, the council was mainly advisory and actually had no authority except for that vested in it by a particular president. Since American presidents had never been placed under any obligation to receive or accept advice, they could make any use they chose—including no use at all—of this organizational setup.

In addition the National Security Council was a purely ad hoc arrangement with no membership from outside the administration; in effect, the NSC was merely another name for the presidency. The listed members were the president, the vice president, the secretaries of State and Defense, the mobilization director and the president's special assistant for national security affairs—eventually, during his rise to prominence, Henry A. Kissinger.

As has been noted, in both the Eisenhower and Kennedy administrations committees of the NSC were formed with power in some cases to act for the president. One of these—originally called the Special Group and later in succession the 303 committee, 40 committee and operations advisory group—did theoretically authorize or disapprove the CIA's covert activities. However, it could be taken for granted that the CIA's most sensitive projects—those to which the Rockefeller commission reported even the agency's own inspector general had no access, for example—never came before this body.

Against Fulbright's powerful and well-organized move were stacked all of the factors that for a generation had enabled the CIA to flourish—to convince successive administrations that acts of violence and overthrowing governments were "related to intelligence," to run circles around Congress and the White House, and to intimidate the courts and the Justice department with implied dangers to national security.

A major supporting pillar of the CIA's political edifice was the conviction on the part of Americans not otherwise extreme in their views that because of international Communism and its police and spy apparatus the United States had to have something equally ruthless and unprincipled in order to survive. The policy was called "fighting fire with fire"; it was typified in a *Saturday Evening Post* article titled, "I'm Glad the CIA Is 'Immoral.'"

The Fulbright move was also unluckily timed in that anti-war sentiment which would soon join forces with anti-CIA feeling had not yet developed to any extent. In mid-1966 there were 267,000 American troops in South Vietnam, half the eventual peak, and sporadic anti-draft and anti-war demonstrations were under way at home. There was a twinge of national conscience when a group of European hospitals offered to assist the United States in providing care for four hundred South Vietnamese children suffering from napalm burns. And there was grumbling when the American command spent $500,000 to provide South Vietnamese Premier Ky with a personal plane equipped with a bar, TV, stereo recordings, and a few other conveniences.

Nevertheless, the war was still popular. It was yet to become clear generally, in terms of mounting casualties and urban and rural ruin, where the Vietnam policy was bound to lead. Instead there was lingering exhilaration surviving from the nation's entry under President Johnson into full-scale war, as well as pride in and concern for the nation's youthful troops.

Under these circumstances Senator Russell was able to hold his forces together on a strictly cold war type of anti-Communist front in the fight against the Fulbright resolution. As far as could be determined from the abbreviated transcript of the debate, this was accomplished with a minimum of oratory on the opposition's side. The CIA and hard-line anti-Communism over the years had become almost synonymous, and as long as sentiment was running in that direction Russell and his supporters had little need to emphasize their well-known identity.

In any case, though a highly successful parliamentarian, the gentleman from Georgia was not much of an orator. The most effective thing about his speaking delivery was the confident and persuasive way in which, after a few disjointed and sometimes wild remarks, he could sit down as though everything had just been settled in his favor—as so often proved to be the fact.

There were references to the Soviet KGB, or State Security Committee, said to have a clandestine arm very similar to the CIA, with some 20,000 employees. (The CIA's manpower was said to be around 15,000.) Former CIA Director Dulles was quoted as saying:

> Any investigation, whether by a congressional committee or any other body, which results in disclosure of our secret activities and operations or uncovers our personnel, will help a potential enemy just as if the enemy had been able to infiltrate his own agents right into our shop.

A statement having a lot more to do with the safety of the nation was provided a year earlier in 1965 by former President Harry Truman, who long after his memoirs were published in 1955–56 was just emerging as a severe critic of the CIA:

> For some time I have been disturbed by the way the CIA has been diverted from its original assignment. It has become an operational and, at times, a policymaking arm of the government. This has led to trouble and may have compounded our difficulties in several explosive areas.

Russell stressed the personal hazards for those engaged in espionage abroad. Referring to the possibility of information leaks that would expose them to further danger he said:

> It would be better to abolish the CIA out of hand than to adopt a theory that such information should be made available to every member of Congress.

That no one was asking for information that would endanger operatives abroad, or suggesting that such information be available to every member of Congress, made no difference. When the debate was over the Senate voted 61 to 28 to consign the Fulbright resolution to its eternal sleep with Armed Services committee.

To judge by the voting alone the Senate had moved hardly an inch in ten years. Even with the loss of fourteen of his co-signers, Mansfield had managed to corral twenty-seven votes for his proposition in 1956. Fulbright, after a procedural stretch scarcely equalled in the history of law-making, had obtained only one vote more than that.

The *New York Times* called the performance "shoddy" and said it had shown "the Senate establishment—the 'Club'—at its stuffy worst." "Senator Russell has brought discredit not upon Senators Fulbright and McCarthy but upon himself," said the *Times*. The conservative press naturally took an opposite view, with the *St. Louis Globe-Democrat* heading its editorial "Brickbats for Fulbright," and declaring that the CIA would have been destroyed if "made subject to the militant doves on Fulbright's committee." For whatever consolation it might be, the Senate soon rallied to Fulbright's support to extract an apology from CIA Director Helms when the latter indiscreetly congratulated the *Globe-Democrat* on its editorial.

Senator Russell's victory was thus complete, except for forces at large in the world over which to his great regret he had no control. In the development of anti-war sentiment during the remainder of the year, these forces rapidly converged against him. Only six months later, in January 1967, he felt obliged to make a gesture toward reversing his field. Avoiding another showdown and acting almost like a dove, he announced that Senators Mansfield, Fulbright, and Bourke B. Hickenlooper, Republican, of Iowa—all members of the Foreign Relations Committee—had been cordially invited to sit with him and the rest of the secret seven in their meetings with the CIA.

A UPI dispatch made the gentleman from Georgia

sound magnanimous, saying he had "acted to end the long dispute over control of the spy agency." But there was nothing in the gesture about making the chairmanship elective. And whereas the Appropriations committee was permitted to select those who would represent it on the watchdog panel, it was to be noted that in the case of Foreign Relations Senator Russell had made that selection in advance (i.e., no militant doves, Mansfield and Fulbright being confirmed liberals but a bit too balanced and mature to fit that description). Also, Russell retained the right to call meetings, including the right to call none.

Still, since the gesture could be considered a welcome recognition of a principle, the members of the Foreign Relations committee accepted the invitations tendered them. For an all-too-brief period it could be considered that something like a stand-off on the Fulbright issue had been achieved, and that perhaps better days were ahead in which the watchdog groups would assume a judicial character and perform a real service.

Then, in a completely anti-climactic development only three years later, the whole matter was rendered academic when Senator John B. Stennis, Democrat, of Mississippi, who had succeeded the by then terminally ill Russell as Armed Services chairman, took advantage of the loophole and firmly discontinued all further meetings of the watchdog panel. In other words, he abolished it.

Stennis had always been one of the Senate's staunchest anti-Communists. He never wavered, or even endured much argument on the subject, from his original decision on the watchdog group. It could hardly be denied that he was recognizing the reality that went on behind a "control" facade when he said:

> If you are going to have an intelligence agency, you have to protect it as such . . . and shut your eyes some, and take what's coming.

One of his measures for dealing with "subversives" was a proposed constitutional amendment to deprive them of the right to a trial. Aside from raising a nice question as to who was being subversive, the Stennis assault on one of the sturdiest of the democratic principles embodied in the Constitution was primarily directed against a group known as the Chicago Seven, one of whom was Tom Hayden, future husband of film actress and anti-Vietnam War activist Jane Fonda. In 1982, after the general turnaround in sentiment on Vietnam, Hayden was elected an Honorable Member of the California State Legislative Assembly.

Yet Stennis was still immensely popular, and after being re-elected that same year at the ripe age of 80 to another six-year term in the Senate, he drew indulgent smiles nationwide by saying for television that he got through his campaign on two aspirin tablets.

The senator from Mississippi is still sitting where the senator from Georgia formerly sat, and the CIA, having survived several subsequent attempts to control it, remains virtually as free of Congressional control as ever.

Judicial Turnover

13

Juri Raus was of Estonian descent and, ostensibly at least, was employed by the Bureau of Public Roads. He was active in Estonian emigré circles, in 1963–64 serving as National Commander of the Legion for Estonian Liberation. Since Estonia was one of the small Baltic countries incorporated into the Soviet Union in World War II, the Legion was strongly anti-Communist and a potential instrument for obtaining information and causing trouble along Soviet borders.

At three meetings of the Legion while he was National Commander, Raus warned the delegates against trafficking with a certain Eerick Heine, an Estonian emigré who insisted on retaining the extra "e" in his first name, and who was employed in a furniture factory near Toronto, Canada. Heine was accustomed to supplementing his income by showing anti-Communist films and delivering anti-Communist lectures in Canada and the United States. Raus claimed to know that the films and lectures were part of Heine's "cover," and that in reality he was "a dispatched Soviet intelligence operative."

Demand for Heine's lectures fell off sharply because of the Raus warnings. When he learned that the laws of the United States provided relief for persons who were untruthfully denounced, especially if this affected their means of livelihood, Heine engaged legal counsel in the District of Columbia and brought a slander suit against Raus, asking $10,000 in compensatory and $100,000 in punitive damages.

Raus was living in suburban Maryland, a state with only one Federal District Court, so the case wound up in Baltimore. Raus filed a demurrer in which he did not deny making the allegedly slanderous statements but claimed that he did so under a "qualified privilege." *The Columbia Law Review*, a publication so conservative in its presentations that the wordage of supporting and temporizing footnotes frequently exceeded that of the articles to which they referred, said his claim of privilege was "apparently grounded on his prerogative as National Commander of the Legion for Estonian Liberation."

When the case came to trial a year later, there was still no indication that Raus was actually a CIA agent. Heine's lawyers were convinced that there was no evidence that their client was a Soviet intelligence operative. They said Heine had an unbroken record of participation in anti-Communist activities both overtly and covertly. There appeared to be a possibility that he had been confused with a man whose name was similar in pronunciation, and that the confusion might have arisen because both had discussed the use of floating balloons for propaganda distribution purposes.

The chances that Raus would be granted a privilege on the basis of heading an emigré organization meanwhile appeared to be slim or nonexistent. At the last minute, disclosing its connection with the case for the first time and despite the tradition that intelligence agents were on their own when they got into trouble, the CIA came to his aid. Deputy Director Helms filed an affidavit revealing that instead of acting in his role as an Estonian patriot, Raus was acting for the CIA when he made the statements in question. The original affidavit said only that "the defendant was acting within the scope of his employment by the Central Intelligence Agency" and that he "had been instructed to disseminate such information to the members of the legion."

On the basis of the affidavit and a supporting statement from CIA Director Raborn, Raus then claimed executive privilege and asked for an immediate judgment in his favor. When Federal Judge Roszel C. Thomsen objected that the CIA affidavit did not contain enough information to enable him to rule, Helms filed a supplement stating specifically that Raus had been "instructed to warn Estonian emigré groups that Eerick Heine was a dispatched Soviet intelligence operative."

Judge Thomsen then entered "a summary judgment in favor of the defendant" on the ground that "he was absolutely privileged when he made the defamatory statements in question." Whether intentionally or not, by placing no qualifying word such as "alleged" in front of "defamatory statements," the judge's ruling was that Heine had indeed been defamed, but that the CIA was "absolutely privileged" to do this.

But how could he so rule when nothing had been heard concerning the merits of the case? The simple truth was—simple in more ways than one—that if the CIA was "absolutely privileged," the merits were in no way involved. A year's carefully prepared evidence went down the drain. And along with everything else the CIA had been granted the right to keep secret its involvement and claim of privilege until that distant day when the case came to trial, and to fail to reimburse litigants for wasted time and effort.

The Columbia Law Review, jarred out of its original somnolence on the subject, carried its account of the decision under a heading which in capital letters—this publication's equivalent of banner headlines—said: SPYING AND SLANDERING: AN ABSOLUTE PRIVILEGE OF THE CIA AGENT. Fred P. Graham, in a *New York Times* article headed "The Spy Who Came into Court," explained that the CIA had succeeded in invoking two controversial decisions in which the Supreme Court by narrow voting in 1959 had greatly expanded the sweep of governmental immunity.

Graham wrote:

The Constitution gives congressmen absolute immunity for any speech in session, and the high court had previously extended similar immunity to judicial officers and to cabinet-rank members of the executive branch. In the 1959 decisions the Supreme Court stretched the privilege further to excuse an acting director of the Office of Rent Stabilization and a Navy captain who was Commander of the Boston Naval Shipyard.

Now the privilege had been extended to a purported employee of the Bureau of Public Roads, representing himself as an independent Estonian patriot, who had presumed to convict and condemn a man without hearing or trial and on the basis of evidence entirely unknown; and whose real employer in these activities was an agency specializing in operations outside the law and common morality.

Graham said the sharply divided 1959 rulings by the high court had caused serious apprehensions even though they applied to normal agencies "where it could be assumed that the government would always act with honorable motives and a sense of fair play." Their extension to the CIA, he said, had "reckoned without the CIA's special claim to operate outside the conventional rules," and had "turned the proceedings into a fiasco."

Despite their frustrating defeat Heine and his attorneys had what seemed to be a brilliant idea. If he was really a Soviet intelligence operative as the CIA had stated in writing and under oath, they reasoned, Heine would have to be considered guilty of failing to register as such under the Federal Foreign Agents Registration Act. With the purpose of provoking a showdown they dispatched letters to this effect to the headquarters of both the FBI and the CIA. Heine then presented himself in Washington, demanding that he be arrested.

The silence was deafening. In an absence of action or explanation it had to be assumed that the FBI and CIA, much as they might feud over matters affecting their bureaucratic status, had had no difficulty in getting together against a mere private individual. Neither agency disputed Heine's obviously valid claim, but no one ever lifted a finger to arrest him.

At the time of Judge Thomsen's decision, on December 8, 1966, it could still be hoped that Heine would be granted relief on appeal. Four years later when his case reached the Supreme Court, however, the case was in a judicially damaged condition. It had been remanded once, only to have the same decision against Heine pronounced again. The truth was that there was no way under the Constitution for the courts to make the distinction Graham had made between the CIA and other government agencies.

After more than five years of frustrating and expensive litigation, by a vote of 7 to 2 and as usual in such denial orders without explanation, the Supreme Court refused to hear the case. This was the end of the road for Heine. And there was no case above the horizon that could reverse the precedent in the foreseeable future.

Not all of the CIA's ventures into the courts were as successful from the CIA's point of view as the one against Heine. Federal Judge William J. Lindberg in 1952 had sentenced two CIA agents using the names Wayne Richardson and Miller Holland to fifteen days in jail for contempt because they refused to testify in a case involving Owen Lattimore, the Far Eastern expert of Johns Hopkins University. The obdurate judge had also refused bail, forcing President Truman to issue full pardons to obtain their release, even though it was a matter of only two weeks.

In general, however, with its spying and communications paraphernalia and its studied posture always implying that the agency was fending off imminent danger, the CIA had its way. At the Justice Department it had been able to negotiate an above-the-law agreement that it would be allowed to decide for itself whether any of its personnel should be prosecuted. And at the Pentagon its legal ascendancy was so great that there was scarcely a peep of protest when the CIA decided on its own that eight Green Berets the army had nailed with maximum charges should not be prosecuted for the cold-blooded murder of an alleged double agent in South Vietnam.

This particular murder had become so celebrated and had been the subject of so many press conferences that little doubt remained as to what had happened. Especially clear was the fate of Thai Khac Chuyen, a Vietnamese who had served the CIA and Green Beret intelligence in the Central Highlands and along both sides of the upper interior borders of South Vietnam. When it appeared that he was spying also for the North Vietnamese, Chuyen had been killed by the Berets and had been given a "wet disposal" at sea.

The CIA and the Green Berets were associated as they had been in Bolivia and elsewhere. This time they were engaged in arming mountain tribesmen and in directing their operations along the borders of Cambodia, Laos, and North Vietnam. The Berets, a 3,000-man outfit, were members of the army's Fifth Special Forces and were commanded by Colonel Robert B. Rheault (pronounced Roe). Serving his second tour of duty in Vietnam, Rheault had an excellent record and a promising career.

According to the Berets, Thai Khac Chuyen had been providing valuable information concerning the numbers and movements of the Communist forces in the Cambodian sanctuaries. Then his sources seemed to dry up, and Chuyen appeared to suffer from a lack of motivation. A sergeant examining a roll of film captured in an unpublicized raid on one of the sanctuaries thought he recognized Chuyen in the company of a known North Vietnamese intelligence officer. The sergeant reported to Rheault that Chuyen apparently was a double agent, and Rheault suggested that the sergeant consult with the CIA on the subject.

The CIA representative at Nhatrang, 260 miles north of Saigon, was asked whether his organization could provide a "safe haven" for Chuyen, meaning a place where he could do no damage. After checking with Saigon the CIA representative replied in the negative and mentioned meaningfully that the Berets themselves might wish to "terminate the relationship with extreme prejudice,"—a way of saying Chuyen might be killed. A Green Beret officer later talked to an agency representative in Saigon and came away convinced that the CIA thought "termination," or "elimination," was the best policy.

Whether the CIA ordered the slaying or merely suggested it as a possibility remained obscure. In any event the Berets concocted a scheme for disposing of Chuyen and covering his absence with a fake story that he had been sent on a dangerous mission from which he did not return.

On June 20, 1969, under a pretext that he was being injected with a truth serum for a lie detector test, Chuyen was given a heavy dose of morphine to knock him out. He was then taken by small boat to a depth of 150 feet offshore where he was shot twice in the head with a .22 caliber revolver. His body was encased in a mail sack, weighted with a heavy chain and tire rims, and dumped overboard. The body was never recovered despite an intensive Navy search, but in view of the Navy's difficulties in locating large solid objects in that much water, such as sunken submarines and the hydrogen bomb that was lost off Palomares, Spain, this could not be considered significant.

General Creighton W. Abrams, commander-in-chief for Vietnam, telephoned Rheault the day after the "disposal." Abrams said he had been advised "routinely" by the CIA of some trouble about a double agent, and asked for a status report. Rheault said the agent had been sent on a dangerous mission, and that he would report further when possible.

It soon became apparent that Abrams was seething, that he knew or sensed a great deal more than he had indicated in his first mention of the subject, that he did not regard the matter as at all "routine," and that he must have made his position forcefully clear to the CIA. The Berets received an urgent teletype from the CIA reading:

Return agent to duty. If unable to do so we must advise Abrams and [Ambassador Ellsworth] Bunker.

Has highest morale and flap potential.

Although too late to save Chuyen, the message survived as an interesting piece of evidence, since how could the CIA have issued such a flat and unequivocal countermanding order if, as was so widely contended afterward, the agency was only indirectly involved?

General Abrams soon had enough information to confirm his worst suspicions. If murder without trial had become standard operating procedure in any part of the United States army, Abrams, who had been General Patton's tank commander in World War II, was decidedly unaware of the fact. In a towering rage he moved with all dispatch and with every resource at his command to bring charges of murder and conspiracy to commit murder against Rheault, two majors, three captains and a warrant officer.

The announcement of the charges was greeted with consternation and indignation in Washington, but Abrams would not be deterred. On September 18 reporters were summoned to a ten P.M. press conference in Saigon and told that a pretrial investigation had been completed and that Rheault and the two majors would be courtmartialed on October 20, with other trial dates to be set later. Army Secretary Stanley Resor, backstopping Abrams in Washington, said he had resisted great pressure from Congress and elsewhere to dismiss the charges or to remove the cases from Abrams's jurisdiction, but that "to have done so would have been unwise and unfair."

Resor and Abrams had failed to reckon with the power of the CIA, which soon notified the army that it would refuse to provide witnesses for the courtmartial proceedings. In a glare of national publicity, the CIA's stand could not have been taken without tacit White House approval, but such approvals were not necessarily difficult to obtain.

Only eleven days after giving Abrams his full support, Resor announced the army's capitulation:

> I have been advised today that the CIA . . . has determined in the interest of national security that it will not make available any of its personnel as witnesses in connection with the pending trials. . . . It is my judgment that under these circumstances the defendants cannot receive a fair trial. Accordingly I have directed that all charges be dismissed immediately. . . . [But] I want to make clear that the acts which were charged, but not proved, represent a fundamental violation of army regulations, orders and principles. The army cannot and will not condone unlawful acts of the kind alleged.

Resor's closing remarks were hollow words under the circumstances, and they were accompanied by dubious official shenanigans. At the Pentagon a pretense was maintained that Resor had reached his decision without consulting Defense Secretary Melvin Laird, while at the White House Press Secretary Ronald Ziegler said President Nixon "did not become involved."

The only high official to speak out forthrightly and to the point was United Nations Ambassador Arthur Goldberg, who said:

> In the widespread relief at the dropping of the charges, and in the preceding political clamor to do so, I note an appalling, indeed frightening, deterioration in our national standards of morality and law. The war in Vietnam cannot justify us as a nation now, for the first time in our history, to tolerate—more, to legitimate—the cold-blooded murder of individuals wholly under the control of our troops.

In an absence of any possibility of prosecution, Robert A. Morasco, of Bloomfield, New Jersey, openly identified himself as the trigger man in the Chuyen slaying. He said he was under the impression that the CIA had issued "an oblique but very, very clear order" for the killing. His statement was greeted without comment by the CIA, although in the similar "termination" of Che Guevara there were doubtful claims that did square with the circumstances that the CIA had tried to spare the adopted Cuban hero for further questioning.[16]

Actually, if the army had pressed ahead with its court-martial proceedings, the CIA probably could not have gotten away with its plan to withhold witnesses. Under a well-established judicial principle restated in passing by the Supreme Court in *Reynolds vs. the United States* in 1953, the government could invoke its evidentiary privileges in criminal cases "only at the price of letting the defendants go free."

Also, the CIA was planning to act in the name of national security, whereas the man in a position to make the determination, General Abrams, had decided that no such security was involved. The only external hazard facing the nation in connection with the Chuyen slaying was the possibility of an attack on the United States by a very small but very indignant widow, Madame Thai Khac Chuyen. Her angry response to Army Secretary Resor's capitulation was: "This means the Americans can kill anyone they want to."

Even so, the government in Washington may later have seemed to the bereaved Madame Chuyen to be preferable to her own in Saigon. Taking advantage of the circumstance that there had been no legal determination of Chuyen's fate, and sparing the CIA from any involvement in an act of decency so foreign to the agency's way of doing things, the American State Department proffered to Madame Chuyen a "missing person's gratuity" of $6,472. By contrast, she was completely ignored in Saigon. In the course of denying that Chuyen could have been a "triple agent"—spying for the South Vietnamese too—President Thieu said: "We have no interest in the matter whatsoever."

Madame Chuyen's gratuity demonstrated that honorable motives still existed in the American government, but there was nothing to answer the baffling question as to why such a government was maintaining an agency universally regarded as evil when the most careful examination of its operations showed only damage upon damage with no compensating benefits for the United States.

Mind Control

14

In order to achieve its self-perceived objectives, the CIA believed that it was not enough to be immune from congressional or judicial control. The agency felt it was also imperative that anti-CIA sentiment, and leftist leanings in general, had to be defused and combatted on every front. To this end, the CIA infiltrated the groves of academe, the missionary corps, the editorial boards of influential journals and book publishers, and any other quarters where public attitudes could be effectively influenced.

The campus revolts in late 1966 provided a springboard for the first big exposure of the CIA's long-secret attempt to guide and control the thinking not only of Americans, but in fact of everyone, everywhere. A typical uprising, sponsored originally by the Students for a Democratic Society (SDS) in November, prevented the CIA from recruiting for employees on the Columbia University campus in New York City.

Initially a total of 500 Columbia students were involved. As a first move a contingent of more than 100 of them went to Dodge Hall and blocked the entrance to the office assigned to a CIA recruiter who had just arrived on the campus after making appointments for employment interviews with twenty-five members of the student body.

After an unsuccessful attempt to persuade the students to leave their stations voluntarily, Columbia authorities declared the office closed for a week of deliberation and called a meeting for that night to discuss the issue.

The entire contingent of 500 demonstrators—chanting, "The CIA Must Go!"—marched two-by-two and arm-in-arm into the ornate rotunda of Low Library a few hours later for a session on the subject with Dr. Grayson Kirk, president of the University.

The students contended that the CIA was engaged in practices that were "morally reprehensible." Dr. Kirk, after replying that the university did not wish to discriminate against any organization or group seeking to recruit on the campus, continued:

> The moment we start making value judgments of this kind I think we endanger perhaps the most precious quality of the university community. It is a place where people meet in an atmosphere of respect for the opinions of others, and wherein free discussion of all matters affecting society is to be held and fostered.

Dr. Kirk proved persuasive and the SDS promptly disowned eighteen students who blocked the entrance of an office assigned for the next CIA attempt to recruit on the campus. "The Columbia chapter of SDS did not endorse the action of the eighteen," said John Fuerst, local chairman. "We are not condemning the group's intentions but we disagree with its tactics."

The handful of persistent dissenters nevertheless prevented the CIA recruiter from operating, and also used their blockade to prevent him from going to lunch. This time the CIA or the university or both gave up. The university announced that no disciplinary action would be taken against the demonstrators. The departing CIA recruiter said that future employment interviews in the area would be conducted through the CIA's field office in New York City. Since New York was one of the places where a telephone number but no address was listed for the CIA, this gave future employment interviews the character of a rendezvous rather than an appointment.

Soon after this incident twenty-three members of the faculty at Vassar in Poughkeepsie, New York, signed an open letter urging students and especially prospective graduates to consider "how subsequent academic employment will be affected by prior employment with the CIA." The letter charged:

> The CIA has undermined the official goals of our foreign policy and has subverted the independence of research in major universities to a point where no American social scientist or scholar can now be above suspicion when he or she goes abroad.

In one of the incidents to which the letter referred the Massachusetts Institute of Technology had revealed and at the same time severed a connection between the CIA and its Center for International Studies. In the unlikely hope that recipients of the money would be willing and able to influence scholars toward anti-Communism, the CIA had provided the center with a $300,000 funding grant in 1951 and for fifteen years had paid a major portion of its $750,000-a-year operating expenses.

Anti-CIA sentiment flared again at the annual meeting of the American Anthropological Society. Dr. Ralph L. Beals of the University of California at Los Angeles revealed that CIA agents had been masquerading abroad as peripatetic American anthropologists. This had its amusing aspects, he admitted, as did reports that during the Michigan State University project in South Vietnam a number of CIA agents had achieved faculty status. On the serious side, however, Dr. Beals contended that mixing academics with spying could be fatal for the scholarly professions:

> Actions which compromise the intellectual integrity and autonomy of research scholars and institutions not only weaken those international understandings essential to our discipline, but in so doing they threaten any contribution anthropology might make to our own society and to the general interests of human welfare. . . . Constraint, deception, and secrecy have no place in science.

Delegates to the annual meeting of the American Federation of Teachers were in a similar mood when they met in Chicago a few weeks after Illinois Governor Otto Kerner had called out National Guard troops to quell antiwar demonstrations. In that connection Dr. Martin Luther King had cancelled a speech scheduled before the World Council of Churches in Geneva, Switzerland, because, as he put it, "Riots now raging in Chicago demand that I remain on the scene."

The teacher-delegates denounced the CIA for having become involved in academics and condemned "the recent tendency to view faculty and student criticism of American foreign policy as unhealthy." They reaffirmed a teacher's right and duty to protest, including his or her right to practice civil disobedience, against "the immoral and unjust practices of a public agency."

All this was before the 1967 blowup in which the CIA was revealed to have secretly subsidized the National Students Association and an astounding list of other organizations and activities. The pent-up force of that spontaneous combustion, remarkable among other reasons because in a country with free speech and a free press the disclosures had been delayed so long, would show that over the years the CIA's ideological and monetary blessings had fallen not only on students but on almost every type of person who could be said to be active in the international field—from labor toughs working the docks to frail philosophers with an interest in human welfare.

The real bombshell was detonated February 14, 1967. On that otherwise peaceful St. Valentine's day the editors of *Ramparts* magazine took full-page advertisements in the *New York Times* and the *Washington Post* to announce that their forthcoming March issue would lift the lid on a fifteen-year-old scandal. The advertisements said:

The CIA has infiltrated and subverted the country's student leadership. It has used students to spy. It has used students to pressure international student organizations into Cold War positions, and it has interfered in a most shocking manner in the internal workings of the nation's oldest and largest student organization.

The March issue more than fulfilled its promise and was followed by a stream of confirmations and additional disclosures. The National Students Association with chapters on 340 campuses conceded that during the period 1952–66 it had received more than $3 million from the CIA, and that the source of this money usually was known only to the association's two top officers. The annual CIA allotments to the association had risen to a peak of $400,000 in the 1950s and as the Cold War grew less intense had dwindled to $50,000 when they were discontinued in 1966.

Eugene Groves, a graduate in physics from the University of Chicago, a Rhodes scholar, and a former president of NSA, said that in the earlier years the organization's leadership had felt that "the existence of heavily financed and totally controlled Soviet front organizations in the international field made it imperative that democratic and progressive organizations maintain a presence abroad that would offer an alternative." Now, he said, the leadership had decided that "covert relationships with government agencies were intolerable in an open democratic organization."

No one was more surprised by the furor than Thomas W. Braden, who had headed the CIA's international activities section during the program's early years (1950–54). He said he still thought the subsidies were a good idea and recalled having delivered $15,000 in cash to Irving Brown of the American Federation of Labor because "Brown needed the money to pay off strong-arm squads in Mediterranean ports so that American supplies could be delivered against the opposition of Communist dock workers." Braden also remembered having bestowed $50,000 in fifty dollar bills on Walter Reuther, president of the United Automobile Workers, in an arrangements under which Reuther's brother Victor distributed the money among West German labor unions.

When Braden's recollections appeared in print there

were many indignant denials, but Reuther apparently was unwilling to become an occasional if not a persistent liar for the sake of $50,000 that had merely passed through his hands. He issued a confirmation of the incident in which he was involved, saying it was a one-shot affair and would not be repeated. Less easily explained was a revelation that the National Students Association had used $140,000 of the CIA's money to pay off the debts of a string of discount textbook stores operated by NSA. In this case the CIA could scarcely even claim that there was an international aspect to the transaction.

Braden disclosed that in addition to its aid for student activities the CIA had been able to place agents and funds in some extremely high-thinking adult intellectual organizations including the Congress for Cultural Freedom, whose most prominent figure was British philosopher Bertrand Russell. The former head of international activities said this worked out to everyone's advantage, and explained:

> The agents could not only propose anti-Communist programs to the official leaders of the cultural organizations but they could also suggest ways and means to solve the inevitable budgetary problems. Why not see whether the money could be obtained from "American Foundations?"

It had to be admitted that the CIA had found an ingenious way to spend an unlimited amount of money with almost no one aware of where the funds were coming from. There were about a dozen of these "foundations," called "conduits" by the CIA. Some were legitimate philanthropic organizations which had agreed to pass along the CIA's money in the way Walter Reuther had done. Others were like the CIA in having no listed addresses, but unlike the CIA in that they existed only on paper. Irving Kristol, who without knowing that the publication was CIA-financed, served for five years as coeditor of the Congress for Cultural Freedom's *Encounter* magazine in London, later recalled in the *New York Times* Sunday magazine section for May 8, 1967:

> Farfield Foundation, our ostensible sponsor . . . was no shadowy or ghostly entity. Its president, Julius (Junky) Fleischmann—whose millions stemmed from yeast, gin and other profitable commodities—would float over to London now and then on his yacht, and Spender [Stephen Spender, the other coeditor] would give a "London literary party" for him. There he would be introduced as "the patron" of *Encounter*, and he would acknowledge the introduction with a gracious modesty that seemed quite becoming. . . .

Kristol, who later sponsored a "New Conservative" movement, said he would not have taken the job if he had known of the CIA financing. In listing his reasons he said that after having served in the United States Army during World War II he had "taken a solemn oath to myself that I would never, never again work as a functionary in a large organization, and especially not for the United States government." But he said there was no observable evidence of the CIA's tampering with *Encounter*'s editorial policy. He and Spender were hired, he said,

> because our views, including of course our political views (anti-Communist liberal) and our talents were congenial to the sponsoring organization. We could always be fired were our services unsatisfactory. Aside from that our freedom was complete.

Kristol's inadvertent lumping of the CIA with other large governmental organizations drew fire in a letter published in a subsequent issue of the *Times*:

> That organization, as has been abundantly documented in the *Times* and elsewhere, has organized the overthrow of popularly elected and supported governments (Iran, Guatemala), has intervened surreptitiously in the affairs of other nations (Indonesia, the Congo, and a half dozen other places), and has engaged in assassination, sabotage and sub-

version—at the same time systematically deceiving the American people whose interests it allegedly was advancing. The CIA, in short, has been conducting a foreign policy indistinguishable from Stalinist Communism. Yet Mr. Kristol, who finds Communism contemptible, considers the CIA no more despicable than the Post Office Department!

The controversy over CIA subsidies went on for months, and branched into areas where there might be no subsidy at all. Eventually ordinary tourists had to ask themselves whether they could be acceptable human beings if they were also potential spies, and American missionaries who might have spotted with joy a few extra dollars in their collection boxes had to consider whether the Lord's work could be done if they were suspected of having dealings with the intelligence agency.

After reports had appeared in the press of "systematic use of American missionaries by the CIA" the magazine *Christian Century* commented:

> Since the CIA specializes in keeping everyone in the dark—friend and foe alike—there is no way to know how widespread the practice has been. . . . However, we would expect that most missionaries would recoil from such dubious double agentry.

The CIA told Senate investigators in 1975 that over the years the agency had made "direct operational use" of twenty-one individuals in its dealing with American missionaries. There was, however, no clear statement as to whether "direct operational use" would include most of the contacts maintained.

Christian Century continued:

> The most disturbing aspect is a sharp difference of opinion in the National Council of Churches' Division of Overseas Missionaries (DOM). True, DOM has put out a policy statement counseling against direct cooperation with the CIA, but the statement is so open-ended as to be virtually without

force. It says it is all right for missionaries to give information to representatives of United States government agencies other than the CIA, and of course the CIA agents are not above posing as diplomats or what-have-you. Further, the more conservative Protestant missionary groups, together with some Roman Catholic missionary orders, seem to see no necessary conflict of interest in having dealings with the United States spy network.

After pointing out the special pitfalls of collaboration with an agency operating outside usual morality, the magazine came out adamantly against use of missionaries in any type of spying:

> Such "cloth and dagger" cooperation constitutes a reversion to the kind of alliances between church and empire builders that existed in the nineteenth century. It makes it impossible for the missionary to be trusted in the country in which he labors. The missionary cannot carry out his tasks . . . while at the same time assisting the United States government in making its determinations . . . as to how the nations should use their freedoms.

Tom Braden, who at this time in the late 1960s was his own program's chief apologist,[17] wrote the *Saturday Evening Post* article titled, "I'm Glad the CIA Is 'Immoral'." In the course of his presentation he made clear that the quotation marks around the word "Immoral" did not mean that he had reservations as to whether or not that was the case. When he asked himself rhetorically whether the CIA's activities were "immoral, wrong and disgraceful," he replied: "Only in the sense that war itself is 'immoral, wrong and disgraceful.'" In effect he answered the question affirmatively and accompanied his reply with an excuse: "For the Cold War is a war, fought with ideas instead of guns."

Yet he did not claim great success for his program. On the contrary he said the Russians had "stolen the great words," and explained:

Years after I left the CIA the then United Nations Ambassador Adlai Stevenson told me how he had been outraged when delegates from the underdeveloped countries, young men who had come to maturity during the Cold War, assumed that everyone who was for "peace" and "justice" and "freedom" must also be for Communism.

Braden was writing seventeen years after his program's inception. When he was with the CIA, artificial earth satellites were only a gleam in Wernher von Braun's eye. Now they were spinning relentlessly over both the Soviet Union and the United States, taking and transmitting reel after reel of photographs with enough resolution to show the numbers and types of vehicles on highways, streets, and construction sites below. Neither country could undertake anything as large-scale as the construction of an underground missile launcher without the other's spotting the activity immediately. Also, before the death of Stalin in 1953 the Soviet Union had been opened to only a few individually invited visitors, whereas now the country was receiving more than a million tourists a year, a large percentage of them Americans.

Nevertheless, the issue in principle remained the same as to whether or not a person could in good conscience travel in the Soviet Union as a tourist and then report back to the CIA. To the surprise of the agency, there was strong resistance to the practice among both conservatives and liberals.

In the first place it was discourteous after having been received as a guest. Just as a scholar could not retain his integrity and a missionary could not perform his mission, it began to look as though a tourist could not observe the common decencies if he opted for the CIA's stance. And the image which the practice tended to generate of a typical American—a sort of shifty-eyed fellow eternally vigilant for a chance to gain a competitive advantage in international intercourse—was not well calculated to be of assistance in recapturing the "great words."

One of the most distinguished recipients of the CIA's ideological largesse was a well-known and highly respected publishing house, Frederick A. Praeger, Inc. According to Praeger, president of the company, the CIA provided financial support for "fifteen or sixteen" Praeger books during the late 1950s. After someone had leaked to the press what Praeger considered to be a distorted version of the arrangement, the publisher called a press conference to "put the matter in perspective."

Praeger said the subsidized volumes constituted only one percent of the books published by his company during the period in question. He added:

> The editorial board of Frederick A. Praeger, Incorporated, passed on the books as books, without any knowledge of where they had come from. The books went through the regular routine with editoral staff and editorial board members, who had no knowledge of any sources of support. The books were developed according to the standards that we applied to all our books.

In the absence of further exposition it had to be assumed that Praeger had used subtle methods, perhaps a word of approval dropped here and there, to make sure that his board members selected the right manuscripts to be brought up to standard. The publisher refused to respond on a point crucial for authors who anticipated royalties, when asked whether the CIA had agreed to purchase substantial numbers of the favored volumes for gift distribution at home and abroad.

E. Howard Hunt told the Senate Intelligence Committee in an unguarded moment that CIA-sponsored books directed against Communist China "had to circulate in the United States because Praeger was a commercial U.S. publisher . . . and we had a bilateral agreement with the British that we wouldn't propagandize their people."

This seemed to be showing a lot of admirable consideration for the British but none at all for Americans. The Senate committee, which seemed to be about half on the side of the CIA in these embarrassing situations, sought in its report to smooth any feelings that might have been ruffled. It explained that in 1967 the CIA had discontinued sponsorship of books, "except abroad," and that "most" of these were in foreign languages.

Although apparently intended to be reassuring, the committee statement's use of the phrase "except abroad" and the word "most" aroused suspicions. It developed that "some 250" CIA books had been published abroad in the nine years since the transfer of patronage, so if only a half dozen or so per year were in English it would still be correct to say that "most" were in foreign languages. And where would those in English circulate? It looked as though the United States might be the only candidate again, although whether any abuses of this kind actually occurred could not be determined.

In addition to being an unabashed statement of intention to propagandize Americans while avoiding such dishonest tactics wherever the Union Jack prevailed, the bilateral agreement was another example of how the CIA acted as its own State Department, concluding solemn agreements usually involving cash with governments and intelligence agencies throughout the world. Such agreements, actually treaties of a sort, were invariably top secret, and no Senate confirmation was required for them.

Another publishing disclosure involved the equally distinguished <u>magazine *Foreign Affairs,*</u> which was supposed to represent a broad and tolerant international viewpoint. The lead article in the magazine's April 1966 issue was found to have been written by a CIA analyst not identified as such. The disclosure this time was triggered by a tip to reporters from Senator Fulbright.

Under the title, "The Faceless Vietcong," there appeared the name George A. Carver, described in the magazine as "a student of political theory and Asian affairs, with degrees from Yale and Oxford; former officer in the United States mission in Saigon; author of *Aesthetics and the Problem of Meaning.*" The editor of *Foreign Affairs* said he would have preferred to include Carver's CIA connection but "the CIA wouldn't stand for it."

Clayton Fritchey, commenting in *Harper's* magazine, wrote:

Carver's article adds up to an elaborate effort to fortify the Administration's charges that the National Liberation Front is a mere puppet of Hanoi. No doubt it reflects his sincere views, but sincere or not it is a powerful piece of pro-administration propaganda. It is simply a camouflaged White Paper. There was no way for the reader to know that Carver was an "interested" party.

While he was at it Fritchey recalled that CIA Director Helms had "foolishly" testified that the agency never tried to influence policy. Fritchey continued:

Later testimony has confirmed what everyone knows, that the CIA not only planned the invasion of Cuba but persuaded John F. Kennedy to go through with it. Even the best of Presidents are suckers for the CIA because it is so seductive to know more, or think you know more, than the general public. Hence the question as to whether the CIA is going to run the country or vice versa ultimately will have to be settled by Congress.

Until 1971 Helms had never delivered a public speech. A closed-door address which he gave before the Business Council at the Homestead Inn in Hot Springs, Virginia, in May 1969, nevertheless was reported through a widely hailed scoop by UPI correspondent James R. Srodes.

Srodes, who stood six feet five inches and weighed 280 pounds, happened to wander to the back of the Inn. When he discovered that the Helms speech was being piped by loudspeaker into the kitchen so that waiters would know when to bring on certain courses, he remained within earshot during the whole of the CIA director's delivery. Accounts of his exploit made interesting reading because of the aura of mystery that always attended the CIA and because of a tantalizing twist of words that labeled the story "Spying on the Master Spy."

As it turned out the method by which it was obtained was the essence of the story, because the Helms speech definitely contained no news. It was no more than an updated version three years later of Carver's article for *For-*

eign Affairs. The best of the Helms quotes that Srodes could scrape together were that Ho Chi Minh was "an utterly coldblooded individual," that the Kremlin leadership and policy were "utterly bankrupt," and that the National Liberation Front had "given up hope of winning on the battlefield."

A little more significance could be attached to the speech later by noting that Helms presented it more than two years after Senator Russell reversed his position in the dispute with the Foreign Relations Committee, and more than a year after the Tet offensive in South Vietnam. That the agency was still voicing such a hard propaganda line this late in the game was enough to refute claims made after the Vietnam effort was in shambles, and based on some exceptions the agency had taken to programs not its own, that the CIA was really a moderating force in that abortive war. On the contrary, as we have seen, the CIA's ten-year pursuit of a policy of brute force in the administration of South Vietnam, and its financial and military support for extremism in the form of President Diem's psychopathic brother Nhu, were the principal factors in the destabilization of Diem, which with much aid from a policy adopted by President Johnson, precipitated the war.

15

Much Ado

Though it might seem reasonable to assume that some of the CIA's operations must have been more successful than those recorded here, research on which this book was based yielded no evidence to support such an assumption. Where CIA operations produced visible results, it was difficult to detect tangible benefits to the United States or serious damage to potential enemies.

A prime example of the emptiness of a so-called CIA "success" was the dissemination by the agency of a falsified version of Khrushchev's famous "de-Stalinization" speech.

In 1956 after obtaining a copy of Khrushchev's speech denouncing the crimes of Stalin, the CIA prepared a false version of the document. The spurious part consisted of thirty-two phony inserts on subjects Khrushchev had not even mentioned and was designed to give the Soviet Union as much diplomatic trouble as possible.

Since Khrushchev had taken a steep and rocky road by exposing evil in his own country instead of spending all his time denouncing imperialism in the usual Communist way, it might have been thought that in this instance he deserved at least grudging gratitude from the West, but no such consideration deterred the CIA operatives.

In explaining the matter many years afterward in the *New York Times* Sunday magazine section for April 18, 1971, Benjamin Welles wrote:

> Among its many tasks Helms's Plans Directorate also runs "disinformation"—strategic deception designed to keep the

KGB off balance. One of the most successful if little known spying adventures of this sort came about after Nikita Khrushchev's celebrated "secret" speech of February 24, 1956, at the Twentieth Party Congress in Moscow. Stalin's death three years earlier had left world Communism leaderless. Finally emerging at the top after a power struggle Khrushchev sprang on a surprised party the epochal "de-Stalinization" speech which was to rend the party and promote the Sino-Soviet split.

As delivered by Khrushchev the speech had contained nothing on foreign policy. Welles continued:

> Helms's men, rapidly assembling Kremlin views on foreign countries acquired through a variety of secret sources, including authentic damning statements made by Soviet leaders about rulers and governments in the non-aligned world, made a total of thirty-two inserts. The real text was printed in the *Times* June 5, 1956, and the CIA leaked its fuller version simultaneously, exactly as though it had been photographed by a Minox spy camera and then enlarged. It was distributed to strategic spots around the world, and for months foreign ministries puzzled over which was the true version. "Eventually most governments decided that the *New York Times* version was that which Moscow had 'sanitized' for foreign Communist parties," recalled one source. "They decided that the other version with its damning references was the real thing. The Kremlin took a long time living that down."

Fortunately for the dignity of the human race, the operation was much less successful than was represented by the source quoted by Welles. In his 1970 memoirs Khrushchev gave no indication that he ever even heard either of the bogus version of his speech or of the CIA's paying a fancy price for his original prose. On other evidence and on the face of things it appeared that the only success the operation could have had, if it ever got off the ground at all—the project actually was canceled in midcourse—must have been in someone's vivid imagination.

The stuff that Welles was writing was really sickening

to anyone who had gotten even a faint glimpse of the truth. There were no such deliberations or decisions in foreign ministries, and if there had been, the participants would have shown a lot more confidence in the *Times* than he appeared to have. A decision that with both versions of the speech obviously available, the *Times* would have chosen or happened to publish the wrong one was just not in the cards. It would have been even less likely that, if such an egregious error had occurred, the newspaper would never have gotten around to correcting the situation.

Meanwhile, in the name of secrecy—the truth was secret but lies were not—writers were permitted to skate all over the lot with the wildest kind of speculation. Leonard Moseley, in *Dulles* (Dial, 1978) actually said the CIA had paid $750,000 for the speech, while Ray S. Cline in *Secrets, Spies and Scholars* (Acropolis, 1976) said "a very handsome price" was paid. Counterintelligence Chief Angleton, who should have known, claimed that the speech was turned over for ideological reasons with no payment whatever, and in this instance he may have been the closest of the three to the truth.

Khrushchev wrote in his memoirs:

> It [the speech] was supposed to have been secret but actually was far from being secret. We took measures to make sure that copies of it circulated to the fraternal Communist parties. . . . That is how the Polish party received a copy. . . . Our document fell into the hands of some Polish comrades who were hostile toward the Soviet Union. They used the speech for their own purposes and made copies of it. I was told it was being sold for very little. So Khrushchev's speech was not appraised as being worth much! Intelligence agents from every country in the world could buy it cheap on the open market. That is how the document came to be published.

So here was the truth at last. What Americans would call zealous Polish patriots were distributing the speech. There was one possibility, however, that somehow didn't seem as unlikely as would at first appear. The possibility was that someone in the CIA did pay quite a bit of money for the speech, not because he needed to but because that would look a lot better on his report. Since the CIA people were not common criminals—though they could become uncommon criminals on short notice—that might have been quite a bit more likely than that someone simply stuck the money in his pocket.

For that matter, the idea that there was anything especially daring, conspiratorial, exclusive, or expensive about the CIA's obtaining a copy of Khrushchev's speech had to be something that developed later, as there was no such pretense at the time it was published. In announcing its forthcoming publication a day in advance the *New York Times* said at the top of its front page: "The text has been in the hands of the United States *and other Western governments* for several days" (italics added). This was certainly saying in plain words that the distribution was general.

For anyone doubting the above, including those who had written so lavishly about this supposedly masterful stroke by the CIA's intelligence geniuses, the film files of the *New York Times* were available even in small libraries such as the one I used at Cocoa, Florida. With a few minutes of instruction the most untrained person could look it up in a jiffy.

When I was a young reporter I was taught that anything, no matter how detailed, explicit, or accurate it might be, was still propaganda if the source was hidden. Later, thanks as much as anything else to the CIA's having succeeded in making virtues of both dishonesty and secrecy, which were in fact very close to being the same thing, the sourceless stuff became the whole meat of what we were getting, when we were getting anything. It was only in later life that I learned you had to ask a person whether you could quote him.

Anyhow, to do the best possible with what was available, according to some of those miserable, sourceless, I-know-something-you-don't-know accounts that were passing for news, CIA Director Dulles had dramatically offered to pay $100,000 for a copy of the speech. In spite of everything there may have been a grain or two of truth in some of these stories, since Dulles was certainly fascinated by the sum of $100,000—a real fortune in his day, though later it would appear that even a sharecropper needed that much investment to get him by.

So it was quite possible that in the speech operation as in the cases of Lumumba and others the CIA men in the field were under great pressure to spend a huge sum of dollars with nothing all-that-expensive around on which to disburse the funds. In these circumstances a person willing to accept money could actually seem a godsend. This was another reason I was not quite ready to abandon the possibility that the CIA did pay a fairly round sum for the text even though it may have been available for little or nothing.

Another odd thing about the publication of Khrushchev's speech, which would later be represented as such a stunning blow to the whole fabric of Soviet society, was that there was nothing especially new in it, because the *Times* and other publications had already pretty well covered its contents. On March 16, 1956, less than a month after its delivery and under the byline of Harrison E. Salisbury, the *Times* had carried a two-column-long summary of the speech. Salisbury, who cited "diplomatic reports," explained:

> Party delegates are now spreading by word of mouth around the country the essence of Mr. Khrushchev's remarks. Some experts suggested that after Soviet opinion had been prepared for the shock the whole case against Stalin might be made public.

The matter was seriously and disturbingly puzzling, as though deception could have been carried to the point of blotting out plain facts and common sense. Cline in his book would describe obtaining a copy of Khrushchev's speech as "one of the CIA's greatest coups of all time," and Allen Dulles in retirement would call it "one of the main coups while I was there." It would be hard to imagine two better authorities on this subject, and yet there was not a shred of evidence to support the implications of those statements. Khrushchev's speech was a big thing in the Soviet Union of course, but this little nibbling around the edges by the CIA was nothing substantial at all.

The insignificant nature of the spurious version's effect, if there was any, can also be judged from the following: during his many years as Foreign Relations Chairman, the matter never came to the attention of Senator Fulbright, who first learned of the falsification of Khrushchev's speech from reading the manuscript for this book.

In contrast with the CIA's attitude toward him, incidentally, Khrushchev was generous in his comments concerning America's slain president, who had handed him the worst defeat of his career. In his memoirs he wrote:

> As for Kennedy, his death was a great loss. He was gifted with the ability to resolve international conflicts by negotiation. Regardless of his youth he was a real statesman. I believe that if Kennedy had lived relations between the Soviet Union and the United States would be much better than they are. Why do I say that? Because Kennedy would never have let his country get bogged down in Vietnam.

After word got around that overthrowing duly elected governments was not such a laudable pastime as had been represented, the CIA's success in predicting the first Chinese nuclear explosion was sometimes placed at the top of its list of positive achievements. The prediction was often called "precise," although on September 29, 1964, nineteen days before the event, Secretary of State Rusk could say only that the test explosion would occur "in the near future."

How the prediction helped the United States or hurt the Chinese was another matter. Since most of the Chinese nuclear scientists were American-educated it was probable that in corresponding with former colleagues in the United States some of them had written letters as informative as the CIA's prediction. Despite secrecy restrictions a professional man would have assumed that he could be frank at least to the extent of Rusk's knowledge.

Intelligence gathered before and during the missile crisis, including the masterful handling of the eccentric Penkovsky and the U–2 photographs that confirmed the worst, were not emphasized on the CIA's list of positive achievements because credit there had to be shared to a considerable extent with the British and with the Air Force. Prediction of Khrushchev's rise to power was a major item on the list but was eventually offset by the agency's failure to obtain the slightest advance indication of his ouster, which came the day before the Chinese nuclear explosion.

One exploit persistently on the CIA's list of "successes" was its 1955 feat in which a six-million-dollar, 24-foot-deep and 600-yard-long tunnel was dug from West to East Berlin so that a tap could be placed on the Russian military telephone system. The episode had merits as an espionage thriller: locating the telephone junction, patiently digging for months, smuggling the dirt out through a fake radar station in boxes marked "ELECTRONIC EQUIPMENT," and installing refrigeration to prevent snow from melting in telltale fashion above the tunnel.

As often as the story was told, however, there was never a hint as to what advantage had accrued to the United States and its allies from the several months of expensive eavesdropping that proved possible before the Soviets "discovered" the tap. Anyone familiar with such matters would have known that if a concrete, understandable benefit could have been injected into such a good story, it would have been leaked.

The truth was that the Russians knew of the tunnel project well before construction started. Their information came from George Blake, a former British vice consul in South Korea, who had been captured and successfully indoctrinated by the Communists during the Korean War, and who at the time of the tunnel's construction, had infiltrated the Berlin command setup. Five years later he pleaded guilty to charges of espionage and was sentenced to forty-two years in prison, from which, no doubt with a helping hand and many expressions of gratitude from the Soviets, he escaped and defected to Moscow in 1966.

Blake's information presented the Russians with an attractive set of options. They could have exposed the matter immediately, but they had no reason to do so. Since they knew about it and would not be putting on the wires anything harmful to themselves, the tunnel had been rendered as harmless as a pussycat as far as they were concerned. They decided to let the tunnel be completed and see if they could make use of it themselves—double-barreled use in fact, since they could no doubt arrange to do some listening as the CIA planned to do, and could also put false information on the wires, which the West would readily accept as real stuff.

This is precisely what happened. The tunnel operated in the Russians' behalf instead of against them for approximately eleven months before the Soviets for whatever reasons—probably because by that time their secret must have been out too—decided to "discover" the telephone system tap. Unfortunately it must also be recorded that so immovably slanted was the viewpoint of those representing the agency that with full knowledge of Blake's treachery Harry Rositzke, in *The CIA's Secret Operations*, still treated the tunnel as a valuable coup scored by the CIA.[18]

And Benjamin Welles, who obviously had been supplied only incomplete information in the same 1971 *Times* article quoted at the beginning of this chapter, could still refer to the tunnel as one of the CIA's "smashing successes," the only other "smashing success" treated in the article having been the falsification of Khrushchev's de-Stalinization speech.

Normally CIA operations could be made to appear to have yielded great benefit only by supposing that something of a calamitous nature would have occurred if the agency had not prevented it. And as nuclear scientist Leo Szilard pointed out in *The Voice of the Dolphins* (Simon and Schuster, 1961) such speculation wasn't paying off. Szilard (the man who wrote the letter to FDR which Einstein

signed and which resulted in the atomic bomb) argued
that the United States was constantly engaged in pouring
its resources into fruitless attempts to control events while
good, bad and calamitous results continued to occur in the
same proportions and with the same regularity as always.
Meanwhile the CIA, using secrecy as a cloak, was permitted to claim all sorts of benefits that did not exist, and to
represent whenever it chose to do so that American foreign policy was the opposite of the one stated publicly and
privately by government leaders.

A prime example of the latter was the CIA's provision
of aid to Israel for achieving the atomic bomb. *New York
Times* writers Tad Szulc and Seymour Hersh reported
separately that this included sending "several" nuclear
scientists to provide technological support in the late
1950s and mid-1960s at Israel's Dimona Atomic Research
Center near Beersheba in the Negev Desert, and that support may have been only the tip of the iceberg. Szulc also
mentioned "other sources"—not his primary informants,
who denied it, but apparently well-versed members of the
intelligence community—who said that "the CIA team
made fissionable material . . . available to the Israelis from
United States stocks." If such was the case it would have
constituted a capital crime, one not likely ever to be admitted by anybody.

Writing in the August 1975, issue of *Penthouse* magazine after he had left the *Times*, Szulc attributed his primary information to "sources close to" former Counterintelligence Chief Angleton, who had the responsibility
for CIA-Israeli relations from 1954 through 1974, and
who had left the agency in a dispute with CIA Director
Colby at the beginning of the publication year.

In explanation of the CIA's providing the A-bomb aid,
Szulc said:

> Although details of the Israeli enterprise are still top se-
> cret, it is known that in the wake of the 1956 Suez war the
> Eisenhower administration resolved to provide Israel with all
> possible aid in developing an atomic weapon. . . . The CIA
> was charged with the responsibility of providing this support.

As everyone in newspaper work knew, "sources close to" usually meant the person himself, who had vouchsafed the information with the understanding that it would not be attributed directly to him, while "it is known" would normally refer to a solemn assurance from the same source. However that may have been, as far as there having been any such policy in the Eisenhower or any other administration was concerned, this was clearly a case of a reporter's being deliberately and badly misled.

John Eisenhower, who was Assistant White House Staff Secretary in 1958–61 and during the next three years assisted in the compilation of his father's memoirs, told me under date of March 10, 1978, that he "never heard of such an idea," and added: "As I recall we were unhappy to get the rumor that Israel was secretly developing such a weapon." Gordon Gray, Eisenhower's Special Assistant for National Security, also assured me that the information given Szulc on this subject was "not correct"; while McGeorge Bundy, the pre-Kissinger Kissinger who served as Special Assistant for National Security under Presidents Kennedy and Johnson, said that during his tenure (1961–66) it was "the explicit and clearly understood policy of the United States that we ought to do everything we could to ensure that the famous reactor at Dimona was not used for military purposes."

The French-built Dimona reactor was capable of producing enough plutonium for about one bomb a year. Since its operation dated back to the late 1950s, that would have been barely enough for the thirteen atomic bombs reported by *Time* magazine of April 12, 1976, to have been assembled by the Israelis and rushed to waiting warplanes during an initial seventy-two-hour period when the battle was going against them in the October 1973 Mideast War.

That activity and the preparations for it, known or suspected from satellite and aerial photographs, caused the Russians to deploy in Egypt twenty Scud missiles with a 185-mile range, and to ship from Odessa through the Bosporus a number of nuclear warheads to be affixed to them. The Soviet maneuver in turn was readily detected by the United States and was connected with an action October 25, 1973, that, to the consternation of almost everyone, placed American armed forces on a worldwide nuclear alert.

The *Time* article, including such details as renderings of long secret and private conversations between Moshe Dayan and Golda Meir (which could hardly have come from anyone except Dayan himself—who was quoted directly on the policy behind such conversations), said that fortunately the battle turned in Israel's favor before any nuclear triggers could be set. Dr. Kissinger was then able to put through the compromise settlement of the war. But it was at least a mini-nuclear confrontation, creating a "mini-Balance of Terror" in the Mideast.

Dayan's contention was that the vastly outnumbered Israelis "had no choice" but to go for the big bomb. "With our manpower," he said, "we cannot physically, financially or economically go on acquiring more and more tanks and more and more planes. Before long you would have all of us maintaining and oiling the tanks."

The Rogue Elephant

16

Hard on the heels of the enormously costly turn of events in Iran (see Chapter 9) came disclosure of the CIA's part in the Watergate affair. In the background this consisted of having set the pattern for Watergate in the first place, having invented and promoted many of the practices involved, and having supplied "ex" personnel for some of the leading players. In the foreground the contribution included furnishing false identification papers and such intriguing items as a false voice box and a soon-to-be-famous red wig for use in burglarizing the office of Daniel Ellsberg's psychiatrist and in other episodes which Attorney General Mitchell called "White House Horrors."

On the whole the CIA's immediate contribution could be described as slight. Actually the "amateurish" performances of the participants in Watergate and the comparatively innocuous nature of their crimes were often laughing matters at the CIA, as became clear after Ambassador Helms was called home from Iran for testimony.

That a number of its former employees were among those caught in the Watergate break-in was a source of some embarrassment to the CIA. On that subject, in answer to a question by Senator Howard Baker, Republican, of Tennessee, Helms testified:

> Well, Senator Baker, I do not know whether these are proper matters for me to discuss in this forum, but I would like to point out something to you. Breaking and entering and not getting caught is a very difficult activity, and for it to

be done properly one has to have trained individuals who do nothing else and who are used to doing this frequently and are trained right up to the minute in how to do it.

Senator Baker: Was [James] McCord [former CIA man caught in Democratic National Headquarters] in that category?

Ambassador Helms: Obviously not. (Laughter).

E. Howard Hunt elaborated the agency's viewpoint in the matter when he described the breaking and entry into the office of Ellsberg's psychiatrist as a "success." Since no evidence of any kind was obtained in that operation, a confused Senator asked, "In what respect?"

Hunt, seeming equally confused that the Senator wouldn't understand, replied: "We got in and out without getting caught."

The good humor with which the Helms testimony was given and received was something foreigners could hardly be expected to share. Even a committee outraged by such practices at home could tolerantly accept the idea that in the CIA's case the frequent breakings and enterings necessary to keep a staff of burglars in trim would be carried out overseas, or at least against unwanted aliens. It was a typical piece of CIA reasoning, with infinite attention for the measly temporary advantages that might be obtained and none for the overall damage such practices could inflict.

The CIA was already on the downward toboggan in public esteem when Senate investigators appeared on the scene in 1975. Americans had been outraged to learn through newspapers that the CIA with other intelligence agencies had compiled a computer index of 300,000 Americans, with separate files on 7,500 of them, because they opposed the Vietnam War. And any remaining doubt that the CIA had been giving the White House the run-around should have been dispelled when CIA Director Colby told the Rockefeller Commission concerning the agency's twenty-year program for opening the mails: "I don't think any president individually knew." The statement seemed to suggest that there was some collective way in which they could have known, but apparently the meaning was more simply that they didn't know about this activity.

The twenty-year program was carried out from 1953 through 1973 at LaGuardia and Kennedy International airports in New York, and was longer than several others in different parts of the country about which the presidents also did not know. The New York operation reflected a good deal more credit on the American public than it did on its perpetrators. Millions of pieces of mail were photographed and computerized, for what purpose would be hard to imagine, and 200,000 letters, mainly but by no means entirely to and from Iron Curtain countries, were opened and read. Yet according to the testimony not a single domestic traitor or foreign spy was ever identified or brought to trial by this method.[19]

The downward trend for the CIA reached a probable low in November of 1975 when a Gallup poll showed only fourteen percent of the citizenry still willing to speak a good word for the agency—as compared to thirty-seven percent still approving a badly mauled FBI. Immediately following the poll came the Senate committee's "Alleged Assassination Plots Involving Foreign Leaders; An Interim Report," dated November 20 and replete with all the medieval evils commonly associated with the Borgias. In addition to bombs, telescopic rifles, the poisoned pen, and poisoned pills and darts, the CIA in "at least eight" attempts to kill Castro was shown to have used an exploding seashell which was to have been placed near his favorite bathing spot, as well as poisoned cigars and a scuba diving suit that had been contaminated with deadly bacteria.

The plots in fact went from the most gruesomely macabre to the absolutely ridiculous. One would have sprayed Castro's broadcasting studio with a chemical which when inhaled would make his speech nonsensical, and another would have coated his shoes with a preparation designed to cause his beard to fall out, the idea being that he would then lose his charismatic appeal for the Cuban people. The plans for the latter specified that Castro's footgear would be coated with thallium salts when he left them outside a hotel room to be shined, and that the depilatory effects of the salts would reach his beard when he bent over to tie his shoes.

From any standpoint, it was by common consent the worst documentation any nation had ever voluntarily published against itself. (Khrushchev's de-Stalinization speech may have been worse but perhaps was not published voluntarily.)

The public's reaction to the assassination report was awaited with bated breath, and turned out to be the opposite of the one expected. Instead of buckling down to the task of rectifying the situation, the nation was like a man who had been foolish enough to inquire into his wife's previous sex life and who, upon learning the truth, had recoiled in stark anguish and shut up like a clam. He was sorry he had learned what he did, and he never wanted to hear anything on that subject again. The House of Representatives resoundingly voted 246–124 to refuse to permit the release of its intelligence committee's findings, and the vote on further disclosures by the Senate group would have been close if the Church committee had not succeeded in avoiding a showdown on the issue.

A large contributing factor was the murder in gangland fashion on December 23, 1975, of Richard S. Welch, the CIA's station chief at Athens, Greece. Welch had been identified as a CIA operative in a book published in East Berlin as far back as 1968, as well as many times since, and it was not even clear that his death had anything to do with his employment, let alone investigative disclosures; but just a CIA suggestion that such might have been the case was enough to cause opprobrium to fall on those daring to expose the agency's iniquities. After President Ford had attended his funeral and made a big thing of the CIA viewpoint in the matter, Welch was succeeded by a man who was identified immediately in both Greek and American publications as the new CIA Station Chief. Even if Welch's murder was related to his employment he would have been either the first CIA Station Chief or the first in a great many years to be slain for that reason. John Stockwell, in *In Search of Enemies*, said: "During my twelve years of service [with the CIA] I knew of no other case officer murdered, although at least twenty State Department, United States Information Service, and Agency for International Development officers had been killed, kidnapped, or suffered harrowing experiences during that period." William R. Corson, in *The Armies of Ignorance*, said Welch "had made no secret of his position," and added: "It is unfair to eulogize him on the improper grounds that he was killed because of leaks and congressional investigations."

The only good thing that could be said of the public's new attitude toward learning the truth was that the attitude couldn't last forever. As 1976 proceeded, a common remark was that the CIA's only remaining difficulty lay in how to avoid an appearance of gloating. Taylor Branch of *Esquire* magazine, in a special article for a September issue of the *New York Times* Sunday magazine section, lamented:

> The CIA bowled over the Pike Committee [in the House] and seduced the Church Committee [in the Senate]. . . . No congressional oversight committee is likely to have a better chance to control the CIA. . . . The agency began these searching investigations hanging on the ropes, and clearly emerged the winner. Its powers, so unique and still largely hidden, remain essentially unchanged.

By the summer, any hope that the Carter administration would act promptly to remedy the situation went glimmering even before the presidential honeymoon was over, when the *Washington Post* disclosed secret CIA payments to King Hussein of Jordan totaling $20 million and amounting to $750,000 for 1976.

Twenty million dollars was a powerful lot of money to have handed a man under the table even over the course of more than two decades, and the fact that nothing concerning this had come to light during a whole generation was enough to raise questions as to what kind of business this country and its news media might be operating. But instead of congratulating the *Post* for having brought the matter to his and the public's attention for the first time, President Carter found that the *Post* had acted irresponsibly in its publication.

Despite a clear provision in the Constitution requiring a regular accounting for "all" public expenditures, President Carter also found nothing illegal or improper in what, as it turned out, was a worldwide pattern of payments to key figures, in a system of institutionalized bribery circling the globe. Professor Arthur S. Miller of the George Washington University School of Law, insisting that the Constitution's "all" must mean *all*, commented in the May 1977, issue of the *Progressive* magazine:

> If there was any doubt that the CIA is, in fact, a "rogue elephant" out of control, as Senator Frank Church once observed, it vanished. . . . The president's reaction indicates that he has already become a prisoner of "the system"—a captive of the weird reasoning that passes for logic where matters of "national security" are concerned.

In the midst of the 1975 disclosures, with millions who disliked the agency still considering it a necessary evil, a Harris poll at the beginning of August showed that the public heavily favored making the CIA more accountable but had rejected by 80 to 6 percent the idea of "abolishing the CIA and leaving the United States with no foreign intelligence agency." At first brush this certainly seemed an overwhelming endorsement of the CIA as an absolute necessity.

On the other hand, considering the way the question was worded, with its emphatically clear implication that such a step would be leaving the United States defenseless before its enemies, it could be considered surprising that even six percent had opted for that choice. No one contended that the disaffected portion of the population was anything like that large, and even if it had been, the country would probably have been unable to operate. In a not too distant day in fact, Jesse James and a disaffected band of thirteen men had very nearly prevented the country from operating over a considerable length of time.

Perhaps the pollsters did not know that the CIA was getting only fifteen percent of the intelligence dollar, and was spending up to eighty percent of that comparatively small portion on activities having nothing to do with intelligence. Also that, except for its monopoly over throwing monkey wrenches into movements not meeting its approval around the world, and the even less commendable endeavors in its Department of Dirty Tricks, it would be difficult to find CIA activities that weren't already being duplicated in at least one if not several ways.

In his advocacy for abolishing the CIA, Tom Braden said he would give its overt intelligence functions to the State Department, its military role to the military, and its propaganda and psychological warfare mission to the Voice of America. He said he would retain "a very few men" in a no-name group to act as deep-cover spies, but would limit their covert activities to "passing money to 'friendlies.'" Perhaps a small White House staff would be needed to prepare the president's daily intelligence report. They would have ample intelligence resources at their disposal, and one highly competent civilian expert, Arthur Schlesinger for example, could be worth a whole army of prowling spies.

Apparently it had to be accepted that the time wasn't right for the kind of clean sweep Braden had in mind, but that day still seemed certain to come. At least if the experience of the Russians was a guide there was no reason why the CIA problem could not ultimately be faced. During their first half century the Soviets had conducted ten more or less thorough intelligence reorganizations. Several infamous outfits had passed into history, and certainly none was ever permitted to develop and pursue its own separate foreign policy. Allen Dulles really belonged back in that day two generations earlier when Bolsheviks were pictured in the American press with long, stand-up hair, with wildly evil and bearded faces, and with bombs bulging from their pockets.

Soviet intelligence shakeups had taken the form of

abolishing one agency and replacing it with another, but the same procedure was not necessarily indicated in the United States. Due to the concentration of all power in the Communist Party the Soviets were accustomed to thinking of intelligence as primarily a civilian function, whereas in America it was still mainly located in the military, where morale for the most part continued to be higher than in the civilian bureaucracy. It was true that military intelligence estimates would always be weighted heavily in the military establishment's favor, but this was an understandable and in some respects a desirable bias, and there were towering historical precedents for making the necessary allowances—such as Defense Secretary Forrestal's statement that the military leaders would fortify the moon if they could obtain an authorization for doing so, and Clemenceau's famous remark that war was too important to be left to the generals.

Considering the extent to which the proliferation of agencies had been carried, it could well be that if one of them were abolished it would not need to be replaced. The Defense Intelligence Agency, it will be recalled, was set up after the Bay of Pigs and assigned to all the legitimate functions of the CIA; and more than twenty years later the DIA had an excellent track record when compared to the CIA in matters involving intelligence. There was no evidence whatever that the existence of a civilian intelligence agency had in any way modified the military reach; on the contrary the CIA almost always took the military point of view and then went beyond it. More important to the present consideration, the huge Defense Department intelligence setup was not threatening the application of a fair-minded foreign policy, whereas the CIA was persistently making such a foreign policy impossible.

Pending a complete recasting of the intelligence community into something considerably more useful, there were a few interim steps that might greatly improve the situation, and might even head off the necessity for more comprehensive measures:

—The CIA somehow insinuated into its particular area of activity the idea that assassination was acceptable if carried out with a certain amount of training or finesse. But it was deeply embedded in the consciousness of almost everyone at home and abroad that the word designated the worst, the most despicable, and the most cowardly form of murder. A dictionary definition of the word appeared to support the prevailing view: "To kill by surprise, or by secret or treacherous assault." The attempted legitimization of the practice had to be stopped, and it would not be stopped as long as assassination was included in training programs.

The clear course for the United States Army therefore appeared to be to rise up in its majesty as General Abrams had done, and this time to tear such ideas and training root and branch forever from its Green Beret program and any other in which such ideas and practices might have gained entry. Then even those nations that didn't like the United States could still if they chose regard this country as a worthy or respectable opponent.

—To cite correctly an example which Allen Dulles so often cited incorrectly, just as British Intelligence was under their Foreign Office, so American civilian intelligence should be placed under the State Department. That department may have seemed a bit tedious at times, but it had generally attempted to act in the country's long-term interest and in accordance with principles in which Americans believed. To have made that statement regarding the CIA would surely have provoked loud and long laughter almost anywhere—perhaps rueful or bitter laughter in some cases.

—If the CIA was going to insist on having a military role it should be able to observe the rules of war as well as they were observed by the regular armed forces. It would be refreshing, and also surprising, to learn that the agency had set up a training program heavily slanted toward their observance. So far as anyone knew, violations of the rules of war did not produce victories anyway, and even if they had, the victories would have been badly tainted. As long as we were alive and functioning only with the permission of the people with their fingers on the nuclear triggers, and probably weren't going to have much to say about our ultimate fate, the best policy seemed to be to live out such time as we might have in a way enabling us to feel comfortable with ourselves and to sleep well at night.

NOTES

1. The Choleric Years

1. A memo for the file dictated by FBI Director J. Edgar Hoover two years later and finally released under the Freedom of Information Act said Giancana was still at large despite this listing "because of Giancana's close relationship with Frank Sinatra who, in turn, claimed to be a close friend of the Kennedy family." Attorney General Kennedy, seeking to obliterate the crime connection, tried to prosecute the mobster for using an illegal wiretap to check on his girlfriend, singer Phyllis McGuire, but was prevented from doing so when it developed the wiretap had been obligingly installed for Giancana, gratis, by the CIA.

3. Caribbean Debacle

2. How Nixon could have misinterpreted Kennedy's remarks as a reference to the coming invasion has remained obscure. In his memoirs (Grosset and Dunlap, 1978, page 220) Nixon said that unspecified afternoon newspapers of the previous day had carried headlines proclaiming "Kennedy Advocates U.S. Intervention in Cuba," but there was no mention of such headlines at the time of his original pronouncement during a television debate October 21, 1960. His reply then was to a statement in that morning's *New York Times* in which Kennedy's strongest words were these: "We must seek to strengthen the non-Batista democratic anti-Castro forces in exile, and in Cuba itself, who offer eventual hope of overthrowing Castro." This was advocating intervention of a kind, no doubt, but scarcely a reference to something that was already large-scale and imminent. Nevertheless, in his memoirs, Nixon said: "In order to protect the secrecy of the planning and the safety of thousands of men and women involved in the operation, I had no choice but to take a

completely opposite stand . . . the most uncomfortable and ironic
duty I have had to perform in any political campaign."

4. *Era of Absolutism*

3. Bernard Diederich in his thoroughly detailed *Trujillo*
(Little, Brown, 1978) accepted the committee version of the carbines' origin in the consulate, but confirmed that they were received by the assassins from the supermarket owner. There did
not appear to have been any reason why the weapons would have
been placed with that individual merely for storage or delivery.
Diederich and the committee agreed that the Smith & Wesson
revolvers passed to the dissidents were brought into the country
by American diplomatic pouch in March 1961, apparently without benefit of a "Pouch Restriction Waiver Request and Certification."

6. *The Sun Rises*

4. See John Stockwell's *In Search of Enemies*, page 101: ". . .
in my twelve years of case officering [for the CIA] I never saw or
heard of a situation in which the KGB attacked or obstructed a
CIA operation." Also, page 238: "In fact CIA and KGB officers
entertain each other frequently in their homes. . . . The Soviets,
Chinese, and even the North Koreans, like the CIA, do not want
the intelligence world to be complicated by James Bond-type be-
havior. It isn't done."

5. As Schlesinger brought out in his *Robert Kennedy and His
Times* (Houghton Mifflin, 1978), the Kennedys in an exchange
with their ambassador in Washington nevertheless gave the Soviets a secret and informal but written commitment to remove the
Turkish missiles, which were in fact removed in about six months.
In the circumstances there appeared to be nothing to lose, although nuclear weapons being what they were the Soviets no
doubt still were glad to get the commitment and the removal.

6. The extent to which Khrushchev contributed personally
to the favorable outcome of the missile crisis was indicated several
months later in a conversation with Norman Cousins, editor of
the *Saturday Review*. As reproduced in the October 15, 1977 issue
of Cousins's magazine, the Soviet premier spoke freely of the missile crisis, saying:

> When I asked the military advisers whether they could
> assure me that holding fast would not result in the death of
> five hundred million people, they looked at me as though I

were out of my mind, or worse, a traitor. The biggest tragedy as they saw it was not that our country might be devastated and everything lost, but that the Chinese or the Albanians would accuse us of appeasement or weakness. So I said to myself, "To Hell with these maniacs. If I can get the United States to assure me that it will not attempt to overthrow the Cuban government, I will remove the missiles." That is what happened. And so now I am being reviled by the Chinese and the Albanians. They say I was afraid to stand up to a paper tiger. It is all such nonsense. What good would it have done me in the last hour of my life to know that though our great country and the United States were in complete ruins, the national honor of the Soviet Union was intact?

7. Such pressure was not always from generals. As David Detzer pointed out in his 1979 *The Brink* (Crowell, page 234), among the telegrams that could be described as trigger-happy that arrived at the White House at the height of the crisis was one reading, "Any further delay in bombing missile sites fails to exploit Soviet uncertainty," from a professor named Zbigniew Brzezinski, who would later be entrusted with our security to the extent it was possible for one appointed man to be so entrusted, as President Carter's Special Assistant for National Security. Brzezinski's position in this instance was identical to that of General Curtis E. LeMay, the firebrand-type officer who then headed the air force. Fortunately their advice was rejected by Kennedy, who argued cogently that if missile sites were bombed and Russians were killed the Soviets would feel compelled to react in a substantial way, and who proceeded with dispatch and double emphasis to avoid the chain of events his conclusion suggested. Even for the invasion of Cuba should one prove necessary, consideration of bombing missile sites as part of that operation was discontinued.

8. Although fear of nuclear war with the United States was overwhelmingly his greatest concern, there were some other considerations propelling Khrushchev toward an accommodation with Washington at almost any price. One of them, seldom mentioned for diplomatic reasons, was undoubtedly the growing political, economic, and even military power of Germany, where there were more nuclear weapons per square mile than in any other country in the world. The truth was that the Germans were fully capable of reunifying and becoming an instant nuclear power any time either Moscow or Washington let down their guard.

The extent to which the above reality could be ignored in day-to-day intercourse was demonstrated later when the Carter administration vigorously protested to Bonn the projected export of $4 billion worth of nuclear material and technology (the Manhattan Project cost only $2 billion) from West Germany to Brazil. In what could be called a reversal of priorities on a gargantuan scale, the protest raised no objection to the existence of such materials and technology in a country that had launched two world wars in the first half of the century and clearly was moving toward a position from which it might precipitate a third. The effort instead was entirely focused on preventing bomb possibilities in an underdeveloped country lacking both the inclination and the resources necessary for propagating global war.

8. Saga of the Orient

9.   Southern Air Transport was sold in 1973 for $6,470,000. The CIA's larger Air America, with assets at one time totaling $50 million, was also in process of liquidation due to American withdrawal from Southeast Asia.

10.   Few American universities later would accept an association of any kind with the CIA. As for individual professors, Harvard University set a precedent by ruling that members of its staff could work for the CIA only if they did so on a nonsecret basis. Although the CIA rejected the policy and made clear that it would continue to seek clandestine relationships at Harvard, the ruling still had the merit of greatly increasing the danger to their professional careers of those who succumbed to the agency's blandishments.

10. Bureaucracy Unlimited

11.   The OSS provided a solid precedent for the kind of trickery later practiced by the CIA, by going behind FDR's back in a 1943 attempt to turn World War II against the Soviet Union. The treacherous enterprise actually got as far as secret negotiations with former German Chancellor Franz von Papen, in which it was agreed that Germany would be awarded the Russian Ukraine among other things, and in fact would have become the principal beneficiary of the war. All this was made clear reluctantly but unambiguously in Anthony Cave Brown's *The Last Hero* (Times Books, 1982). The writer felt forced to conclude that if Donovan was a hero it might be just as well if he turned out to have been the last one.

12.   An obvious exception, along with his associates, was Ed-

win P. Wilson, who became a millionaire while working for the CIA between 1967 and 1972, and later a multimillionaire but finally a prison inmate after years of exporting terrorist weapons, explosives, and training personnel mainly to Libya. In this connection it is worth noting that when oil-wealthy Libyan Dictator Moammar Khadafy decided to go in for some sophisticated terrorism, with heavy emphasis on assassination, he sought his assistance from the American CIA and its fringes rather than from the similar arm of his military supplier, the Soviet KGB.

12. *Cold War Magic*

13. The watchdog panel nevertheless was referred to semiofficially from time to time as "The Joint Armed Services-Appropriations Subcommittee on Intelligence." A similar watchdog group, also excluding the Foreign Affairs Committee in that body, functioned for a number of years in the House of Representatives. In other words, in the beginning at least, and even though it was mainly a civilian agency, the CIA was regarded by both houses of Congress as having much to do with military planning and precautions and little or nothing to do with foreign relations. This was perhaps natural since, if the CIA had one original assignment overriding all others, it was to "prevent another Pearl Harbor," where surprise resulted not so much from lack of intelligence information as from failure to interpret the information correctly. But strangely enough, this firm initial purpose so strongly indicated in Congress was later one of the areas in which no progress whatever could be cited with confidence, as Pulitzer Prize-winning author Thomas Powers pointed out in a penetrating analysis in his 1979 *The Man Who Kept the Secrets* (Knopf, pages 355–56). Powers wrote:

> Perhaps the most interesting thing I discovered about the Agency, in fact, is the probability that it would fail to predict even a major attack upon the United States. . . . It is hard to escape the conclusion that if surprise offers an advantage in nuclear war, it's there for the taking.

14. During the session's preliminaries Senator Claiborne Pell, Democrat, of Rhode Island, sometimes described as one of the half dozen richest men in the Senate, but a man with sympathies for those less fortunate than himself, rose to call attention to the historical coincidence.

Pell recalled that there was a time during America's infancy when French officials and court favorites could have people imprisoned in the Bastille "with no record available as to what had become of the unfortunate persons." He added:

> Hatred of oppression, represented by this building, caused the people to storm the fortress. The attack on this symbol of all the cruel and despotic aspects of the then traditional order in Europe helped to open the floodgates of revolution, which in time spread to almost all the nations of the Continent.

Pell's denunciation of secrecy and an infamous institution was considered to have heralded the day's proceedings.

15. This incident occurred when the London-owned and Soviet-chartered freighter *Streatham Hill* was damaged in transit and with a bent propeller was forced to put into the port of San Juan for repairs. To raise the ship higher in the water, a total of 14,135 hundred-pound sacks of sugar were off-loaded and stored in a warehouse at the Isla Grande pier, where with CIA connivance, the contamination took place.

When Kennedy learned of the matter he issued flat orders that the contaminated sugar must not leave the territory of the United States. This forced the CIA to instigate litigation to prevent the sugar's being reloaded while the *Streathem Hill* was still waiting in port, and then to buy up and dispose of the damaged consignment to prevent its being innocently sold on the open market in New York.

The cost of purchasing the contaminated sugar was $141,350 at ten cents a pound, plus $149,223 in storage bills which had accumulated. The cost of the litigation seeking an attachment on the sugar could not be estimated, but it involved four appeals, three of them to the Supreme Court of Puerto Rico and one to the United States Circuit Court of Appeals in Boston. Eventually the litigation went against the CIA and a sale of the sugar to unsuspecting parties ominously impended.

In the windup of the affair, William Standard, a New York lawyer representing the Soviets' Prodintorg import agency, handled the sale of the worthless sugar to a group of men claiming to represent a well-known American import firm. Standard knew nothing of the contamination or what the excitement was about at the time, and still seemed a little puzzled ten years later when he told me:

> I never saw people so anxious to buy sugar. They called me at my home in Connecticut on a Sunday and wanted me

to get to work on it right away. I sold them the sugar at the going rate the next day, and have no idea what they did with it. They may have dumped it in the ocean for all I know.

13. Judicial Turnover

16.   As will be recalled the CIA at the time of Guevara's execution was definitely in the driver's seat and was issuing orders right and left—orders that could be countermanded "only by the Commander-in-Chief of the Armed Forces." In these circumstances the Bolivians could have carried out the summary executions of Guevara and his companions either on direct orders from or in concert with the CIA, but not over CIA objections.

14. Mind Control

17.   For other reasons, chiefly the arrogance generated in its officials by the exercise of too much secret power, Braden later concluded that the CIA had become a "monster," and that investigating committees would only "prop up the monster." In an article for the April 5, 1975, issue of the *Saturday Review* he advocated complete abolition of the agency.

15. Much Ado

18.   It should be noted that as a former employee Rositzke was under contract to submit his material to the CIA for clearance, and he would never have gotten this item past the agency's censors if he had treated it any other way. Under the circumstances, he no doubt deserves credit for having shoehorned the facts concerning Blake's treachery into his account.

Rositzke also argued that the Soviets, knowingly it seemed, had given away an intelligence bonanza, in efforts to spare Blake from exposure. This may have been persuasive to the censors but seemed unlikely to pass muster anywhere else. The Soviets were in an intelligence driver's seat—they knew and the CIA didn't know they knew—and as long as that situation obtained they had attractive possibilities before them.

16. The Rogue Elephant

19.   CIA Director James Schlesinger in May 1973, asked the agency's employees to report to him any of its activities which they considered either illegal, improper or both, of which opening the mails was a prime example. In response he received memoranda totaling 700 pages, enough for a fat book. When the release of all

or any part of this material was requested under the Freedom of Information Act, however, the request was denied *in toto* on the ground that this would reveal "intelligence sources and methods." The still-secret memoranda have become known as "the family jewels."

**UNITED STATES COVERT ACTION ABROAD TO
IMPOSE OR RESTORE FAVORABLE POLITICAL
CONDITIONS, 1946–1983.**
Partial List.

A Chronology BY TOM GERVASI

1946: Greece. Restore monarch after overthrow of Metaxas government. Successful.

1946–1955: West Germany. Average of $6 million annually to support former Nazi intelligence network of General Reinhard Gehlen. Successful.

1948–1968: Italy. Average of $30 million annually in payments to political and labor leaders to support anti-Communist candidates in Italian elections. Successful.

1949: Greece. Military assistance to anti-Communist forces in Greek civil war. Successful.

1949–1953: Ukraine. Organize and support a Ukrainian resistance movement. Unsuccessful.

1949–1961: Burma. Support 12,000 Nationalist China troops in Burma under General Li Mi as an incursion force into People's Republic of China. Unsuccessful.

1950–1952: Poland. Financial and military assistance for Polish Freedom and Independence Movement. Unsuccessful.

1950: Albania. Overthrow government of Enver Hoxha. Unsuccessful.

1951–1954: China. Airdrop guerrilla teams into People's Republic of China. Unsuccessful.

1953: Iran. Overthrow Mossadegh government and install Zahedi. Cost: $10 million. Successful.

1953: Philippines. Assassination and propaganda campaign to overcome Huk resistance and install government of Ramon Magsaysay. Successful.

1953: Costa Rica. Overthrow government of José Figueres. Unsuccessful.

1954: South Vietnam. Install government of Ngo Dinh Diem. Successful.

1954: West Germany. Arrange abduction and discreditation of West German intelligence chief Otto John, and replace with Reinhard Gehlen. Successful.

1954: Guatemala. Overthrow government of Jacobo Arbenz Guzmán and replace with Carlos Castillo Armas. Successful.

1955: China. Assassinate Zhou Enlai en route to Bandung Conference. Unsuccessful.

1956: Hungary. Financial and military assistance to organize and support a Hungarian resistance movement, and broad propaganda campaign to encourage it. Unsuccessful.

1956: Cuba. Establish anti-Communist police force, Buro de Represion Actividades Communistas (BRAC) under Batista regime. Successful.

1956: Egypt. Overthrow Nasser government. Unsuccessful.

1956: Syria. Overthrow Ghazzi government. Aborted by Israeli invasion of Egypt.

1956–1957: Jordan. Average of $750,000 annually in personal payments to King Hussein. According to United States government, payments ceased when disclosed in 1976.

1957: Lebanon. Financial assistance for the election of pro-American candidates to Lebanese Parliament. Successful.

1958: Indonesia. Financial and military assistance, including B–26 bombers, for rebel forces attempting to overthrow Sukarno government. Unsuccessful.

1958–1961: Tibet. Infiltrate Tibetan guerrillas trained in United States to fight Chinese Communists. Unsuccessful.

1959: Cambodia. Assassinate Prince Norodom Sihanouk. Unsuccessful.

1960: Guatemala. Military assistance, including the use of B–26 bombers, for government of Miguel Ydígoras Fuentes to defeat rebel forces. Successful.

1960: Angola. Financial and military assistance to rebel forces of Holden Roberto. Inconclusive.

1960: Laos. Military assistance, including 400 United States Special Forces troops, to deny the Plain of Jars and Mekong Basin to Pathet Lao. Inconclusive.

1961–1965: Laos. Average of $300 million annually to recruit and maintain L'Armée Clandestine of 35,000 Hmong and Meo tribesmen and 17,000 Thai mercenaries in support of government of Phoumi Nosavan to resist Pathet Lao. Successful.

1961–1963: Cuba. Assassinate Fidel Castro. Six attempts in this period. Unsuccessful.

1961: Cuba. Train and support invasion force of Cuban exiles to overthrow Castro government, and assist their invasion at the Bay of Pigs. Cost: $62 million. Unsuccessful.

1961: Ecuador. Overthrow government of José Velasco Ibarra. Successful.

1961: Congo. Precipitate conditions leading to assassination of Patrice Lumumba. Successful.

1961: Dominican Republic. Precipitate conditions leading to assassination of Rafael Trujillo. Successful.

1961–1966: Cuba. Broad sabotage program, including terrorist attacks on coastal targets and bacteriological warfare, in effort to weaken Castro government. Unsuccessful.

1962: Thailand. Brigade of 5,000 United States Marines to resist threat to Thai government from Pathet Lao. Successful.

1962–1964: British Guiana. Organize labor strikes and riots to overthrow government of Cheddi Jagan. Successful.

1962–1964: Brazil. Organize campaign of labor strikes and propaganda to overthrow government of João Goulart. Successful.

1963: Dominican Republic. Overthrow government of Juan Bosch in military coup. Successful.

1963: South Vietnam. Precipitate conditions leading to assassination of Ngo Dinh Diem. Successful.

1963: Ecuador. Overthrow government of Carlos Julio Arosemena. Successful.

1963–1984: El Salvador. Organize ORDEN and ANSESAL domestic intelligence networks under direction of General José Alberto Medrano and Colonel Nicolas Carranza, and provide intelligence support and training in surveillance, interrogation and assassination techniques. Successful.

1963–1973: Iraq. Financial and military assistance for Freedom Party of M˙ 'la Mustafa al Barzani in effort to establish independent Kurdistan. Unsuccessful.

1964: Chile. $20 million in assistance for Eduardo Frei to defeat Salvador Allende in Chilean elections. Successful.

1964: Brazil, Guatemala, Uruguay, Dominican Republic. Provide training in assassination and interrogation techniques for police and intelligence personnel. Inconclusive.

1964: Congo. Financial and military assistance, including B–26 and T–28 aircraft, and American and exiled Cuban pilots, for Joseph Mobutu and Cyril Adoula, and later for Moise Tshombe in Katanga, to defeat rebel forces loyal to Lumumba. Successful.

1964–1967: South Vietnam. Phoenix Program to eliminate Viet Cong political infrastructure through more than 20,000 assassinations. Infiltrated by Viet Cong and only partially successful.

1964–1971: North Vietnam. Sabotage and ambush missions under Operations Plan 34A by United States Special Forces and Nung tribesmen. Inconclusive.

1965–1971: Laos. Under Operations Shining Brass and Prairie Fire, sabotage and ambush missions by United States Special Forces personnel and Nung and Meo tribesmen under General Vang Pao. Inconclusive.

1965: Thailand. Recruit 17,000 mercenaries to support Laotian government of Phoumi Nosavan resisting Pathet Lao. Successful.

1965: Peru. Provide training in assassination and interrogation techniques for Peruvian police and intelligence personnel, similiar to training given in Uruguay, Brazil and Dominican Republic, in effort to defeat resistance movement. Unsuccessful.

1965: Indonesia. Organize campaign of propaganda to overthrow Sukarno government, and precipitate conditions leading to massacre of more than 500,000 members of Indonesian Communist Party, in order to eliminate opposition to new Suharto government. Successful.

1967: Bolivia. Assist government in capture of Ernesto Ché Guevara. Successful.

1967: Greece. Overthrow government of George Papandreou and install military government of Colonel George Papadopoulos after abdication of King Constantine. Successful.

1967–1971: Cambodia. Under Projects Daniel Boone and Salem House, sabotage and ambush missions by United States Special Forces personnel and Meo tribesmen. Inconclusive.

1969–1970: Cambodia. Bombing campaign to crush Viet Cong sanctuaries in Cambodia. Unsuccessful.

1970: Cambodia. Overthrow government of Prince Norodom Sihanouk. Successful.

1970–1973: Chile. Campaign of assassinations, propaganda, labor strikes and demonstrations to overthrow government of Salvador Allende. Successful. Cost: $8,400,000.

1973–1978: Afghanistan. Military and financial assistance to government of Mohammed Daud to resist rise to power of Noor Mohammed Taraki. Unsuccessful.

1975: Portugal. Overthrow government of General Vasco dos Santos Gonçalves. Successful.

1975: Angola. Military assistance to forces of Holden Roberto and Jonas Savimbi to defeat forces of Popular Movement for the Liberation of Angola (MPLA) during Angolan civil war, and prevent MPLA from forming new government. Unsuccessful.

1975: Australia. Propaganda and political pressure to force dissolution of labor government of Gough Whitlam. Successful.

1976: Jamaica. Military coup to overthrow government of Michael Manley. Unsuccessful.

1976–1979: Jamaica. Assassinate Michael Manley. Three attempts in this period. Unsuccessful.

1976–1984: Angola. Financial and military assistance to forces of Jonas Savimbi to harrass and destabilize Neto and succeeding governments. Inconclusive.

1979: Iran. Install military government to replace Shah and resist growth of Moslem fundamentalism. Unsuccessful.

1979–1980: Jamaica. Financial pressure to destabilize government of Michael Manley, and campaign of propaganda and demonstrations to defeat it in elections. Successful.

1979: Afghanistan. Military aid to rebel forces of Zia Nezri, Zia Khan Nassry, Gulbuddin Hekmatyar, Sayed Ahmed Gailani and conservative mullahs to overthrow government of Hafizullah Amin. Aborted by Soviet intervention and installation of new government.

1980–1984: Afghanistan. Continuing military aid to same rebel groups to harrass Soviet occupation forces and challenge legitimacy of government of Babrak Karmal.

1979: Seychelles. Destabilize government of France Albert René. Unsuccessful.

✓ **1980: Grenada.** Mercenary coup to overthrow government of Maurice Bishop. Unsuccessful.

1980: Dominica. Financial support to Freedom Party of Eugenia Charles to defeat Oliver Seraphim in Dominican elections. Successful.

1980: Guyana. Assassinate opposition leader Walter Rodney to consolidate power of government of Forbes Burnham. Successful.

1980–1984: Nicaragua. Military assistance to Adolfo Calero Portocarrero, Alfonso Robelo, Alfonso Callejas, Fernando Chamorro Rappacioli, Edén Pastora Gomez, Adrianna Guillen, Steadman Fagoth and former Somozan National Guard officers, to recruit, train and equip anti-Sandinist forces for sabotage and terrorist incursions into Nicaragua from sanctuaries in Honduras and Costa Rica, in effort to destabilize government of Daniel Ortega Saavedra.

1981: Seychelles. Military coup to overthrow government of France Albert René. Unsuccessful.

1981–1982: Mauritius. Financial support to Seewoosagar Ramgoolam to bring him to power in 1982 elections. Unsuccessful.

1981–1984: Libya. Broad campaign of economic pressure, propaganda, military maneuvers in Egypt, Sudan and Gulf of Sidra, and organization of Libyan Liberation Front exiles to destabilize government of Muammar Quaddafi. Inconclusive.

1982: Chad. Military assistance to Hissen Habré to overthrow government of Goukouni Oueddei. Successful.

1982: Guatemala. Military coup to overthrow government of Angel Aníbal Guevara. Successful.

1982: Bolivia. Military coup to overthrow government of Celso Torrelio. Successful.

1982: Jordan. Military assistance to equip and train two Jordanian brigades as an Arab strike force to implement United States policy objectives without Israeli assistance.

1982–1983: Surinam. Overthrow government of Colonel Desi Bouterse. Three attempts in this period. Unsuccessful.

1984: El Salvador. $1.4 million in financial support for the Presidential election campaign of José Napoleon Duarte. Successful.

SOURCES ✓

Philip Agee and Louis Wolf, editors, *Dirty Work: The CIA in Western Europe*, Secaucus, Lyle Stuart, 1978.

Philip Agee, *Inside The Company: CIA Diary*, New York, Stonehill, 1975.

Bradley Earl Ayers, *The War That Never Was*, Indianapolis/New York, Bobbs-Merrill, 1976.

Robert L. Borosage and John Marks, editors, *The CIA File*, New York, Grossman, 1976.

Frank Brodhead and Edward S. Herman, *Demonstration Elections: U. S.-Staged Elections in The Dominican Republic, Vietnam, and El Salvador*, Boston, South End Press, 1984.

Noam Chomsky and Edward S. Herman, *The Washington Connection and Third World Fascism*, Boston, South End Press, 1979.

William Colby, *Honorable Men: My Life in the CIA*, New York, Simon and Schuster, 1978.

Concerned Citizen's Committee on Jamaica, *Report on the Destabilization of Jamaica*, Washington, D.C., 1980.

William R. Corson, *The Armies of Ignorance*, New York, Dial Press/James Wade, 1967.

CounterSpy, Washington, D.C.

Covert Action Information Bulletin, Washington, D.C.

Wilbur Crane Eveland, *Ropes of Sand*, New York, Norton, 1980.

Jonathan L. Fried, Marvin E. Gettleman, Deborah T. Levenson and Nancy Peckenham, editors, *Guatemala in Rebellion: Unfinished History*, New York, Grove, 1983.

Andre Fontaine, *History of the Cold War*, New York, Pantheon, 1968 and 1969.

G. Heinze and H. Donnay, *Lumumba: The Last Fifty Days*, New York, Grove, 1969.

Edward S. Herman, *The Real Terror Network*, Boston, South End Press, 1982.

Richard H. Immerman, *The CIA in Guatemala*, Austin, University of Texas, 1982.

Otto John, *Twice Through the Lines*, London, Macmillan, 1970.

Madeleine G. Kalb, *The Congo Cables*, New York, Macmillan, 1982.

Jonathan Kwitney, *Endless Enemies: The Making of an Unfriendly World*, New York, Congdon & Weed, 1984.

A. J. Langguth, *Hidden Terrors*, New York, Pantheon, 1978.

Penny Lernoux, "Blood Money," *Penthouse*, April 1984.

Michael Manley, *Jamaica: Struggle in the Periphery*, London, Writers and Readers Publishing Cooperative Society, 1982.

Victor Marchetti and John D. Marks, *The CIA and the Cult of Intelligence*, New York, Knopf, 1974.

✓ Ralph W. McGehee, *Deadly Deceits: My 25 Years in the CIA*, New York, Sheridan Square, 1983.

Allan Nairn, "Behind the Death Squads," *The Progressive*, May 1984.

John M. Orman, *Presidential Secrecy and Deception: Beyond the Power to Persuade*, Westport, Greenwood Press, 1980.

Jenny Pearce, *Under the Eagle: U. S. Intervention in Central America and the Caribbean*, Boston, South End Press, 1982.

David Atlee Phillips, *The Night Watch: 25 Years of Peculiar Service*, New York, Atheneum, 1977.

Thomas Powers, *The Man Who Kept the Secrets: Richard Helms and the CIA*, New York, Knopf, 1979.

Ellen Ray, William Schaap, Karl Van Meter and Louis Wolf, editors, *Dirty Work: The CIA in Africa*, Secaucus, Lyle Stuart, 1979.

Kermit Roosevelt, *Countercoup*, New York, McGraw-Hill, 1979.

✓ Harry Rositzke, *The CIA'S Secret Operations*, New York, Reader's Digest Press, 1977.

Peter Rosset and John Vandermeer, editors, *The Nicaragua*

Reader: Documents of a Revolution Under Fire, New York, Grove, 1983.

Christopher Robbins, *Air America: The Story of the CIA's Secret Airlines*, New York, Putnam's, 1979.

Chris Searle, *Grenada: The Struggle Against Destabilization*, London, Writers and Readers Publishing Cooperative Society, 1983.

Theodore Shackley, *The Third Option: An American View of Counterinsurgency Operations*, New York, McGraw-Hill/Reader's Digest Press, 1981.

Stewart Steven, *Operation Splinter Factor*, Philadelphia/New York, Lippincott, 1974.

✓ John Stockwell, *In Search of Enemies: A CIA Story*, New York, Norton, 1978.

✓ Frank Snepp, *Decent Interval*, New York, Random House, 1977.

Joseph B. Smith, *Portrait of a Cold Warrior*, New York, Putnam's, 1976.

Shelby L. Stanton, *Vietnam: Order of Battle*, Washington, D. C., U. S. News Books, 1981.

Vernon A. Walters, *Silent Missions*, New York, Doubleday, 1978.

Richard Alan White, *The Morass: United States Intervention in Central America*, New York, Harper & Row, 1984.

David Wise and Thomas B. Ross, *The Invisible Government*, New York, Random House, 1964.

David Wise, *The Politics of Lying: Government Deception, Secrecy, and Power*, New York, Random House, 1973.

Peter Wyden, *Bay of Pigs: The Untold Story*, New York, Simon & Schuster, 1979.

United States Senate, Select Committee to Study Governmental Operations with Respect to Intelligence Activities, *Foreign and Military Intelligence: Final Report*, Books I, II, III, and IV, 94th Congress, 2nd Session, Washington, D. C., 1976.

INDEX

Selected Grove Press Paperbacks

62480-7   ACKER, KATHY / Great Expectations: A Novel / $6.95

17458-5   ALLEN, DONALD & BUTTERICK, GEORGE F., eds. / The Postmoderns: The New American Poetry Revised / $9.95

17397-X   ANONYMOUS / My Secret Life / $4.95

62433-5   BARASH, D. and LIPTON, J. / Stop Nuclear War! A Handbook / $7.95

17087-3   BARNES, JOHN / Evita—First Lady: A Biography of Eva Peron / $4.95

17208-6   BECKETT, SAMUEL / Endgame / $3.50

17299-X   BECKETT, SAMUEL / Three Novels: Molloy, Malone Dies and The Unnamable / $6.95

17204-3   BECKETT, SAMUEL / Waiting for Godot / $3.50

62064-X   BECKETT, SAMUEL / Worstward Ho / $5.95

17244-2   BORGES, JORGE LUIS / Ficciones / $6.95

17112-8   BRECHT, BERTOLT / Galileo / $2.95

17106-3   BRECHT, BERTOLT / Mother Courage and Her Children / $2.45

17393-7   BRETON ANDRE / Nadja / $5.95

17439-9   BULGAKOV, MIKHAIL / The Master and Margarita / $4.95

17108-X   BURROUGHS, WILLIAM S. / Naked Lunch / $4.95

17749-5   BURROUGHS, WILLIAM S. / The Soft Machine, Nova Express, The Wild Boys: Three Novels / $5.95

62488-2   CLARK, AL, ed. / The Film Year Book 1984 / $12.95

17535-2   COWARD, NOEL / Three Plays (Private Lives, Hay Fever, Blithe Spirit) / $7.95

17219-1   CUMMINGS, E.E. / 100 Selected Poems / $2.95

17327-9   FANON, FRANZ / The Wretched of the Earth / $4.95

17483-6   FROMM, ERICH / The Forgotten Language / $6.95

17390-2   GENET, JEAN / The Maids and Deathwatch: Two Plays / $6.95

17838-6   GENET, JEAN / Querelle / $4.95

17662-6   GERVASI, TOM / Arsenal of Democracy II / $12.95

17956-0   GETTLEMAN, MARVIN, et.al. eds. / El Salvador: Central America in the New Cold War / $9.95

17648-0   GIRODIAS, MAURICE, ed. / The Olympia Reader / $5.95

62490-4   GUITAR PLAYER MAGAZINE / The Guitar Player Book (Revised and Updated Edition) $11.95

62003-8 ✓ HITLER, ADOLF / Hitler's Secret Book / $7.95

17125-X   HOCHHUTH, ROLF / The Deputy / $7.95

62115-8   HOLMES, BURTON / The Olympian Games in Athens, 1896 / $6.95

17209-4 IONESCO, EUGENE / Four Plays (The Bald Soprano, The Lesson, The Chairs, and Jack or The Submission) / $6.95

17226-4 IONESCO, EUGENE / Rhinocerous / $5.95

62123-9 JOHNSON, CHARLES / Oxherding Tale / $6.95

17254-X KEENE, DONALD, ed. / Modern Japanese Literature / $12.50

17952-8 KEROUAC, JACK / The Subterraneans / $3.50

62424-6 LAWRENCE, D.H. / Lady Chatterley's Lover / $3.95

17016-4 MAMET, DAVID / American Buffalo / $4.95

17760-6 MILLER, HENRY / Tropic of Cancer / $4.95

17295-7 MILLER, HENRY / Tropic of Capricorn / $3.95

17869-6 NERUDA, PABLO / Five Decades: Poems 1925-1970. Bilingual ed. / $12.50

17092-X ODETS, CLIFFORD / Six Plays (Waiting for Lefty, Awake and Sing, Golden Boy, Rocket to the Moon, Till the Day I Die, Paradise Lost) / $7.95

17650-2 OE, KENZABURO / A Personal Matter / $6.95

17232-9 PINTER, HAROLD / The Birthday Party & The Room / $6.95

17251-5 PINTER, HAROLD / The Homecoming / $5.95

17539-5 POMERANCE, BERNARD / The Elephant Man / $4.25

17827-0 RAHULA, WALPOLA / What the Buddha Taught / $6.95

17658-8 REAGE, PAULINE / The Story of O, Part II; Return to the Chateau / $3.95

62169-7 RECHY, JOHN / City of Night / $4.50

62001-1 ROSSET, BARNEY and JORDAN, FRED, eds. / Evergreen Review No. 98 / $5.95

62498-X ROSSET, PETER and VANDERMEER, JOHN / The Nicaragua Reader / $8.95

17119-5 SADE, MARQUIS DE / The 120 Days of Sodom and Other Writings / $12.50

62009-7 SEGALL, J. PETER / Deduct This Book: How Not to Pay Taxes While Ronald Reagan is President / $6.95

17467-4 SELBY, HUBERT / Last Exit to Brooklyn / $2.95

17948-X SHAWN, WALLACE, and GREGORY, ANDRE / My Dinner with Andre / $5.95

17797-5 SNOW, EDGAR / Red Star Over China / $9.95

17260-4 STOPPARD, TOM / Rosencrantz and Guildenstern Are Dead / $3.95

17474-7 SUZUKI, D.T. / Introduction to Zen Buddhism / $3.95

17599-9 THELWELL, MICHAEL / The Harder They Come: A Novel about Jamaica / $7.95

17969-2 TOOLE, JOHN KENNEDY / A Confederacy of Dunces / $4.50

17418-6 WATTS, ALAN W. / The Spirit of Zen / $3.95

GROVE PRESS, INC., 196 West Houston St., New York, N.Y. 10014